160

AF652523

HUMAN RIGHTS

About the Author

Dr. K. Mohanasundaram after his graduation in History in Sri Palani Andavar Arts College, Palani did his M.A. History in Annamalai University and M.A. Political Science at Sri Venkateshwara University, Tirupati. He did his Ph.D. on 'Indo-Sri Lanka Relations with Reference to the Tamils in Sri Lanka". At present he teaches History and guiding research in Islamiah College, Vaniyambadi, Tamil Nadu. He has published a book on "Dynamics of Tamil Nadu Politics in Sri Lankan Ethnicity" and contributed text and study materials for a number of universities at the Post Graduate level in areas such as 'Intellectual History of Tamil Nadu' and 'Human Rights'. He has contributed number of articles in national and international journals that includes issues on coalition politics. He is a regular contributor to conferences besides chairing sessions in seminars and workshops.

HUMAN RIGHTS
Theories and Practice

K. Mohanasundaram
Associate Professor in History
Islamiah College
Vaniyambadi

CONCEPT PUBLISHING COMPANY PVT. LTD.,
NEW DELHI-110059

© K. Mohanasundaram

All rights reserved. No part of this work may be reproduced, stored, adapted, or transmitted in any form or by any means, electronic, mechanical, photocopying, micro-filming recording or otherwise, or translated in any language, without the prior written permission of the copyright owner and the publisher. The book is sold subject to the condition that it shall not, by way of trade or otherwise, be lent, resold, hired out, or otherwise circulated without the prior publisher's written consent in any form of binding or cover other than that in which it is published.

The views and opinions expressed in this book are author(s) own and the facts reported by him/her have been verified to the extent possible, and the publishers are not in any way liable for the same.

ISBN 978-81-8069-917-7 (HB)
PB)

First Published 2013

Published and Printed by

Concept Publishing Company Pvt. Ltd.
A/15-16, Commercial Block, Mohan Garden
New Delhi-110059 (India)
T: 25351460, 25351794, *F*: 091-11-25357109
E: publishing@conceptpub.com, W: www.conceptpub.com
Editorial Office: H-13, Bali Nagar, New Delhi-110 015, India.

Cataloging in Publication Data--*Courtesy:* D.K. Agencies (P) Ltd. <docinfo@dkagencies.com>

Mohanasundaram, K.
Human rights : theories and practice / K. Mohanasundaram.
p. cm.
Includes bibliographical references (p.) and index.
ISBN 9788180699177 (hb.)
ISBN 9788180699375 (pbk.)

1. Human rights—India. 2. Human rights. I. Title.

DDC 323.0954 23

Preface

Human right as a study is gaining importance in the recent years. Awareness of human rights is a requirement to protect one's own rights as well as the rights of the others. Indian Universities introduced this subject in Undergraduate and Postgraduate courses. In some states, this subject is taught at the high school levels and there is a demand for its introduction at the early stage of education to inculcate the values of human rights. A plethora of literature is available on the subject covering various facets of human rights and its operation. However, the general reader or student pursuing his studies has to refer several books and search for other published materials to get a fair view on issues pertaining to human rights. At the higher education level, students from different faculties are in need of a comprehensive book on human rights covering all the key topics that includes basic theories, documents and contemporary issues. This work is a modest attempt to fill the gap by providing the theories of human rights as well as its application in day-to day life with latest reference details.

As Ramachandra Guha has rightly pointed out that those writing contemporary history and issues face a challenge from the readers. The issues discussed by the author are fresh in their memory and they may have their own serious opinion about it. An attempt is made to incorporate several contemporary events and its effect on human rights concept through the explanation of case studies that may be very familiar to the common reader who follows the media focus on such matters.

The work is broadly divided into two major divisions incorporating the evolution of human rights concept and other international endeavour to establish human rights norms at the global level. The creation of UNO and other international agencies as well as all important human rights declarations and related documents formed the first part. Some of the most pressing contemporary human rights issues that includes the rights of women, children, Dalits, bonded labour, refugees, transgender groups, capital punishment, environmental challenges to human rights, Law enforcing agencies role in human rights protection, terrorism and human rights and issues related to HIV/AIDS affected persons are incorporated with necessary case study details. The development of human rights concept in India also finds its place in the second part.

To facilitate the student readers, a 'points to remember' section is included at the end of every chapter. In addition, model questions and objective type questions with key are given. To help the general reader who wishes to utilize the services of Human Rights Commissions in India for the protection of the rights of individuals, the basic guideline and format is given with address. The redressal mechanisms available in India and the rights of the persons arrested by the police also found its place.

I borrowed materials liberally from a number of authors and institutions. I am indebted to them and I quoted the source of my information at appropriate places in the book. However, I am alone responsible for any commissions and omissions and the views expressed in the work.

Several libraries and individuals helped me in the preparation of this work. I owe my sincere thanks to the librarians and others for their support in completion of the work. I thank my guide and mentor Dr. S. Baskaran, former Member-Secretary, Tamil Nadu State Council for Higher Education (TANSCHE), Chennai, who is a source of inspiration and support. My thanks are due to the management of Vaniyambadi Muslim Educational Society, for the encouragement I am receiving for my acdemic pursuits. My wife Kumudha and daughter Rudrappriya provided the necessary ambiance to complete the book and I am indebted to them for their patience and support. I thank M. Saravanan for his assistance in organising the manuscript.

Contents

1

Human Rights and Its Historical Development

Introduction

Human Rights are natural rights that belong to the people simply because they are human beings. Human Rights are generally defined as the rights which every human being is entitled to enjoy. Human rights are inherent because human beings born with them. The rights of every individual should be protected. If we go to the pages of history we can come to the conclusion that every society and culture has this right in one form or the other. Some of these rights and principles which evolved over the years should be respected and is considered universal in nature. The struggle for the recognition of Human Rights was an integral part of human history.

In the 20th century the birth of UNO is an important event that is linked with the observance of Human Rights all-over the world. Human Rights enable the human beings to enjoy the life in its full capacity and also enhance one's own personality. Due to international consent and efforts, the observation of Human Rights in every society is carefully monitored. Countries like India passed Human Rights Act and incorporates Human Rights in their respective constitutions. The Human Rights may be classified under civil, political, economic, social and cultural rights categories. A number of theories on Human Rights exist to cover the various aspects of Human Rights.[1] These theories evolved over the millennia due to the exposure of human race to the vagaries of violations on the rights of men. Advancement of civilizations also stimulated the elite to produce these theories. These theories touch upon different aspects of human rights.

Meaning of Human Rights

There is a close relation between the human rights and the legal rights. Human Rights are mostly a subject of legal discussion. Basically it stresses that human beings are entitled for several inviolable legal rights.[2] The concept Human Rights is difficult to understand and complex in nature. To simply put, these rights are given to every individual human being because they are human beings. It protects them from the Government and its officials as well as from the encroachment on their rights by others. Human Rights are equally given to all human beings because they are human beings. Before understanding Human Rights we must understand Rights in its proper perspective.

According to Allen, Right is nothing but a legal guarantee given to enjoy a benefit legally. To Holland, Right can be enjoyed with the concurrence and the support of Government to control the activities of others. Holmes argued that Right is a kind of permission to use some natural powers and to recover the lost Rights and the permission to get relief. Right is a legally protected one and the legal duty is to respect it. If Rights are not respected that is legally wrong is the general impression one may get from the existing literature on Human Rights. Barker pointed out that the state is the immediate source of rights.[3] All these definitions stress that individual's welfare and their power should be honoured by the Law and the Government. Generally speaking individual Rights should be recognized and protected by Government. But some scholars argue that Human Rights are not depending upon the Government.

Human History is full of episodes in which individuals struggled against nature and fellow-men. Since 'might is right' individuals suffered a lot. Hence, rules and regulations were framed to safeguard the interest of the weaker sections of the society. During ancient times Human Rights were not respected much. Only in the recent past the terminology Human Rights gained much importance. Human Rights enhance the dignity of the individual. During the early and medieval period the awareness on Human Rights was negligible since theories on Human Rights are not existed as of now. The concept of Human Rights evolved from the concept of Natural Rights which was fundamental to all the rights that emerged later.

Nature and Scope of Human Rights

Every human being is entitled for the application of Human Rights for the pursuit of happiness. It covers the entire mankind irrespective of any individual difference. Human Rights are naturally endowed upon human beings. It was termed as natural rights earlier. Human Rights are not acquired, nor can they be transferred, disposed of or extinguished by any act or event since these rights are universally inherent in all human beings. Regarding the duties that connected with Human Rights the states enforce them through the rule of Law. The rule of Law stresses that all are equal before Law irrespective of their social status. Efforts are also made to provide remedies for the violation of Human Rights.

Without enforcement one cannot enjoy the fruits of human rights. Human Rights can be enforced with the help of law. Hence, they are subject to the interpretation of the court, law. If Human Rights are enshrined in the Constitution, the courts can implement them. At the regional level organisations such as the European Council looked after the implementation of Human Rights. At the global level the UNO and the International Charters play the same role. Rights are emerging from the society and reflect the culture of the society. Without a society the rights cannot be enjoyed in isolation. Every right is linked with a related duty. In a sense rights and duties are the two sides of a coin. A man cannot demand his rights without the obligation of duties on his part. The rights should be such that respects the welfare of everyone in the society. The rights should be moral based and their aim should be general welfare of the society.

In fact, the rights are not created by the state. But the state only gives legal status to the rights that were recognized by the society in the interest of all. Any welfare measure that is not protected by law cannot become a right. The right should be definite so that there should be no confusion in its interpretation. Clarity of rights alone can help a person to approach the law enforcing agencies for the redressal of any grievances over the violation of his rights.

In the 20th century, due to the outbreak of two world wars, human rights violations reached an alarming level. Naturally, the leaders paid great attention to protect it from further onslaught. The creation of UNO in 1945 was a major step in this direction. Protection of Human Rights became a global concern. Both Government and Non-Governmental Organisations (NGOs) are taking lot of pain in protecting the rights of Human beings. Under the guidance of UNO, efforts are taken to define Human Rights of individuals and groups. A systematic effort was being made to cover even the minute details of Human Rights. The comity of nations should endorse these rights and implement them in their respective boundaries. Consequently, almost all the countries incorporated these Human Rights in their constitutions.

Awareness of Human Rights is essential for its effective implementation. Hence countries all-over the world are taking efforts to make its own people understand the basics of Human Rights. By introducing Human Rights as a subject in the curricula of the schools and colleges, its awareness may reach even the common man in every society. With this objective Human Rights as a subject is introduced as a compulsory subject in some universities and colleges. At present, several universities are introducing this subject as a compulsory subject at the postgraduate level. Human Rights is also introduced as a undergraduate and Postgraduate degree course in some universities. The Supreme Court of India is also stressing the importance of its introduction in the curricula of schools, colleges and Universities. In the 21st century, Human Rights as a subject gained much importance.

Three Generation of Human Rights

As we all know, the rights were not introduced in one day or by any individual ruler. The contemporary concept of Human Rights evolved over the years. They may be broadly classified into three generations of Human Rights. The first generation Rights are mostly related with the civil and political rights of the individual or the liberty oriented rights. These were meant to impose negative obligations on governments to desist from interfering with the exercise of individual liberty.[4] Since the 19th century, these rights were among the major concerns of all liberal and democratic movements all-over the world.

It is realized that social, economic and cultural rights are also equally important for the well-being of individuals and the society. The second generation rights are those which can be said to be 'security-oriented' and provide for social, economic and cultural rights. These rights are more positive in nature. It is the duty of the state to ensure that these rights should be realized. The Universal Declaration of Human Rights contains the essence of these two generation rights. It was passed by the UNO in 1948 and was an important landmark in the history of human rights.

The third generations of Human Rights are of relatively recent origin. They have evolved in recent years in response to new concerns in which the international consensus has emerged. They mainly focus on environmental, cultural and developmental rights.[5] They are concerned with rights of groups and peoples rather than of individuals. It includes the right to self-determination and the right to development. The developing countries have played an important role in bringing these rights into focus. The Declaration on the Right to Development adopted by the UN General Assembly in 1986 is the most important example in this direction.

Importance of Rights and Duties

One must understand that rights and duties are inseparable. In fact, the Rights and Duties are interrelated and are the two sides of a coin. If duty is the foundation, the rights are the superstructure constructed above that foundation. Duties can be broadly classified into moral duties and legal duties. Moral duties cannot be imposed on the individual through a court of law since it is only an expectation. Social service, maintenance of environment, having compassion towards fellow beings, helping others in distress are some of the examples of moral duties. One can expect these qualities from an individual but cannot punish anyone in the court of law if they do not follow these duties. But if anyone violates a legal duty he can be punished by the Government. Every right has a corresponding obligation or duty. Without duties there can be no rights. One can enjoy his rights only when he respects the rights of others.

While individuals are interested in protecting their rights they have some obligation to the state. There are certain important duties related to Government and a citizen is expected to adhere to these duties. Allegiance to state is an important duty of a citizen. Cooperating with the government, protecting the motherland during war time, helping the state to maintain law and order are some of the duties the people should perform. To obey the law of the land respecting the national flag and national anthem is also regarded as an important duty. Protecting the sovereignty, unity and integrity of India, respecting women, preservation of our composite culture and Protecting the natural environment are other important duties. Even though people have right to oppose a law that is against their interest, they are normally expected to cooperate with the Government. Properly evaluating the policies and functions of any Government is also the duty of the people. Properly paying tax to the Government is also an important duty.

Earlier, the government is concerned mostly with the maintenance of law and order.[6] As time passes on, most of the Governments are concerned with the welfare of its citizens. These welfare Governments plans a lot and needs a vast financial resources. The people must pay their taxes properly to support monetary needs of their Governments. The proper exercise of franchise and holding public office is another important duty. In a democracy, exercise of voting right is essential. The vote ultimately determines the formation of any Government and the voter must carefully exercise his option. Unfortunately, in countries like India, only 45 to 60 per cent of voters are normally exercising their right of voting in every election. The percentage decreases considerably in Metropolitan cities. The apathy of the voter may affect the winning chances of good candidates and consequently a good Government. Likewise, the people must join important public offices as a member to exercise his duties. These are some of the important duties that must be performed by the citizens.

Theories of Human Rights

As we discussed earlier, the theories of human rights evolved over a period of time. Different scholars belong to different countries and time recorded their perception of human rights. Thus, in the evolution of human history, several theories on Human Rights emerged. The following are some of the important theories that can be analyzed for understanding the contents of rights:

(i) The Theory of Natural Rights
(ii) The Legal Theory of Rights
(iii) The Historical Theory of Rights
(iv) The Idealistic Theory of Rights
(v) The Social Welfare Theory of Rights
(vi) The Economic Theory of Rights.

Theory of Natural Rights

Among the number of existing theories, Natural rights theory is the earliest theory on Human Rights. It is simple in explanation. It stress that certain rights are so essential to personal life that they are termed as 'Natural'. It is based on the belief that nature as an original creating force gave to every man the power of finding the right principles on which anyone can organize his life. It is believed that these principles are based upon the universal law, the law of nature, and are common to all people residing in various parts of the world. This theory emphasize that it is the product of human nature, that is, all men are born with certain rights. It must be noted here that these rights are inalienable. It is believed that it cannot be separated from the human beings by any force on earth.

The concept of natural rights actually originated in ancient Rome. It discovered that men of all races and countries living under the control of Roman rule seemed to have some common rules of life. This body of principles common to all men was termed as Natural Law by the Romans. Considerable part of their legislation was based upon these Natural Laws. Cicero is an important scholar who propounded the theory of Natural Rights. In the middle Ages, Natural Law was associated with the Law of God and of the Church. The hold of Church lost its grip after eighteenth century. Locke argues that certain rights were natural and approved by God. The Law of Nature, according to Locke stands as an eternal rule to all men, legislators as well as others. The need for a civil society was felt because of the presence of certain inconveniences in the state of nature and men agreed to transfer some of the rights in order to safeguard the remaining natural rights.[7] They were life, liberty and property. The American Declaration of Rights and the Declaration of French National Assembly during the French Revolution gave a new emphasis to the doctrine of Natural Rights.[8] But Bentham rejected the concept of Natural Rights. To him Natural Rights are 'simple nonsense'. Thus Bentham made an end of Natural Rights. Bentham opposed the concept of natural rights on the plea that every right has a corresponding duty. Each duty has some sanctions behind it like legal, moral or religious. But there is no such thing as a natural sanction behind any duty. Hence, there is no such thing as 'natural duty' and therefore, there are no natural right was his argument.

Legal Theory of Rights

Contrary to our understanding of Natural Rights the scholars argue that there are no rights which inherent in man. To them, laws are created and maintained by the state and neither they are prior nor anterior to the state. Normally, the state formulates and defines rights. It has rights to restrict their scope and provide guarantees for their enjoyment by men. State is the source of all rights and hence there can be no rights without or against the state. To have rights against the state is equal to saying that the individual has no rights at all. But such a theory of rights is not acceptable to many scholars. Laski argued that the state does not create rights, but only recognizes them. A system of rights derived purely from law cannot be permanent. It stressed that Law is not the only source of rights. The real source of rights is our conception of right and wrong. With this different argument, the legal theory does not give us a satisfactory explanation of rights. But all the arguements of the supporters of legal theory cannot be set aside. Rights which are not supported by the Laws of the state remain only as a claim. According to Barker, the state is the immediate source of rights. Laski rightly pointed out that "every state is known by the rights it maintains". Therefore, a right has both a moral and legal reference.

Historical Theory of Rights

According to Historical theory of Rights, the rights are the product of history. Ritchie pointed out that "those rights which people think they ought to have are just those rights which they have been accustomed to have, or which they have a tradition of having once possessed". Edmond Burke maintained that the French Revolution was based on the abstract rights of men, whereas the English Revolution is based on the customary rights of people of England. One can accept that there is much truth in the historical theory of rights and many of our rights really can be traced back from the primitive customs. Rights change with the facts of time and place. Therefore, history, as such is not the only basis of rights and the customs do not provide an absolute right.

Idealistic Theory of Rights

This theory is popularly known as the Personality Theory. By this theory, rights are the external conditions essential to men's real development. According to Heinrici, a right is really necessary to the maintenance of material conditions essential to the existence of human personality.[9] The Idealistic theory reiterates the creation of those conditions which helps man to reach the fullest level of his personality. The Idealistic theory of Rights appeals to the moral and democratic rights of man, as it relates right to morality rather than reality. It does not subordinate the self-development of man to the social whole.

Social Welfare Theory of Rights

The scholars like Jeremy Bentham and J.S. Mill hold that rights are conditions of social welfare. They are the creation of the society. Hence, law, customs, traditions and the natural rights should yield to what is socially useful.[10] The right to property does not mean the right of few people to prosper at the cost of many individuals. Bentham and Mill are the real exponents of the Social Welfare Theory of Rights. They formulated the principle of the greatest of happiness of greatest number and made it the criterion of utility. One's rights are built upon his contribution to the well-being of society and one cannot have rights against the public welfare. Rights, as such, are built upon the utility to the individual and the community they live. But there is criticism against the theory that any social system which ignores individual personality and glorifies the common interest of society cannot prosper.

Economic Theory of Rights

Regarding the economic theory of rights, the contribution of Karl Marx is noteworthy. The teachings of Karl Marx inspire the economic theory of rights. It rejects the concept of Natural and inalienable rights and other rights as an explanation of the nature of rights. Marx regards that the state as a coercive agency, safeguards the interest of the dominant group in the society. Marx explained the political, social, religious and other institutions of any given historical period are determined by economic factors, which is essentially the mode of production. He pointed out that in every system of production one can see the rise of two opposing classes, the exploiters and exploited.[11] The clash between the two classes is inevitable and it is a continuing process in human history.

The idea of Marx coincides with the thought process of Laski. The laws made by the governing class are aimed to protect the interest of this group alone. Hence, rights are as such neither the product of human nature nor their origin traced by the customs. The economic structure of the society is the foundation on which the political system of a country is built and legal framework created. Karl Marx believes that rights can exist only in a classless society. He dismissed all talk of rights in a capitalistic society. There is truth in the argument of Karl Marx. But all that Karl Marx argues is not acceptable. The laws of the state are the outcome of different sources and not the work of economic class alone. The communist countries reflected the concept of economic rights in their constitutions, but the civil rights were subordinated to economic rights.

The above analysis clearly indicates that there is not one single theory which can sufficiently explain the origin and nature of rights. Each theory is the product of its own time. It relates to the genius of the scholars who formulated such theories. We will accept that there is some element of truth in all these theories. We should not forget one eternal truth that the individual good and social good goes together. Society is an organic unity and the welfare of the community is built upon the welfare of the individual. Both go hand in hand and complement each other. This is the essence of rights.

We understood that the Human Rights are essential for the fullest possible development of one's own personality and for his happiness. The modern concept of Human Rights does not exist in the ancient societies. But in one form or the other, some rights exist in almost all the societies at different points of time. These rights are considered as natural and inalienable. As human civilization advances, the concept of human rights also advances. The Medieval Era gives importance to God and Church and thereby relegated the rights of man to oblivion. That was why Will Durant termed the period as the 'Age of Faith'. One can trace the origin of the three generation of rights and their respective importance to the advancement of humanity. The different theories on human rights represent different dimensions of human rights and each theory contains some valid truth. There is no single theory that can represent all the ingredient of human rights.

Historical Development of Human Rights

The Human Right as we understood today evolved with the advancement of civilization. It was a slow and painful process. All countries do not enjoy Human Rights equally at any given period of time. At the beginning, the rights enjoyed by men were termed as

Natural Rights. Almost all societies and cultures give some sort of rights to its people. Since kingship was mostly the order of the day, king was the final authority in anything. He can give or take away any right as he pleases. The Greeks realized the importance of rights among their citizens. In the middle age which was the 'Age of Faith', religion determines everything including the individual's right. Only after the seventeenth and eighteenth century, scholars openly favoured the importance of individual's rights.

In England, the people asserted their right through Magna Carta and Bill of Rights.[12] The American Declaration of Independence and the French Declaration of the Rights of Man and Citizen also represented the desire of people to have their freedom and rights. Changes witnessed in industrial and agrarian front changed the mode of production and consequently a new social order sets in. The Labour uprisings and related developments slowly changed the outlook on individual's right. Finally, the two world wars exhibit the gross violation of Human Rights in an unprecedented scale.[13] A systematic effort was made to protect human rights all-over the world through agencies like UNO. It heralded a new era in the history of human rights. As such from early times, the concept of human rights evolved slowly in accordance with the changing needs of time.

Evolution of Human Rights in England

Magna Carta (1215 A.D.)

In the History of Human Rights, the first call for right was raised in England. King John II of England who ruled during the early part of 13th century was a most unpopular king. He was known for treachery, cruelty and cowardliness. He never bothered about the welfare of his people. He earned the wrath of not only the common man but also the nobles and clergy. Hence, people decided to establish their rights. After considerable struggle and pressure the king was forced to obey the popular will. Finally, in June 15, 1215 A.D., he met the people and their leaders and signed the document prepared by them. This popular document is referred to as the Magna Carta.

The Magna Carta established the rights of the public over the authority of their ruler.[14] It was considered as a Great Document uplifting the rights of the subjects. Its impact was felt not only in England but all-over the world. This document contains 63 subdivisions elaborating on the rights of English citizens and regulated the arbitrary power of the British monarch. It became guidelines to the future rulers of England. It implied that even though the king enjoys absolute power he cannot encroach upon the rights of individuals too much. Magna Carta stress that the king should not tax the public without the concurrence of the Parliament. He should not imprison anyone without valid reason. He must deliver justice impartially. The people also regained their right to prayer in the Churches. If the king deviate from the path of justice people can set right his course of action.

Since Magna Carta was created by the people's movement it led to the emergence of democracy in England. In the field of justice, equality, and in the customs and conventions people proved that they have the power to control the authority of their ruler. It was such a major event happened for the first time in history that led to the healthy development of democratic institutions. This document is considered as a foundation to the rights of the people and guaranteed its implementation to the succeeding generations. Hence, it is termed as Magna Carta. (Great Charter)

Petition of Rights (1628 A.D.)

Charles I, the king of England was proud and strongly believed in the Divine Right of Kings. In Europe, the Divine Right of King underlined the importance of king as the representative of God. Hence, he should not be questioned by anyone and be treated almost like the God. Even though Charles I made several promises to his people and the Parliament, he never fulfilled them. His foreign policy was a total failure. He was forced to send an expedition to La Rochelle under the command of Buckingham to help the French Protestants (Huguenots) who had been attacked by the French king. The expedition failed and the Huguenots surrounded to the French Government. This offended the English and their Parliament. The people disliked the king's favourites like Buckingham. This period witnessed the struggle between the Parliament and the king of England.[15] Charles I needed money but his second Parliament refused to grant him any money till he redressed its grievances. It also expected him to improve his qualities.

The House of Commons, headed by Sir John Eliot accused Buckingham of wasting money and neglected the interests of the country. Since he abused power the Parliament wanted to impeach him. But Charles I dissolved the Parliament to save Buckingham. Since the Parliament refused to grant him money he decided to make use of illegal ways to raise money. By 'forced loan' he demanded money from five Knights. When they refused payment he imprisoned these respectable persons. The ordinary people were forced to serve as soldiers. He forced the public to provide free food and shelter to his soldiers (billeting). The disputes between soldiers and civilians were not tried in the ordinary courts of England. But instead it was tried by a military court under a military officer. Even the court was forced to obey the improper orders of the king even though they were against the legal system. Despite these unconstitutional means Charles could not get the money he needed. Charles I called his third Parliament in 1628 A.D. to meet his financial needs. But the Parliament refused to grant him money till he carries on the government in accordance with the law of the land. The Parliament determined to check the king's attempt of encroachment on the rights and liberties of the people.

Provisions and Its Importance

The English Parliament drew up the Petition of Rights with several clauses to protect the rights of the public:

- (i) It stressed that the levying of taxes or loans by the king without the consent of Parliament was illegal.
- (ii) All arbitrary imprisonment of free men was illegal.
- (iii) The king should not impose any martial law in times of peace.
- (iv) The private citizens should not be forced to provide food and shelter to soldiers and sailors of soldiers.
- (v) The petition incorporated the four cardinal points—arbitrary taxation, arbitrary imprisonment, martial law and billeting.

These conditions were unacceptable to King Charles I. Though he was hesitant to give his consent to the petition, he needed the money very badly. He knew that he cannot raise it without the consent of the Parliament. In the compelling circumstances he signed the petition of Right and the Parliament granted him the money he needed. Charles I accepted the petition and promised to abide by its clauses. But he violated every clause of the petition with deliberate intention later.

The Petition of Rights was a great landmark in the constitutional history of England. It was regarded as the Second Great Charter of English liberties; the first was the Magna Carta and the third The Bill of Rights. It limited the powers of the king and safeguarded the rights and liberties of the people of England. The illegal powers of the arbitrary government were checked. Since he violated the clauses of the document, he paid a heavy price of his life for this mistake. He foolishly sacrificed himself for the sake of arbitrary power and prestige. All the developments related to the petition of Rights show how people was eager to protect their own rights despite the threat from their own ruler. They struggled to establish the will of common man over the arbitrary authority of their king. In the evolution of Human Rights these attempts strengthened the resolve of the people to uphold their rights above everything.

Bill of Rights and Its Provisions (1689 A.D.)

The struggle between the king and the Parliament which represented the people of England continued even during the reign of James II. The king wanted to establish the Divine Right of Kings and wanted to rule as an absolute monarch. In taxation, foreign policy making and in religious view he wanted to impose his will. It was challenged by the people. It led to the Glorious Revolution which was termed as the Bloodless Revolution. It ended the despotism of the king and heralded the victory of Parliamentary Government. After the flight of King James II, the Parliament declared that he abdicated the throne which falls vacant. It was jointly offered to William III and Marry.

In the Declaration of Rights, the conditions on which the throne was offered to William and Marry were clearly spelt. William and Marry agreed the conditions and became King and Queen of England. The crown was jointly accepted by them on their binding themselves by the terms given in the declaration. The convention Parliament enacted the Declaration of Rights as the Bill of Rights. It rejected the illegal claims and actions of James II. It also set forth the conditions under which England was to be governed by William and Marry and also by the future rulers of England.

1. The suspending and dispensing powers of King are illegal.
2. The prerogative courts to dispense justice like the Ecclesiastical Commission court, etc. are illegal.

3. Without the consent of the Parliament the king cannot raise or maintain a standing army in time of peace.
4. Without consent of Parliament the King cannot levy taxes and raise money.
5. The King should not interfere in the elections of the Parliament. The Members of Parliament should enjoy freedom of speech and debate. The Parliament must meet frequently to do its business.
6. The people have the right to petition the King.
7. Excessive fines and cruel punishments should not be inflicted.
8. Jurymen must be honestly chosen.
9. The Protestants may keep arms for purpose of self-defence as permitted under the Law of England.
10. No Roman Catholic King or Queen or a person marrying a Roman Catholic shall in future possess or inherit the crown.

The Bill of Rights was an important document that completed the work began by the Magna Carta and forms the third Great Charter of liberties of the English people. It established the supremacy of Parliament and limited the powers of the monarchy. From the Human Rights point of view, it safeguarded the popular rights and liberties.

The Act of Atlainder, which was passed in England in 1641, declared that the special courts of King were not beyond the jurisdiction of common law of the land. It established Rule of Law and demonstrated that the law is above the authority of the King. Another important development that protects the rights of the people of England was the passage of *Habeas Corpus*. It stresses that anyone who is arrested should be produced before the judge and should be explained the reasons for his arrest. If a person is released he should not be arrested again for the same crime for which he was arrested earlier. The official who violates this provision should also be punished. This Act protected the individual's liberty. Even today this *Habeas Corpus* is effectively used by those who were arrested arbitrarily in countries like India. It is a shield of protection for individual liberty from the arbitrary power of state and individuals.

Hugo Grotis, almost during the same period, wrote on the development of Natural Rights theory. He stressed that all men are equal and independent and they must respect rights of others and the law among nations. The next stage in the evolution of Human Rights was the Social Contract Theory of Rousseau, who was a popular political philosopher of France. His popular quote that *man was born free and found everywhere in chains* changed the fate of several countries. It has its influence on the American Declaration of Independence and the French Revolution.

Significance of American Declaration of Independence (1776 A.D.)

Driven by the spirit of liberty, the migrants from England created a new economic system in USA. The lifestyle evolved in USA was totally different from the English life. In course of time, the emigrants thought that they will prosper only if they liberate from the clutches of England. Due to variety of factors writers, clergymen, lawyers and other sections of the society joined together with those who wanted to liberate from English control. The movement which is popularly referred to as the sons of liberty expanded the struggle against the British. In 1774 A.D., twelve colonies passed the Declaration of Rights and Grievances. It pinpointed the flaws in the English Constitution and stressed the rights of American people. The writings of several prominent writers like Thomas Paine stimulated the feeling of independence. When the British Government failed to redress the grievances of the colonies they declared independence on June 7, 1776 A.D. The Declaration was drafted mostly by Thomas Jefferson, and represented the passion for freedom that was in the hearts of many other Americans.[16]

The Third Continental Congress attended by delegates from English colonies in North America on 4th July, 1776 adopted the *Declaration of Independence.* The war of independence had already started and was to continue for another six years. The Declaration, however, was an official declaration of independence by the American colonies and formation of the United States of America. The significance of the Declaration goes beyond an expression of the colonies' reasons for proclaiming their independence from Britain. 'Its worldwide significance lies in the assertion that all men are created equal, that they are endowed by their Creator with certain unalienable rights that among these, are Life, Liberty, and the pursuit of Happiness'. Excerpts from the Declaration are given below:

> When, in the course of human events, it becomes necessary for one people to dissolve the political bonds which have

> connected them with another, and to assume, among the powers of the earth, the separate and equal station to which the laws of nature and of Nature's God entitle them, a decent respect to the opinions of mankind requires that they should declare the causes which impel them to the separation.
>
> We hold these truths to be self-evident, that all men are created equal, that they are endowed by their Creator with certain unalienable rights that among these are Life, Liberty, and the pursuit of Happiness. That to secure these rights, governments are instituted among Men, deriving their just powers from the consent of the governed, That whenever any Form of Government becomes destructive of these ends, it is the Right of the people to alter or to abolish these ends, and to institute a new Government, laying its foundation on such principles, and organizing its powers in such form, as to them shall seem most likely to effect their Safety and Happiness, Prudence, indeed, will dictate that Governments long established, should not be changed for light and transient causes; and accordingly all experience hath shown, that mankind are more disposed to suffer, while evils are sufferable, than to right themselves by abolishing the forms to which they are accustomed. But when a long train of abuses and usurpations, pursuing invariably the same Object, evinces a design to reduce them under absolute Despotism, it is their right, it is their duty, to throw off such Government and to provide new Guards for their future security. Such has been the patient sufferance of these Colonies, and such is now the necessity which constraints them to alter their former Systems of Government. The history of the present King of Great Britain is a history of repeated injuries and usurpations, all having, in direct object, the establishment of an absolute Tyranny over these States...

The Declaration of American Independence was an important document in the evolution of political freedom. This declaration is known for clarity of thought, and forceful expression of ideas. It is divided into five sections. The Preamble, a succinct statement of underlying political theories, various charges against the King of Britain, the failed attempts to secure redressal of grievances within the empire and an assertion of the independent status of thirteen states were included in these five broad divisions. In the evolution of Human Rights, it plays a significant part like the declarations made during the French Revolution.

Contribution of French Revolution to Human Rights (1789 A.D.)

In 1789 A.D., the French Revolution broke out. The storming of the fortress of Bastille, a state prison, by the people of Paris on 14th July that year symbolized the end of autocracy and of the old regime in France. The National Assembly of France which had started meeting in June 1789 adopted the Declaration of the Rights of Man and Citizen on 26th August, 1789 as a preamble to the new constitution that it was framing for France. This Declaration was truly international in its appeal and inspired revolutionary and democratic movements in almost every country of Europe and in Central and South America and later, in Asia and Africa. It proclaimed that "all men being born equal should have equal rights."[17]

The French Revolution occupies an important place in the world history. The revolution not only changed the fate of France but also acted as a catalyst in changing the political structure of several other countries. 'Liberty, Equality and Fraternity' were the three magic words that heralded the beginning of new era in individual freedom and right. Men born free and have equal rights. It is the duty of the Government to provide protection to the individual from exploitation. He must enjoy liberty, inheritance and protection from the Government. He must be given the right to oppose any attempt of suppression of his rights. Sovereignty is vested only with the people. An individual or an organisation cannot execute power without the due sanction from the public will. The law of the land should be recognized by the legislature. These abovesaid ideas were reflected in the Constitution of France which was passed after the French Revolution in 1791.

The French Declaration of the Rights of Man and Citizen is one of the basic charters of human liberties which inspire the French Revolution. The document contains 17 articles which were adopted in 1789 by the National Assembly of France. It was also served as the preamble to the Constitution of 1791. Later, it was followed by another Constitution in 1793 in which the declaration became the preamble. It was re-titled as the Declaration of the Rights of Men. Again in the Constitution of 1795, the Declaration was used as the preamble. It was also re-titled as the Declaration of the Rights and Duties of Man and the Citizen. The text of the declaration is given below:

> The representatives of the French people, constituted as a National Assembly, considering that ignorance, disregard or contempt of the rights of man are the sole causes of public misfortunes and governmental corruption, have resolved to set forth a solemn declaration of the natural, inalienable and sacred rights of man: in order that this declaration, by being constantly present to all members of the social body, may keep them at all times aware of their rights and duties: that the acts of both the legislative and executive powers, by being liable at every moment to comparison with the aim of all political institutions, may be the more fully respected: and that demands of the citizens by being founded henceforward on simple and incontestable principles, may always rebound to the maintenance of the constitution and the general welfare.

The Assembly consequently recognizes and declares, in the presence and under the auspices of the Supreme Being, the following rights of man and the citizen:

1. Men are born and remain free and equal in rights. Social distinctions may be based only on common utility.
2. The aim of all political association is to preserve the natural and inprescriptible rights of man. These rights are liberty, property, security and resistance to oppression.
3. The principle of all sovereignty rests essentially in the nation. No body and no individuals may exercise authority which does not emanate from the nation expressly.
4. Liberty consists in the ability to do whatever does not harm another: hence the exercise of the natural rights of each man has no limits except those which assure to other members of society the enjoyment of the same rights. These limits can only be determined by law.
5. Law may rightfully prohibit only those actions which are injurious to society. No hindrance should be put in the way of anything not prohibited by law, nor may any man be forced to do what the law does not require.

6. Law is the expression of the general will. All citizens have the right to take part, in person or by their representatives, in its formation. It must be the same for all whether it protects or penalizes. All citizens being equal in its eyes are equally admissible to all public dignities, offices and employments, according to their capacity, and with no other distinction than that of their virtues and talents.
7. No man may be indicted, arrested or detained except in cases determined by law and according to the forms which it has prescribed. Those who instigate, expedite, execute or cause to be executed arbitrary orders should be punished; but any citizen summoned or seized by virtue of the law should obey instantly, and renders himself guilty by resistance.
8. Only strictly necessary punishments may be established by law, and no one may be punished except by virtue of a law established and promulgated before the time of the offence, and legally put into force.
9. Every man being presumed innocent until judged guilty, if it is deemed indispensable to keep him under arrest, all rigours not necessary to secure his person should be severely repressed by law.
10. No one may be disturbed for his opinions, even in religion, provided that their manifestation does not trouble public order as established by law.
11. Free communication of thought and opinion is one of the most precious of the rights of man. Every citizen may therefore speak, write and print freely, on his own responsibility for abuse of this liberty in cases determined by law.
12. Preservation of the rights of man and the citizen requires the existence of public force. These forces are therefore instituted for the advantage of all, not for the private benefit of those of whom they are entrusted.
13. For maintenance of public forces and for expenses of administration common taxation is necessary. It should be apportioned equally among all citizens according to their capacity to pay.
14. All citizens have the right, by themselves or through their representatives, to have demonstrated to them the necessity of public taxes, to consent to them freely, to follow the use

made of the proceeds and to determine the shares to be paid, the means of assessment and collection and the duration.

15. Society has the right to hold accountable every public agent of administration.
16. Any society in which guarantee of rights is not assured or the separation of powers not determined has no constitution.
17. Property being an invincible and sacred right, no one may be deprived of it except for an obvious requirement of public necessity, certified by law, and then on condition of a just compensation in advance.[18]

Industrial and Agrarian Revolution and Human Rights

Industrial Revolution

Industrial Revolution changed many things in the world. It created a new kind of opportunities for a few and led to the exploitations of millions of people all-over the world. In the later half of the eighteenth century remarkable inventions led to increased production and it changed the character of British Industry. The essence of industrial revolution was the use of power driven machinery for large scale production. It needs huge capital and organized gangs of wage earning hands. Machineries in spinning and weaving steam engines revolutionized the industrial scenario. This invention threw million of people out of work. The machinery which substituted labourers increased the output of production at cheaper cost. The people cannot escape the impact of industrial revolution.[19] Large scale human right violations became the order of the day when the people moved to the cities in search of job in factories. In course of time, the suffering working class started organizing labour unions to fight for their rights. In the evolution of human rights it was another important development. In a sense, industrialization heralded human rights.

In the history of Human Rights, the industrial revolution had momentous consequences. England became the leading manufacturing country of the world. Goods were manufactured on a large scale and the owners of the factory were eager to find new markets to sell their goods. British coal was supplied to various parts of the world. Introduction of machinery took the work out of the hands of the people and destroyed the native system of industry. Many people who survived with manual labour were thrown out of work.

Their condition became very pathetic. Due to competition those who used outdated tools were driven out of the market by their competitors. Big capitalists minted money and became more influential.

The industrial revolution had its effect on the distribution of wealth which became more unequal than before. Underpaid workers starved under the wealthy industrialist. These developments created two hostile camps—'Haves and Have-nots'. People started migration towards the north and west of England where iron and coal, essential raw material for industrial production was available in plenty. New cities were created with all the attendant problems. Another important development was the struggle between the capitalist and the workers. The workers who had to work in workshop for longer hours were not properly paid. They pay only very poor wages despite the heavy work extracted from them. Unemployment, distress and poverty followed suit. Naturally, all these led to a struggle between capital and labour. Consequently, a class of men known as socialists emerged in the industrial front. They demanded reforms and wanted to improve their conditions.

The factory owners preferred women and child labour because of their cheaper wages. Their miserable condition and violation of Human Rights led to the passage of many factory laws later. The labourers realized that their owners becoming richer and richer by systematically exploiting them. In order to improve their living conditions they started forming trade unions. Trade unions are organized to protect the working class through collective bargaining. One another social effect of the industrial revolution was the widespread unemployment which created many problems for the industrialized countries. An entirely new set of problems arose out of factory system. The workers demanded shorter working hours and got them after much struggle and sacrifice. When the factory workers demanded reasonable working hours with other basic rights they were fired upon by the police in USA. Several workers died in this incident which took place on 1st day of May. The workers got some of the rights which were demanded and the day was remembered and celebrated all-over the world as 'May Day'. The industrial revolution led to many changes and the emerging working class demanded their own rights and obtained them in a painful process. Due to some political changes, some of these rights were plucked away in some countries later.

Despite advancement of civilization in several parts of the world, including USA, reeled under the horrors of slavery. In the 19th century, attempts were made for the abolition of slavery. There was growing sensitiveness on the moral evil of this institution. The child labour and the way in which children were ill-treated created a strong sense of injustice. It was felt that the moral atmosphere in which the children worked was harmful in the extreme. Physically, intellectually, morally, the result could only be the creation of stunted human beings. This evil system was defended by political economists, manufactures and statesman in the name of individual liberty. Finally, the Factory Act of 1833 was passed by the efforts of English humanitarians. It prohibited the employment of children below nine years of age in spinning and weaving factories. In course of time, several such Acts were passed to improve the condition of the workers. In the evolution of Human Rights, the industrial revolution and the agrarian revolution had its impact in shaping the concept of Human Rights.

Agrarian Revolution

Greater production was achieved in the field of agriculture due to a number of improvements and changes in the later part of 18th century. Ultimately, these developments in England led to the agrarian revolution. Better tools were invented and farming was done more scientifically. Jethro Tull invented a machine for sowing seed. The breed of sheep and cattle improved. A new breed of sheep was introduced that gave both wool and mutton. Rotation of crops was introduced which increased the quantity and quality of the agricultural products. New forms of manure were discovered and an improved method of drainage was introduced that increased productivity. Wastelands were reclaimed and made useful for agriculture. Areas of common land and open fields were permitted to enclose by the individuals through Acts of Parliament. It increased the production manifold.

For the small farmers the new scientific method of cultivation was not possible. Hence, they sold their lands and migrated to new towns to work in factories. The countryside suffered a severe drain in manpower. The importance of the capitalist agriculture increased. The small landowners and the labourers suffered a lot due to enclosure system, which prevented their cattle to graze on the common pastures on account of enclosures. Unable to survive in the countryside, the poor workers migrated to the new industrial sectors. The wages of landless labourers did not rise with prices. It led to starvation.

Generally speaking, the agrarian revolution rewarded rich landlord while punishing the poor worker and small landholders. Their migration created many problems. They lost their livelihood options in their own land and were forced to seek employment elsewhere. They joined with other migrating groups in the new towns. These developments seriously encroached upon the rights of millions of poor labourers. They suffered in silence.

Uprising of Labourers

The factories and industries became a major source of employment. Hence, the people in the country side slowly moved towards the new towns where these factories were located. Since the industrial revolution also created unemployment there was pressure to join in these industries. Their service conditions were not regulated. The producers with the help of Government authority exploited the workers to the core. Long hours of work coupled with poor working conditions in ill-ventilated factories affected the health and morale of the worker. Women and child labour were exploited without any sense of shame. Even though the workers migrated to the industrial areas with the hope of finding permanent employment, they were thrown out as sucked orange. The monotonous nature of long hours of work sapped their energy. They wanted to improve their condition through some action. But the workers were not organized. In such a situation, the trade unions and labour organisations made their presence felt. Slowly the workers were convinced about the need for trade unions.

The labourers struggle forced the factory management and the Government to look into their pressing problems. Everywhere the factory owners are not interested in the welfare of the workers. They are only interested in making quick profit through the exploitation of labour force. Such a state of affair cannot go unnoticed for a long time. The labourers learned the bitter lesson of fighting for their rights and survival through the labour uprising. Such uprising of workers was not an easy task considering their pathetic life.

Emergence of Trade Unionism

The industrial revolution led to the development of larger cities and increased the production manifold. But it also created a very difficult situation for the workforce. One of the evil effects of the industrial revolution was that it has made the condition of workmen in factories and workshops very deplorable. Their condition was all the more miserable on account over work, less pay, no educational and other opportunities of life and bad treatment by their masters. The industrial revolutions have divided the nations into two hostile camps: Wage payers and Wage earners. The workers thought it was impossible to live without some strong organizational support to solve their problems. Consequently, trade unions were founded. Weble rightly defined a trade union as a continuous association of wage earners with a view to maintain or improve their condition or employment through common action. The workers hoped that with the help of trade unions they can bargain with the management for better working condition and reasonable wages.

The owners who invested their capital in the factories were not amused by the emergence of trade unions. The labourers were treated very harshly by their masters. When all peaceful and persuasive methods failed, the workers resorted to strikes. The employers were very much offended by these strikes. They made the Parliament to pass Anti-combination Acts in 1799-1800 A.D. which declared the trade unions illegal and prevented any combination of workers to redress their grievances against the law of the state. Those who organized the strikes were regarded as the conspirators against the state and were heavily punished.

A strong and organized movement was set in motion to repeal the anti-combination laws. Francis led the agitation peacefully and got the support of several members of the Parliament of Great Britain. His efforts and protests led to the repeal of anti-combination laws in 1824 A.D. The workers were permitted to collectively settle their problems with the factory owners. But they could not use strike as a weapon. Robert Owen led the trade union movement successfully. In 1834, he was able to organize nearly half million men working in different trades under the banner of "Grand National Consolidated Trade Union". A general strike of the workers was tried but failed. It led to the split up of this union into number of smaller unions representing their own particular class. Because the labourers felt that within the working class there were different groups representing different types of workforce. Their interest may not coincide with each other. Hence, several smaller unions started functioning from different parts of Europe.

In their struggle for better wages and living condition the legislation brought out by the government also helped the workers. The Reform Bill of 1867 gave voting right to the workers in the towns. It helped them to improve their conditions. The Trade Union Congress was founded to look after the demands of workers. The government passed Trade Union Act of 1871 A.D. which served the charter of liberties. The Trade Unions were declared legal and the strikes were no longer regarded as a crime against the state. Hereafter, the trade unions became a powerful force in the country. In 1875, Employers and Workmen Act was passed which permitted peaceful picketing. In 1889, a large number of poor unskilled labourers organized a strike in the London docks and successfully settled their demands. Following this strike, the movement took a new turn in which new trade unions were formed with labourers as well as artisans as its members. Unionism became more democratic. The unionist favour vigorous strike and action through the Parliament. In course of time, several Factory Acts were passed in 1802, 1819, and 1833. The Mines Act in 1842 and Factory and Workshop Act of 1891 and 1931 were passed to improve the condition of the workers. Their working hours, leave, leisure, compensation and wages were effectively settled through legal means. These pioneering efforts of trade unions in England helped the workers of other countries to fight for their rights.

Following the success of Trade Unions in England, workers all-over the world started organizing trade unions and movements to protect their rights. In India also workers organized themselves in the textile unions in the 1920s and used strike as a means to settle their problem with the factory management. Later, workers of all other trades also started organizing the trade unions to protect the interest of workers. In Bombay and Madras, Trade Unions were started for the ship workers as well as for the textile labourers. The swadeshi leaders were active in helping the creation of worker's organisations and were instrumental in several strikes. Their contribution was notable in Railways, Jute Industry and in Government Press.[20]

Human Rights Violations During World Wars

As a consequence to Industrial Revolution several forces were unleashed. The industrial revolution also led to competition in many other fields. Industrialized nations of Europe and America are searching for markets as well as colonies to procure raw materials for industries. Search for colonies led to intense rivalry that led to building up of arms and ammunitions. Great powers like Britain, Germany, France and Russia started building up powerful armies and joined hands with other countries to form alliance against rival powers. It inevitably led to the First World War in 1914 which lasted up to 1918. It affected vast sections of people all-over the world.

In several ways, not only the countries participated in the war were affected but also the countries which were not part to this war were also affected. Millions of people were displaced due to the war and nine million people died and at least twenty million people were seriously wounded. The human rights violation was unimaginable. Children, women and elderly were not spared the horrors of war. Innocent people's rights were violated without any botheration on human dignity and civilization. Millions of people became stateless and wandered aimlessly in hostile environment. Following First World War, a great economic depression affected the entire world. Even richer countries like USA were not spared. Economic slowdown coupled with unemployment drastically affected the living standards of people. This indirect effect of world war also led to gross violation of human rights in the economic front. Starvation, famine and industrial stagnations killed millions of people.

The right to self-determination benefited only the big powers which finalized the Treaty of Paris in 1919. For smaller countries such benefits were only a distant dream. Unfortunately, Woodrow Wilson, the author of Fourteen Points was kept out of the League of Nations. The league was a major attempt to protect the world from another world war. This global organisation miserably failed in its primary goal and in preventing the violations of human rights.

The great powers miserably failed in keeping the spirit and purpose of this organisation. Their duplicity, hypocrisy and under hand dealings led to the outbreak of another world war which was more serious and dangerous in nature. The development of science and technology was directed towards invention of deadlier weapons of mass destruction. People suffered a lot during and after the world wars. In the Second World War, an estimated Twenty-five million people were died and fifty million people were wounded. Due to starvation, decease and destruction of properties the people were put to immense hardship. Acute scarcity of food, cloth, petrol, salt and cement created miserable condition. The birth rate fell during the world war. Thousand million dollars worth amount was wasted in the war. The spine-chilling atrocities created a doubt on the sanity of man. He behaved worse than the Stone Age man. The brutality and savageness of the 20th century men shocked the conscience of several right thinking people.

Hitler and Human Rights Violations

The German dictator, Adolph Hitler during the Second War systematically followed a policy of 'ethnic cleansing'. His war machine directed its entire attention in occupying several countries to realize his dream of global German empire. His secret police arrested millions of Jewish people as well as people from other occupied countries. They were brought to the Nazi concentration camps at Datchu, Auswitz and other places. They were tortured to death in the gas chambers, where poisonous gas was administered. Cruel methods of execution on mass scale were invented in these camps. Children and women were not spared the gallows of death.

Prisoners were forced to do many things which a normal human being would refuse to oblige. They prepared the ground for mass burial in which they themselves were buried later. When the large scale executions produced large number of corpses burial method was abandoned. Instead, in large ovens normally used in big bakeries, the dead bodies were burned to ashes. These details were kept secret till the end of war. Only when the Russian army entered in these camps surprisingly the truth came out. The German officials had limited time to destroy all the evidences in these concentration camps. It was shocking and the world leaders were unable to believe the methods and range of execution perpetrated under the Nazi leadership. Nearly 6 miilion Jews and other prisoners were mercilessly executed in these torture chambers.

When prisoners were moved from one place to another in cramped railway wagons they died due to lack of ventilation and proper food. They were killed like cattle for no offense committed. The inmates of these prisons were slowly starved to death. They were forced to do hard work beyond their capabilities. Even for fun and frolic they were killed by the German secret police. The horrors of Nazi camp stirred the conscience of people all-over the world. Consequently, films like 'The Scindler's list' were produced by Jewish directors like Steven Spielberg, to record these human right violations that were etched in the collective memory of the survivors of the Nazi camps. The concentration camps and the fate of the prisoners had profound impact on future steps towards realizing the goals of human rights. In order to punish the guilty, the Nuremberg War Crimes Tribunal enquired the crimes and punished them. It introduced the subject of gross violations of human rights in the main currents of international relations.[21]

Human Rights Violations by Japan

In the Asian front Japanese also committed serious human rights violations in the countries they have occupied. In Korea and other places, they forcibly abducted young women to satisfy the carnal pleasures of the Japanese soldiers. They were termed as 'pleasure woman' and were sexually exploited till the end of the war. The Japanese scientists used the innocent prisoners of war as a Guinea pig to conduct very dangerous experiments. Poisonous substances were injected on women and infants to test how they die under its administration. Rabies and other deadly viruses were also injected to study its effect on individuals. Instead of animals, human beings were directly used as a specimen to conduct various inhuman experiments. These experiments were carried out in Camp Ten and the details were destroyed after Second World War to avoid embarrassment to the Japanese Government. But till now the Japanese Government is facing hostile reception from the affected countries whenever the leaders visited those countries.

When Italy and Germany were defeated, the allied powers wanted to end the war at the earliest. But the Japanese continued their fighting. USA dropped atom bombs in Hiroshima on 6th August, 1945 followed by Nagasaki on 9th August, 1945 to make the Japanese surrender unconditionally. The effects of atom bomb were far reaching. The two cities were reduced to rubbles and lakh of people died in few seconds. The after effects of the atom bomb still trouble the people of Japan. The radiation fall out and its related health hazards affected thousands of people. It affected the fertility behaviour and seriously disturbed the genetic make-up of the people of these regions. Even though the bomb was dropped to end the war quickly it violated the human rights of hundreds and thousands of people in Japan. It was a bitter lesson to the Japanese people and their constitution drafted after the Second World War denounced war as a means to settle any dispute with other countries. Still Japan opposes testing of nuclear weapons by non-nuclear powers.

During the final stages of Second World War, the great leaders of England, USA and Soviet Union decided to create a world body to preserve world peace for ever. The horrors of human rights violations in Nazi Germany and other places made these leaders to pledge for the perseverance of human rights everywhere. Consequently, the UNO was formed and it became the champion of human rights. Eleanor Roosevelt, the wife of American President, F.D Roosevelt, played a very constructive role in preparing the Universal Declaration of Human Rights. The UNO and number of NGOs are playing very useful role in the perseverance of human rights at the global level.

The two world wars played a very important role in the evolution of human rights. Even though human rights were respected in one form or the other in the history of humanity, only after the Second World War a systematic effort was made to conceptualize the core of human rights with all its definitions and interpretations. A thorough study was made on human rights practices in different parts of the world and a systematic compilation of these rights were made. Nations were asked to endorse it and to implement it by embodying them in their respective Constitutions. It became an obligation and sometimes mandatory on the nations to respect and preserve these rights. Irrespective of the types of Government, the human rights became an integral part of every constitution. The UNO observes the human rights violations everywhere and through suitable legal, economic measures controls them.[22] If necessary, even war is also used as a means to make a country to respect human rights. While invading Iraq, one of a major reason cited by USA was the human right violation by Saddam Hussain on the minority Kurdish population though there were other ulterior motives for such step. The US legitimized its action on the ground of human rights violations by Saddam Hussain.

A look at the World History reveals the painful process through which human rights evolved. The human rights evolved with the growth of civilization. But its growth was not uniform. Depending upon the quality of kingship rights were given to their subjects. Human Rights were regarded as Natural Rights earlier as they were regarded as naturally endowed upon the human beings. No one can take away some of these basic rights was the idea of scholars earlier. As times pass on, the thought process on human rights also underwent several changes.

Through their Parliament the people of England fought for their rights and got them endorsed in their unwritten Constitution. The Magna Carta, the Petition of Rights and Bill of Rights followed by the Habeas Corpus Acts shows the determination of English people to fight for justice and for their rights. They fought against their Monarchs and forced them to heed to the popular will of the people. These attempts slowly restricted the unlimited powers of the Emperors under Divine Right theory and elevated the rights of the individuals in the pedestal. It was a great achievement.

In America, the people fought against the domination of their English Colonial masters. The American Declaration of Independence contained the essence of human rights prevailed at that time. The idea of several great scholars on human rights, found its place in the declaration as well as in the American Constitution. The breakout of French Revolution due to the tyranny of Louis XVI led to the French Declaration of the Rights of Man and Citizen. The three eternal principles 'Liberty, Equality and Fraternity' revolutionize human rights everywhere. The Industrial and Agrarian revolutions followed suit. These revolutions created many upheavals in the society and large scale migrations to new towns and cities created further problems. The exploitation of working class led to the formation of trade unions and workers, organisations to fight for their rights. In a painful process the workers negotiated for reasonable hours of work, wages, leave and other conditions by employing strikes as a weapon. The sacrifice of the lives of several workers in US on May 1 is remembered even today as 'May Day' (Worker's Day).

The concept of rights and its importance percolated slowly to the downtrodden people. The 20th century which was regarded as the 'Century of Human Rights' witnessed the outbreak of two world wars. The people suffered all type of human rights violations in its cruellest forms. Ultimately reason dawned on the great leaders who decided to put an end to these violations. A global organisation UNO was formed to protect the rights and dignity of human beings. It was an important event in the history of human rights and a systematic effort was made to conceptualize human rights with suitable interpretations. Countries were made to incorporate these rights in their constitutions and they must respect and observe these rights. This process was supervised by UNO and by several NGOs on human rights.

Questions

1. What is meant by Human Rights?
2. Examine the nature and scope of Human Rights.
3. Briefly define the rights and duties.
4. Examine theories on Human Rights.
5. Write a note on Magna Carta.
6. Bring out the significance of Petition of Rights.
7. How the American Declaration of Human Rights contributed for Human Rights?
8. Bring out the significance of French Revolution for upholding human rights.
9. Trace the relationship between Industrial Revolution and Human Rights.
10. Write a note on the emergence of Trade Unionism.
11. Write an essay on Human Rights violations during the World Wars.
12. Write an essay on the evolution of Human Rights.

Objective Questions

1. During the early periods Human Rights was termed as ....
   (a) Civil Rights (b) Social Rights
   (c) Natural Rights (d) Fundamental Rights.
2. Human Rights are ....
   (a) Inherited (b) Natural
   (c) Inalienable (d) All the above.
3. .... century was regarded as the century of human rights.
   (a) 18th (b) 19th
   (c) 20th (d) 21st.
4. The declaration of the Rights of Man and the Citizen was issued in the year ....
   (a) 1783 (b) 1789
   (c) 1919 (d) 1945.
5. To which scholar Natural Rights are 'simple nonsense'?
   (a) Bentham (b) John Locke
   (c) Cicero (d) Laski.

Key to Objective Questions

1. c 2. d 3. c 4. b 5 a.

NOTES

1. Arjun Dev, Indira Arjun Dev and Gupta Das, ed. *Human Rights: A Source Book* (New Delhi: National Council of Educational Research and Training, 1996), 27-126.
2. Peush Nag, "Human Rights: Meaning and History," in *Human Rights and Reforming the Law,* ed. B. Goswami (Jaipur: Raj Publishing House, 2008), 6-34.
3. A.C. Kapoor, *Principles of Political Science* (New Delhi: S. Chand & Co. Ltd., 1995), 234.
4. Arjun Dev, xiii.
5. Prakash Chander and Prem Arora, *Comparative Politics and International Relations* [Gurgaon: Cosmos Bookhive (P) Ltd., N.Y.], 496-98.
6. The British in India were concerned only about the protection of law and order and in the collection of taxes rather than the creation of a welfare society, see, Irfan Habib, *Essays in Indian History—towards a Marxist perception* (Aligarh: Tulika Books, 1995), 299-300.
7. William T. Bluhm, *Theories of the Political System* (New Delhi: Prentice-Hall of India Pvt. Ltd., 1981), 305-306.
8. Grant and Temperley, *Europe in the Nineteenth and Twentieth Centuries 1789-1950* (London: Longman Group Limited, 1976), 11.
9. A.C. Kapoor, 235.
10. David E. Apter, *Introduction to Political Analysis* (New Delhi: Prentice Hall of India, 1981), 98-102.
11. C.D.M. Ketelbey, *A History of Modern Times from 1789* (Bombay: Oxford University Press, 1976), 351.
12. Vincent A. Smith, *The Oxford History of England* (London: Oxford University Press, 1933), 220.
13. Besides the brutalities of war, Adolf Hitler and his 'Race theory' in practice led to the elimination of millions of Jews and other prisoners of war in concentration camps. George W. Southgate, *A Text book of Modern European History 1789-1960* (London: J.M. Dent and Sons Ltd., 1974), 216-217; and for the race theory and perception of Hitler see, Adolf Hitler, *Mein Kampf,* (*My Struggle*) (New Delhi: Adarsh Books, 2003), 295-297.
14. Vincent A. Smith, 68-69.
15. Wishan Das, *History of Great Britain* (*1485-1952*) (New Delhi: S. Chand & Co, (Pvt.) Ltd., 1975), 157.
16. C.P. Hill, *A History of the United States* [London: Edward Arnold (Publishers) Ltd., 1966], 30-31.
17. C.D.M. Ketelbey, 59.

18. Will and Ariel Durant, *The Lessons of History* (New York: Simon and Schuster, 1968), 39.
19. Bipan Chandra, Mridula Mukherjee and K.N. Panikkar, *India's Struggle for Independence* (New Delhi: Penguin Books, 1989), 212-214.
20. S.K. Sharma, *World Crisis in Human Rights* (Jaipur: Sublime Publications, 2007), 43-44.
21. Vinod Sharma, *Human Rights Violation: A Global Phenomenon* (New Delhi: A.P.H. Publishing Corporation, 2002), 224-225.

2

U.N.O. and International Human Rights

Human Rights exist in one form or the other in different parts of the world from the historical times. It evolved over the millennia and great scholars contributed for the wealth of knowledge on this subject. They gave different interpretations on the rights of men. But in reality mostly in the 20th century, human rights gained much importance. The first half of the 20th century witnessed several changes. During this period of history, several countries suffered under colonial rule and authoritarian rulers. Fascism and Nazism emerged as a challenge to democratic institutions. One can observe the rise of national liberation movements and movement for democracy in colonies during this period.

Enforcement of Human Rights up to World War II

During the period between the First World War and the Second World War several turbulences were witnessed. Hence the period was aptly described as the 'Age of Catastrophe'. The human rights violations were frequently occurred in a massive scale during these periods. Despite centuries of development and civilization men failed to honour rights of other men and violated it without any sense of guilt. The large scale violation of human rights covering millions of people during the war time shocked the conscience of the people. Great leaders of that time pondered over this issue and wanted to create a mechanism to protect human rights. They also wanted to find ways and means to prevent the outbreak of another world war. In the era of atom bomb they know the dangers of the outbreak of another world war that would annihilate the human race from the face of the earth.

After 1945, various developments in relation to the issues discussed above led to the conceptualization and articulation of human rights in their present meaning. The most significant feature of the new conceptualization was its universality. Even though the attempt made at the end of First World War in the form of League of Nations failed, the leaders were determined to protect the human rights and human dignity through a more powerful world body. The birth of UNO heralded a new era in the history of human rights. From this point of history, a systematic attempt was made to preserve human rights in all parts of the world irrespective of national boundaries. The leaders wanted to create a mechanism to look after all the works on human rights. An elaborate arrangement was made to collect documents and details related to human rights from various parts of the world. Experts and legal specialists on human rights issues discussed these documents and practices followed in several countries. Eleanor Roosevelt, the first lady of USA played a significant role in the drafting of Universal Declaration of Human Rights.

The Universal Declaration of Human Rights was proclaimed in 1948. It contained an elaborate list of human rights intended as 'a common standard of achievement for all peoples and all nations'. These rights are universally applicable. It was only a statement of principles and not a legal agreement between countries of the world. In other words, it is not a binding legal document. But the UDHR considerably influences the constitutions and legal systems of many countries including India. It was treated as a standard guideline on the issues involving human rights.

In the earlier chapters, the contemporary concepts of human rights evolved into three generation of rights were described. Several documents were brought into force on civil and political rights and on the economic, social and cultural rights. These documents and the creation of the League of Nations and the UNO are discussed briefly in this chapter.

League of Nations

The First World War, a major war conducted on global scale for several years destroyed the hope of millions of people. The large scale violations of human rights and senseless killings during the war stirred the conscience of leaders like Woodrow Wilson. They felt the need for an International machinery to prevent the outbreak of another major war. Earlier the Hague Conference of 1889, 1907 had settled the problem of eleven states through the verdict of Court of Arbitration. Woodrow Wilson, the President of USA prepared the ground for the League of Nations in his fourteen points. Through the treaty of Versailles in January 1920, 27 nations formed the League at first. Some of the important aims of the League were as follows:

1. There should be no outbreak of war in future.
2. The obligation of the League is prevention of war.
3. Providing cooperation for international peace and security.
4. Recognizing the international law as binding on the conduct of countries involved.
5. The League of Nations should uphold International Justice and honour the treaties.
6. The League makes necessary arrangements for peace treaties, Mandate system and to protect the National Minorities.

For the purpose of preventing the outbreak of war the League was created. It was a voluntary association of states.[1] It had no sovereignty, army or navy. The League functions through four organs namely the League Assembly, the League Council, the Secretariat-General and the Permanent Court of International Justice. The League Assembly was the biggest organ in which each state had one vote. A state can send not more than three representatives. Unanimous decision is necessary for non-procedural matters. The Assembly meets at least once in a year. Special sessions can be convened depending upon the necessity of the situation.

Among the various organs of the League of Nations the League Council was the most powerful organ. But the decision should be unanimous. There were five permanent and four non-permanent members in the council. Due to internal opposition, the USA stayed out of the League. Britain, France, Japan and Italy were the permanent members. In 1926, Germany was admitted as the permanent member. The Council normally convenes for four sessions in a year. The routine official work was looked after by the Secretariat-General. The Permanent Court of International Justice was looked after by nine judges and four deputy judges. One of the important special organisations of the League was the International Labour Office (ILO). It played a crucial role in solving the problems of the workers all-over the world.

Functioning of League

If we evaluate the functioning of League, which failed to achieve its primary goal of preventing the outbreak of another world war, we can find several shortcomings. The League functioned with heavy responsibility without adequate power. It followed an indirect method of action through investigation, reporting, mediation and publicity. Penalty for non-compliance was cutting of commercial relations with that country by other member states. The League succeeded in settling small disputes between various countries. The International Court of Justice did a commendable work by settling 27 cases and gave advisory opinion in several others. The International Labour Organisation did much in improving the working conditions of the labourers. The data gathered on the workers by ILO was useful in deciding several issues on labourers.

In countries like Austria, Hungary and Greece, the League did rehabilitation work. It took preventive steps to check the traffic in opium and made arrangements for the exchange of prisoners of war. It controls the spread of Malaria and suppressed traffic of women and children through various constructive steps. In 1923, the Permanent Slave (Eradication) Commission was constituted by the League. It also promoted intellectual cooperation among the nations. A considerable part of the constructive work did by the League involve human rights protection. But unfortunately, the League failed in its prime objective of preventing the outbreak of another major war. When the Second World War broke out in 1939, the League of Nations collapsed. The League property was taken over by the UNO later.

On non-political and non-military issues the League of Nations did commendable work. It facilitated international cooperation in education, science, labour and in cultural promotion. The failure of League was a warning and a lesson to the world community. Especially, one must appreciate the good work of the League in protecting the rights of women, children, refugees and labour.

Human Rights and U.N.O.

On October 24, 1945, the United Nations Organisation came into being. Nearly four years of planning led to the creation of this international organisation. It was designed to end war and promote peace, justice and better living condition for all mankind. The United

Nations Charter contains 111 articles, covering the purposes and principles of United Nations. The preamble clearly stipulated the guiding spirit of the United Nations. The basic aims of the United Nations are as follows:

1. To save succeeding generations from the horrors of war;
2. To reaffirm faith in fundamental human rights;
3. To establish justice and respect for the obligation arising from treaties and other sources of International Law; and
4. To promote social progress and better standards of life.

The UNO clearly stipulated the punishment for member states in extraordinary situations. Its Charter provides for the suspension and expulsion of members, but no provision has been made for withdrawal from membership. If a member state continuously violates the principle of the Charter it may be expelled from the UN Assembly on the recommendation of the Security Council. The Security Council has the power to restore these rights.

The Charter establishes six organs for the United Nations. They are the General Assembly, the Security Council, the Economic and Social Council (ECOSOC), the Trusteeship Council, the International Court of Justice and the Secretariat.

The General Assembly is the largest organ of UNO. It discusses every matter within the scope of the Charter. The member states can send up to five representatives but they can exercise only one vote. Important questions are decided by two-thirds majority of the members present and voting. All other questions are decided by simple majority of those voting. Normally, the Assembly has to meet once in a year in September but special session can be arranged. Six working committees and seven Vice Presidents under the President, look after the affairs for each session.

The non-permanent members of the Security Council are elected for two years by the Assembly. It also chooses all the eighteen members of the various councils of UNO and elects the 15 judges of the International Court of Justice. The General Assembly is given wide powers to initiate studies for promoting international cooperation in various fields. In promoting international cooperation in economic, social, cultural, education and health matters, the Assembly works mostly through the Economic and Social Council. The budget of UNO is considered and approved by the General Assembly.

The Security Council's main responsibility is the maintenance of international peace. The UK, USA, Russia, France and China are the five permanent members of this council. Six non-permanent members are elected for two years. Each member has one vote but the unanimous opinion of the Big Five members is essential in every case. These Big Five members were given veto power to say 'no' to a proposal. It is the most powerful organ of the UNO.

The Economic and Social Council consists of 27 members elected for a period of three years by the General Assembly. It mainly focuses its attention on making studies and reports on international economic, social, cultural, educational and health related matters. The activities of the specialized agencies are coordinated by ECOSOC.

The Trusteeship Council has to consider reports submitted by the administering authority. The mandatory system of the League has been improved as the Trusteeship system. This council ensures the political, economic, social and educational advancement of people living in any Trust Territories.

The International Court of Justice consists of 15 judges elected for a nine years term. After every three years five judges retire and new judges are appointed. Its Headquarters is at The Hague. This court decides those cases which involves two or more states. It also gives its advisory opinion on legal matters to various organs of the UNO.

The Secretariat is headed by the Secretary General of UNO. He is appointed by the General Assembly in consultation of the Security Council. He is the Chief Executive Officer. A large number of officials are assisting him in looking after the administration of UNO. The Secretariat is practically handling the entire administrative machinery of the UN effectively.

To deal with specific International Problems fourteen specialized agencies are operating in the UN. The International Labour Organisation (ILO), Food and Agricultural Organisation (FAO), U.N. Educational, Scientific and Cultural Organisation (UNESCO), International Monetary Fund (IMF), International Bank for Reconstruction and Development and World Health Organisation (WHO) are some of the important specialized agencies. Some of these agencies are playing a very crucial role in the maintenance of peace, decolonization and stimulating economic cooperation between the rich and poor nations. It tries to provide at least a square meal a day to the people of poor countries and is trying to provide opportunity for growth, education and freedom from disease. It is a major challenging task involving several complicated problems and funding issues.

Regarding the maintenance of human rights by the member countries, the UN plays a crucial role.[2] United Nations concern for human rights begins with the provision for the right to self-determination. By its covenant on Civil and Political Rights (1966), all people have right of determination. The UN takes the initiative for the International Conference on Human Rights in 1968. This conference resolved to protect and promote human rights all-over the world.

With the help of several National Organisations, the ECOSOC is doing great service for the protection of human rights. Several specialized agencies of UN were coordinated for this purpose. The ECOSOC has set-up the Commission on human rights in 1946. It prepared a detailed report for the implementation of the Charter on human rights. In 1967, the Council recommended the establishment of a UN High Commissioner's office for human rights. In course of time, the guidelines of UN on human rights were accepted as guiding principle by several governments. The Commission also investigates the violation of human rights by member states.[3] It takes suitable actions to change the situation in favour of those who are affected. Several countries including India have established National Human Rights Commission for the protection of human rights.

Evaluation of U.N.O.

After the end of Second World War, the cold war politics between the capitalistic countries under USA and the communist bloc under USSR created lot of tension. There was fear on the possibilities of another world war. But UNO played a constructive role during the critical years. In comparison to the League of Nations, the UNO played a crucial role in preventing the outbreak of another world war for more than six decades. Its role in the decolonization of the world is noteworthy. The end of Apartheid in South Africa is an important achievement from the human rights point of view. It resolved conflicts in several areas by negotiations and sending UN peace keeping force. Though slow, the economic and social issues handled by UN helped the poor all-over the world. Especially in Africa which is strife torn, the UN provided food and relief supplies. In Afghanistan also, it provides assistance to the internally displaced people. For the prevention and treatment of dreaded disease AIDS, the UN is doing good work. Conferences and suitable follow-up actions were taken by the UN on population and women issues. Its course of action to protect the environment and ecological balance needs special appreciation. Its another success story is the signing of Universal treaty to outlaw the production and use of chemical and biological weapons. One way or the other, these works involve human right protection.

On the other hand, the UNO was not successful in solving several other problems. One major issue is the monitoring of the observance of U.N. treaties on human rights by the signatory nations. The monitoring agencies have limited power to compel the states to comply. Recent studies concludes "the gap between universal right and remedy... threatening the integrity of the international human rights legal regime." [4] It was partly because of power politics and partly due to its internal weakness. Over the years, the UN has grown unwieldy as a result of the creation of too many agencies. The high cost of peace keeping had its effect on the finances of UN. Of late cases of corruption and maladministration are reported from within the UNO. The Security Council is still unbalanced due to the importance given to Europe and industrialized nations for membership. Countries of Asia and Africa were neglected even after six decades of development. Countries like India, Japan and Germany are demanding their inclusion in the Security Council which was not heeded so far. Serious fund shortage was another important problem of the UNO. The USA contributes considerably for the UN budget. Hence, it practically controls the activities of UNO in its favour. In Iraq, the US forced UNO for a war with Saddam Hussain citing production of mass destructive weapons by Iraq. Later, the weapons of mass destruction allegation turned out as a false propaganda by the US to eliminate Saddam Hussain. Due to funds shortage its activities were restricted in the recent years. Despite these shortcomings, the UNO is playing a key role in the upliftment of human rights. For effective working of this great organisation it also needs repair like an older vessel.

Universal Declaration of Human Rights

The Universal Declaration of Human Rights was adopted and

proclaimed on 10th December, 1948 in the General Assembly of the United Nations. It contains a list of human rights to be respected and observed by all the people and all nations. Due to its very important nature, the full text of this historic document is given below:

Preamble

Whereas, recognition of the inherent dignity and of the equal and inalienable rights of all members of the human family is the foundation of freedom, justice and peace in the world,

Whereas, disregard and contempt for human rights have resulted in barbarous acts which have outraged the conscience of mankind, and the advent of a world in which human beings shall enjoy freedom of speech and belief and freedom from fear and want has been proclaimed as the highest aspiration of the common people,

Whereas, it is essential, if man is not to be compelled to have recourse, as a last resort, to rebellion against tyranny and oppression, that human rights should be protected by the rule of law,

Whereas, it is essential to promote the development of friendly relations between nations,

Whereas, the peoples of the United Nations have in the Charter reaffirmed their faith in fundamental human rights, in the dignity and worth of the human person and in the equal right of men and women have determined to promote social progress and better standard of life in larger freedom,

Whereas, Member States have pledged themselves to achieve, in cooperation with the United Nations, the promotion of universal respect for and observance of human rights and fundamental freedoms.

Whereas, a common understanding of these rights and freedom is of the greatest importance for the full realization of this pledge,

Now, therefore,

The General Assembly

Proclaims this Universal Declaration of Human Rights as a common standard of achievement for all peoples and all nations, to the end that every individual and every organ of society, keeping this Declaration constantly in mind, shall strive by teaching and education to promote respect for these rights and freedoms and by progressive measures, national and international, to secure their universal and effective recognition and observance, both among the peoples of Member States themselves and among the peoples of territories under their jurisdiction.

Article 1

All human beings are born free and equal in dignity and rights. They are endowed with reason and conscience and should act towards one another in a spirit of brotherhood.

Article 2

Everyone is entitled to all the rights and freedoms set forth in this Declaration, without distinction of any kind, such as race, colour, sex, language, religion, political or other opinion, national or social origin, property, birth or other status. Furthermore, no distinction shall be made on the basis of the political, jurisdictional or international status of the country or territory to which a person belongs, whether it is independent, trust, non-self-government or under any other limitation of sovereignty.

Article 3

Everyone has the right to life, liberty and security of person.

Article 4

No one shall be held in slavery or servitude; slavery and the slave trade shall be prohibited in all their forms.

Article 5

No one shall be subjected to torture or to cruel, inhuman or degrading treatment or punishment.

Article 6

Everyone has the right to recognition everywhere as a person before the law.

Article 7

All are equal before the law and are entitled without any discrimination to equal protection of the law. All are entitled to equal protection against any discrimination in violation of this Declaration and against any incitement to such discrimination.

Article 8

Everyone has the right to an effective remedy by the competent national tribunals for acts violating the fundamental rights granted him by the constitution or by law.

Article 9

No one shall be subjected to arbitrary arrest, detention or exile.

Article 10

Everyone is entitled in full equality to a fair and public hearing by an independent and impartial tribunal, in the determination of his rights and obligations and of any criminal charge against him.

Article 11

1. Everyone charged with a penal offence has the right to be presumed innocent until proved guilty according to law in a public trial at which he has had all the guarantees necessary for his defence.
2. No one shall be held guilty of any penal offence on account of any act or omission which did not constitutes a penal offence, under national or international law, at the time when it was committed. Nor shall a heavier penalty be imposed than the one that was applicable at the time the penal offence was committed.

Article 12

No one shall be subjected to arbitrary interference with his privacy, family, home or correspondence, nor to attacks upon his honour and reputation. Everyone has the right to the protection of the law against such interference or attacks.

Article 13

1. Everyone has the right to freedom of movement and residence within the borders of each State.
2. Everyone has the right to leave any country, including his own, and to return to his country.

Article 14

1. Everyone has the right to seek and to enjoy in other countries asylum from persecution.
2. This right may not be invoked in the case of prosecutions genuinely arising from non-political crimes or from acts contrary to the purposes and principles of the United Nations.

Article 15

1. Everyone has the right to a nationality.
2. No one shall be arbitrarily deprived of his nationality nor denied the right to change his nationality.

Article 16

1. Men and Women of full age, without any limitation due to race, nationality or religion, have the right to marry and to found a family. They are entitled to equal rights as to marriage, during marriage and at its dissolution.
2. Marriage shall be entered into only with the free and full consent of the intending spouses.
3. The family is the natural and fundamental group unit of society and is entitled to protection by society and the State.

Article 17

1. Everyone has the right to own property alone as well as in association with others.
2. No one shall be arbitrarily deprived of his property.

Article 18

Everyone has the right to freedom of thought, conscience and religion; this right includes freedom to change his religion or belief, and freedom, either alone or in community with others and in public or private, to manifest his religion or belief in teaching, practice, worship and observance.

Article 19

Everyone has the right to freedom of opinion and expression; this right includes freedom to hold opinions without interference and to seek, receive and impart information and ideas through any media and regardless of frontiers.

Article 20

1. Everyone has the right to freedom of peaceful assembly and association.
2. No one may be compelled to belong to an association.

Article 21

1. Everyone has the right to take part in the government of his country, directly or through freely chosen representatives.
2. Everyone has the right to equal access to public services in his country.
3. The will of the people shall be the basis of the authority of government; this will shall be expressed in periodic and genuine elections which shall be by universal and equal suffrage and shall be held by secret vote or by equivalent free voting procedures.

Article 22

Everyone, as a member of society, has the right to social security and is entitled to realisation, through national effort and international cooperation and in accordance with the organisation and resources of each State, of the economic, social and cultural rights indispensable for his dignity and the free development of his personality.

Article 23

1. Everyone has the right to work, to free choice of employment, to just and favourable conditions of work and to protection against unemployment.
2. Everyone, without any discrimination, has the right to equal pay for equal work.
3. Everyone who works has the right to just and favourable remuneration ensuring for himself and his family an existence worthy of human dignity, and supplemented, if necessary, by other means of a social protection.
4. Everyone has the right to form and to join trade unions for the protection of his interests.

Article 24

Everyone has the right to rest and leisure, including reasonable limitation of working hours and periodic holidays with pay.

Article 25

1. Everyone has the right to a standard of living adequate for the health and well-being of himself and of his family, including food, clothing, and housing and medical care and necessary social services, and the right to security in the event of unemployment, sickness, disability, widowhood, old age or other lack of livelihood in circumstances beyond his control.
2. Motherhood and childhood are entitled to special care and assistance. All children, whether born in or out of wedlock, shall enjoy the same social protection.

Article 26

1. Everyone has the right to education; Education shall be free, at least in the elementary and fundamental stages. Elementary education shall be compulsory. Technical and professional education shall be made generally available and higher education shall be equally accessible to all on the basis of merit.

2. Education shall be directed to the full development of the human personality and to the strengthening of respect for human rights and fundamental freedom. It shall promote understanding, tolerance and friendship among the nations, racial or religious groups, and shall further the activities of the United Nations for the maintenance of peace.
3. Parents have a prior right to choose the kind of education that shall be given to their children.

Article 27

1. Everyone has the right freely to participate in the cultural life of the community, to enjoy the arts and to share in scientific advancement and its benefits.
2. Everyone has the right to the protection of the moral and material interests resulting from any scientific, literary or artistic production of which he is the author.

Article 28

Everyone is entitled to a social and international order in which the rights and freedoms set forth in this Declaration can be fully realized.

Article 29

1. Everyone has duties to the community in which alone the free and full development of his personality is possible.
2. In the exercise of his rights and freedoms, everyone shall be subject only to such limitations as are determined by law solely for the purpose of securing due recognition and respect for the rights and freedoms of others and of meeting the just requirements of morality, public order and the general welfare in a democratic society.
3. These rights and freedoms may in no case be exercised contrary to the purposes and principles of the United Nations.

Article 30

Nothing in this Declaration be interpreted as implying for any State. group of person any right to engage in any activity or to perform any act aimed at the destruction of any of the rights and freedoms set forth herein.

International Covenant on Civil and Political Rights

The International Covenant on Civil and Political Rights was adopted by the General Assembly of the UNO on 16th, December, 1966 and came into force on 23rd, March 1976.[5]

Preamble

The States Parties to the present Covenant.

Considering that, in accordance with the principles proclaimed in the Charter of the United Nations, recognition of the inherent dignity and of the equal and inalienable rights of all members of the human family is the foundation of freedom, justice and peace in the world,

Recognizing that these rights derive from the inherent dignity of the human person,

Recognizing that, in accordance with the Universal Declaration of Human Rights, the ideal of free human beings enjoying civil and political freedom and freedom from fear and want can only be achieved if conditions are created whereby everyone may enjoy his civil and political rights, as well as his economic, social and cultural rights,

Considering the obligation of States under the Charter of the United Nations to promote universal respect for, and observance of, human rights and freedoms,

Realizing that the individual, having duties to other individuals and to the community to which he belongs, is under a responsibility to strive for the promotion and observance of the rights recognized in the present Covenant.

Agree upon the following Articles:

PART 1

Article 1

1. All peoples have the right of self-determination. By virtue of that right they freely determine their political status and

freely pursue their economic, social and cultural development.

2. All peoples may, for their own ends freely dispose of their natural wealth and resources without prejudice to any obligations arising out of international economic cooperation based upon the principle of mutual benefit, and international law. In no case may a people be deprived of its own means of subsistence.
3. The States Parties to the present Covenant, including those having responsibility for the administration of Non-Self-Governing and Trust Territories, shall promote the realization of the right of self-determination, and shall respect the right, in conformity with the provisions of the Charter of the United Nations.

PART 2

Article 2

1. Each State Party to the present Covenant undertakes to respect and to ensure to all individuals within its territory and subject to its jurisdiction the rights recognized in the present Covenant, without distinction of any kind, such as race, colour, sex, language, religion, political or other opinion, national or social origin, property, birth or other status.
2. Where not already provided for by existing legislative or other measures, each State Party to the present Covenant undertakes to take the necessary steps, in accordance with its constitutional processes and with the provisions of the present Covenant, to adopt such legislative or other measures as may be necessary to give effect to the rights recognized in the present Covenant.
3. Each State Party to the present Covenant undertakes:
   (a) To ensure that any person whose rights or freedoms as herein recognized are violated shall have an effective remedy, notwithstanding that the violation has been committed by persons acting in an official capacity;
   (b) To ensure that any person claiming such a remedy shall have his right thereto determined by competent, judicial,

administrative or legislative authorities, or by any other competent authority provided for by the legal system of the State, and to develop the possibilities of judicial remedy;

Article 3

The States Parties to the present Covenant undertake to ensure the equal right of men and women to the enjoyment of all civil and political rights set forth in the present Covenant.

Article 4

1. In time of public emergency which threatens the life of the nation and the existence of which is officially proclaimed, the States Parties to the present Covenant may take measures derogating from, their obligation under the present Covenant to the extent strictly required by the exigencies of the situation, provided that such measures are not inconsistent with their other obligations under international law and do not involve discrimination solely on the ground of race, colour, sex, language, religion or social origin

....

PART 3

Article 6

1. Every human being has the inherent right to life. This right shall be protected by law. No one shall be arbitrarily deprived of his life.
2. In countries which have not abolished the death penalty, sentence of death may be imposed only for the most serious crimes in accordance with the law in force at the time of the commission of the crime and not contrary to the provisions of the present Covenant and to the Convention on the Prevention and Punishment of the Crime of Genocide....
4. Anyone sentenced to death shall have the right to seek pardon or commutation of the sentence. Amnesty, pardon or commutation of the sentence of death may be granted in all cases.

5. Sentence of death shall not be imposed for crimes committed by persons below eighteen years of age and shall not be carried out on pregnant women....

Article 7

1. No one shall be subjected to torture or to cruel, inhuman or degrading treatment or punishment. In particular, no one shall be subjected without his free consent to medical or scientific experimentation.

Article 8

1. No one shall be held in slavery; slavery and the slave trade in all their forms shall be prohibited.
2. No one shall be held in servitude.
3. No one shall be required to perform forced or compulsory labour....

Article 9

1. Everyone has the right to liberty and security of person. No one shall be subjected to arbitrary arrest or detention. No one shall be deprived of his liberty except on such grounds and in accordance with such procedure as are established by law.
2. Anyone who is arrested shall be informed, at the time of arrest, of the reasons for his arrest and shall be promptly informed of any charges against him.
3. Anyone arrested or detained on a criminal charge shall be brought promptly before a judge or other officer authorized by law to exercise judicial power and shall be entitled to trial within a reasonable time or to release...
4. Anyone who is deprived of his liberty by arrest or detention shall be entitled to take proceedings before a court, in order that court may decide without delay on the lawfulness of his detention and order his release if the detention is not lawful.
5. Anyone who has been the victim of unlawful arrest or detention shall have an enforceable right to compensation.

Article 10

1. All persons derived of their liberty shall be treated with humanity and with respect for the inherent dignity of the human person.
2. (a) Accused persons shall, save in exceptional circumstances, be segregated from convicted persons and shall be subject to separate treatment appropriate to their status as unconvicted persons;
   (b) Accused juvenile persons shall be separated from adults and brought as speedily as possible for adjudication.
3. The penitentiary system shall comprise treatment of prisoners, the essential aim of which shall be their reformation and social rehabilitation. Juvenile offenders shall be segregated from adults and be accorded treatment appropriate to their age and legal status.

Article 12

1. Everyone lawfully within the territory of a State shall, within that territory, have the right to liberty of movement and freedom to choose his residence.
2. Everyone shall be free to leave any country, including his own.
3. The above-mentioned rights shall not be subject to any restrictions except those which are provided by law, are necessary to protect national security, public order (*ordre public*), public health or morals or the rights and freedoms of others, and are consistent with the other rights recognized in the present Covenant.
4. No one shall be arbitrarily deprived of the right to enter his own country.

Article 14

1. All persons shall be equal before the courts and tribunals. In the determination of any criminal charge against him, or of his rights and obligations in a suit at law, everyone shall be entitled to a fair and public hearing by a competent, independent and impartial tribunal established by law…

2. Everyone charged with a criminal offence shall have the right to be presumed innocent until proved guilty according to law.
3. In the determination of any criminal charge against him, everyone shall be entitled to the following minimum guarantees, in full equality:
   (a) To be informed promptly and in detail in a language which he understands of the nature and cause of the charge against him;
   (b) To have adequate time and facilities for the preparation of his defense and to communicate with counsel of his own choosing;
   (c) To be tried without undue delay;
   To be tried in his present, and to defend himself in person or through legal assistance of his own choosing
   ....
   (g) Not to be compelled to testify against himself or to confess guilt.
4. In the case of juvenile persons, the procedure shall be such as will take account of their age and the desirability of prompting their rehabilitation

....

Article 16

Everyone shall have the right to recognition everywhere a person before the law.

Article 17

1. No one shall be subjected to arbitrary or unlawful interference with his privacy, family, home or correspondence, nor to unlawful attacks on his honour and reputation.
2. Everyone has the right to the protection of the law against such interference or attacks.

Article 18

1. Everyone shall have the right to freedom of thought, conscience and religion. This right shall include freedom to

have or to adopt a religion or belief of his choice, and freedom, either individually or in community with others and in public or private, to manifest his religion or belief in worship, observance, practice and teaching.

2. No one shall be subject to coercion which would impair his freedom to have or to adopt a religion or belief of his choice.
3. Freedom to manifest one's religion or beliefs may be subject only to such limitations as are prescribed by law and are necessary to protect public safety, order, health, or morals or the fundamental rights and freedoms of others.
4. The State Parties to the present Covenant undertake to have respect for the liberty of parents and, when applicable, legal guardians to ensure the religious and moral education of their children in conformity with their own convictions.

Article 19

1. Everyone shall have the right to hold opinions without interference.
2. Everyone shall have the right to freedom of expression; this right shall include freedom to seek, receive and impart information and ideas of all kinds, regardless of frontiers, either orally, in writing or in print, in the form of art, or through any other media of his choice.
3. The exercise of the rights provided for in paragraph 2 of this Article carries with it special duties and responsibilities. It may therefore be subject to certain restrictions, but these shall only be such as are provided by law and are necessary:
   (a) For respect of the rights or reputations of others;
   (b) For the protection of national security or of public order (*ordre public*), or of public health or morals.

Article 20

1. Any propaganda for war shall be prohibited by law.
2. Any advocacy of national, racial or religious hatred that constitutes incitement to discrimination, hostility or violence shall be prohibited by law.

Article 21

The right of peaceful assembly shall be recognized. No restrictions may be placed on the exercise of this right other than those imposed in conformity with the law and which are necessary in a democratic society in the interests of national security or public safety, public order (*ordre public*), the protection of public health or morals or the protection of the rights and freedoms of others.

Article 22

Everyone shall have the right to freedom of association with others, including the right to form and join trade unions for the protection of his interests.

....

Article 23

1. The family is the natural and fundamental group unit of society and is entitled to protection by society and the State.
2. The right of men and women of marriageable age to marry and to found a family shall be recognized.
3. No marriage shall be entered into without the free and full consent of the intending spouses.
4. States Parties to the present Covenant shall take appropriate steps to ensure equality of rights and responsibilities of spouses as to marriage, during marriage and at its dissolution. In the case of dissolution, provision shall be made for the necessary protection of any children.

Article 24

1. Every child shall have, without any discrimination as to race, colour, sex, language, religion, national or social origin, property or birth, the right to such measures of protection as are required by his status as minor, on the part of his family, society and the State.
2. Every child shall be registered immediately after birth and shall have a name.
3. Every child has the right to acquire a nationality.

Article 25

Every citizen shall have the right and the opportunity, without any of the distinctions mentioned in Article 2 and without unreasonable restrictions:

(a) To take part in the conduct of public affairs, directly or through freely chosen representatives;
(b) To vote and to be elected at genuine periodic elections which shall be by universal and equal suffrage and shall be held by secret ballot, guaranteeing the free expressions of the will of the electors;
(c) To have access, on general terms of equality, to public service in his country.

Article 26

All persons are equal before the law and are entitled without any discrimination to the equal protection of the law. In this respect, the law shall prohibit any discrimination and guarantee to all persons equal and effective protection against discrimination on any ground such as race, colour, sex, language, religion, political or other opinion, national or social origin, property, birth or other status.

Article 27

In those States in which ethnic, religious or linguistic minorities exist, persons belonging to such minorities shall not be denied the right, in community with the other members of their group, to enjoy their own culture, to profess and practice their own religion, or to use their own language.

....

PART 4

Article 40

1. The States Parties to the present Covenant undertake to submit reports on the measures they have adopted which give effect to the rights recognized herein and on the progress made in the enjoyment of those rights.

International Covenant on Economic, Social and Cultural Rights

The International Covenant on Economic, Social and Cultural Rights is an important document. It is a part of the International Bill of Human Rights. It is one of the fundamental documents which lay the basis for the protection and promotion of human rights throughout the world. It was adopted in the UNO on 16th December, 1966 and came into force on 3rd January, 1976. The excerpts from this covenant are reproduced below:

Preamble

The States Parties to the present Covenant

Considering that, in accordance with the principles proclaimed in the Charter of the United Nations, recognition of the inherent dignity and of the equal and inalienable rights of all members of the human family is the foundation of freedom, justice and peace in the world,

Recognizing that, these rights derive from the inherent dignity of the human person,

Recognizing that, in accordance with the Universal Declaration of Human Rights, the ideal of free human beings enjoying freedom from fear and want can only be achieved if conditions are created whereby everyone may enjoy his economic, social and cultural rights, as well as his civil and political rights,

Considering the obligation of States under the Charter of the United Nations to promote universal respect for, and observance of, human rights and freedoms,

Realizing that the individual, having to other individuals and to the community to which he belongs, is under a responsibility to strive for the promotion and observance of the rights recognized in the present Covenant,

Agree upon the following Articles:

PART 1

Article 1

1. All peoples have the right of self-determination. By virtue of that right they freely determine their political status and

freely pursue their economic, social and cultural development.

2. All peoples may, for their own ends, freely dispose of their natural wealth and resources without prejudice to any obligations arising out of international economic cooperation, based upon the principle of mutual benefit, and international law. In no case may a people be deprived of its own means of subsistence.

....

PART 2

Article 2

1. Each State Party to the present Covenant undertakes to take steps, individually and through international assistance and cooperation, especially economic and technical, to the maximum of its available resources, with a view to achieving progressively the full realization of the rights recognized in the present Covenant by all appropriate means, including particularly the adoption of legislative measures.
2. The States Parties to the present Covenant undertake to guarantee that the rights enunciated in the present Covenant will be exercised without discrimination of any kind as to race, colour, sex, language, religion, political or other opinion, national or social origin, property, birth or other status.
3. Developing countries, with due regard to human rights and their national economy, may determine to what extent they would guarantee the economic rights recognized in the present Covenant to non-nationals.

Article 3

The States Parties to the present Covenant undertake to ensure the equal right of men and women to the enjoyment of all economic, social and cultural rights set forth in the present Covenant.

Article 4

The States Parties to the present Covenant recognize that, in the enjoyment of those rights provided by the State in conformity with the present Covenant, the State may subject such rights only to such limitations as are determined by law only in so far as this may be compatible with the nature of these rights and solely for the purpose of promoting the general welfare in a democratic society.

....

PART 3

Article 6

1. The States Parties to the present Covenant recognize the right to work, which includes the right of everyone to the opportunity to gain his living by work which he freely chooses or accepts, and will take appropriate steps to safeguard this right.
2. The steps to be taken by a State Party to the present Covenant to achieve the full realization of this right shall include technical and vocational guidance and training programmes, policies and techniques to achieve steady economic, social and cultural development and full and productive employment under conditions safeguarding fundamental political and economic freedoms to the individual.

Article 7

The States Parties to the present Covenant recognize the right of everyone to the enjoyment of just and favourable conditions of work which ensure, in particular:

(a) Remuneration which provides all worker, as a minimum, with:

(i) Fair wages and equal remuneration for work of equal value without distinction of any kind, in particular women being guaranteed conditions of work not inferior to those enjoyed by men, with equal pay for equal work;

(ii) A decent living for themselves and their families in accordance with the provisions of the present Covenant;

(b) Safe and healthy working conditions;

(c) Equal opportunity for everyone to be promoted in his employment to an appropriate higher level, subject to no considerations other than those of seniority and competence;

(d) Rest, leisure and reasonable limitation of working hours and periodic holidays with pay, as well as remuneration for public holidays.

Article 8

1. The States Parties to the present Covenant undertake to ensure:
   (a) The right of everyone to form trade unions and join the trade union of his choice, subject only to the rules of the organisation concerned, for the promotion and protection of his economic and social interests....
   (b) The right of trade unions to establish national federations or confederations and the right of the latter to form or join international trade union organizations;
   (c) The right of trade unions to function freely subject to no limitations other than those prescribed by law and which are necessary in a democratic society in the interests of national security or public order or for the protection of the rights and freedoms of others;
   (d) The right to strike provided that it is exercised in conformity with the laws of the particular country....

Article 9

The States Parties to the present Covenant recognize the right of everyone to social security, including social insurance.

Article 10

The States Parties to the present Covenant recognize that:

1. The widest possible protection and assistance should be accorded to the family, which is the natural fundamental group unit of society, particularly for its establishment and while it is responsible for the care and education of dependent children. Marriage must be entered into with the free consent of the intending spouses.

2. Special protection should be accorded to mothers during a reasonable period before and after childbirth. During such period working mother should be accorded paid leave or leave with adequate social security benefits.
3. Special measures of protection and assistance should be taken on behalf of all children and young persons without any discrimination for reasons of parentage or other conditions. Children and young persons should be protected from economic and social exploitation. Their employment in work harmful to their morals or health or dangerous to life or likely to hamper their normal development should be punishable by law. States should also set age limits below which the paid employment of child labour should be prohibited and punishable by law.

Article 11

1. The States Parties to the present Covenant recognize the right of everyone to an adequate standard of living for himself and his family, including adequate food, clothing and housing, and to the continuous improvement of living conditions. The States Parties will take appropriate steps to ensure the realization of this right, recognizing to this effect the essential importance of international cooperation based on free consent.
2. The States Parties to the present Covenant, recognizing the fundamental right of everyone to be free from hunger, shall take, individually and through international cooperation, the measures, including specific programmes, which are needed:
   (a) To improve methods of production, conservation and distribution of food by making full use of technical and scientific knowledge. By disseminating knowledge of the principles of nutrition and by developing or reforming agrarian systems in such a way as to achieve the most efficient development and utilization of natural resources;
   (b) Taking into account the problems for both food-importing and food-exporting countries, to ensure and equitable distribution of world food supplies in relation to need.

Article 12

1. The States Parties to the present Covenant recognize the right of everyone to the enjoyment of the highest attainable standard of physical and mental health.
2. The steps to be taken by the States Parties to the present Covenant to achieve the full realization of this right shall include those necessary for:
   (a) The provision for the reduction of the stillbirth-rate and of infant mortality and for the healthy development of the child;
   (b) The improvement of all aspects of environmental and industrial hygiene;
   (c) The prevention, treatment and control of epidemic, endemic, occupational and other diseases;
   (d) The creation of conditions which would assure to all medical services and medical attention in the event of sickness.

Article 13

1. The States Parties to the present Covenant recognize the right of everyone to education. They agree that education shall be directed to the full development of the human personality and the sense of its dignity, and shall strengthen the respect for human rights and fundamental freedoms. They further agree that education shall enable all persons to participate effectively in a free society, promote understanding, tolerance and friendship among all nations and all racial, ethnic or religious groups, and further the activities of the United Nations for the maintenance of peace.
2. The States Parties to the present Covenant recognize that, with a view to achieving the full realization of this right:
   (a) Primary education shall be compulsory and available free to all;
   (b) Secondary education in its different forms, including technical and vocational secondary education, shall be made generally available and accessible to all by every appropriate means, and in particular by the progressive introduction of free education;

(c) Higher education shall be made equally accessible to all, on the basis of capacity, by every appropriate means, and in particular by the progressive introduction of free education;

(d) Fundamental education shall be encouraged or intensified as far as possible for those persons who have not received or completed the whole period of their primary education;

(e) The development of a system of schools at all levels shall be actively pursued, an adequate fellowship system shall be established, and the material conditions of teaching staff shall be continuously improved.

3. The States Parties to the present Covenant undertake to have respect for the liberty of parents and, when applicable, legal guardians to choose for their children schools, other than those established by the public authorities, which conform to such minimum educational standards as may be laid down or approved by the State and to ensure the religious and moral education of their children in conformity with their own convictions.

4. No part of this Article shall be construed so as to interfere with the liberty of individuals and bodies to establish and direct educational institutions, subject always to the observance of the principles set forth in paragraph 1 of this Article and to the requirement that the education given in such institutions shall conform to such minimum standards as may be laid down by the State.

....

Article 15

1. The States Parties to the present Covenant recognize the right of everyone:
   (a) To take part in cultural life;
   (b) To enjoy the benefits of scientific progress and its applications;
   (c) To benefit from the protection of the moral and material interests resulting from any scientific, literary or artistic production of which he is the author.

2. The steps to be taken by the States Parties to the present Covenant to achieve the full realization of this right shall include those necessary for the conservation, the development and the diffusion of science and culture.
3. The States Parties to the present Covenant undertake to respect the freedom indispensable for scientific research and creative activity.
4. The States Parties to the present Covenant recognize the benefits to be derived from the encouragement and development of international contacts and cooperation in the scientific and cultural fields.

......

In comparison to the earlier centuries the 20th century witnessed many turbulences and political upheavals. The two world wars within a span of two decades show the degradation of humanity. In the name of war all sorts of atrocities were committed on the fellow beings. The horrors of Second World War and human rights violations led to another development. The leaders of that time wanted to create a mechanism to prevent the outbreak of another major war. They also wished to protect the rights of individuals and the dignity of humanity. The creation of the League of Nations and later the UNO were attempts in this direction. The League, despites its success in protecting the rights of minorities and other groups failed to achieve its main aim of preventing the outbreak of another major war.

To protect the rights of working class, the ILO was created. The I.L.O. has been the pioneer in the protection of economic and social rights globally.[6] It was a positive step in the right direction. But due to several other factors the League failed to prevent the outbreak of Second World War and collapsed. Even during the final stages of Second World War, the great leaders discussed the ways to maintain universal peace and human rights. The birth of UNO is a great turning point in the evolution of human rights. It stressed the importance of protecting human rights and the dignity of individual. An elaborate attempt was made to gather, analyse and present details on human rights. These attempts led to the Universal Declaration of Human Rights followed by three generation of rights. The International Covenants on Civil and Political Rights and the International Covenant on Economic, Social and Cultural Rights were adopted by the UNO. All these documents were collectively termed as the International Bill of Human Rights.

Questions

1. Write a note on the humanitarian work of the League of Nations.
2. Write an essay on the contribution of UNO to human rights.
3. Examine the significance of Universal Declaration of Human Rights.
4. Write a note on International Labour Organisation.

Objective Type Questions

1. Which First Lady of USA played a key role in the drafting of Universal Declaration of the Human Rights?
   (a) Eleanor Roosevelt (b) Jacqueline Kennedy
   (c) Hilary Clinton (d) None of the above.
2. The League of Nations was the brain child of ....
   (a) Winston Churchill (b) F.D. Roosevelt
   (c) Woodrow Wilson (d) Abraham Lincoln.
3. In which year the UNO came into being?
   (a) 1939 (b) 1940
   (c) 1942 (d) 1945
4. The Headquarters of the International Court of Justice is located at ....
   (a) London (b) New York (c) Rome (d) The Hague.
5. The Universal Declaration of Human Rights was adopted on ....
   (a) 26th January, 1947 (b) 10th November, 1947
   (c) 10th December, 1948 (d) None of the above.
6. The Universal Declaration of Human Rights was issued by the
   (a) American freedom fighters (b) French Revolutionaries
   (c) Russian Revolutionaries (d) UNO.

Key to the Objective Type Questions

1. a 2. c. 3. d. 4. d. 5. c. 6. d.

NOTES

1. George W. Southgate, 218-26.
2. L.N. Basu, *Human Rights in a Global Perspective* (Jaipur: Aavishkar Publishers, 2003), 154-56.
3. R.C. Ramphal, *Perspectives in Human Rights* (New Delhi: Rajat Publications, 2001), 56-57.
4. Sally Engle Merry, *Human Rights and Gender Violence* (New Delhi: Oxford University Press, 2009), 72.
5. Arjun Dev, 46-57.
6. Ashima Sahu, *Human Rights Violations and the Law* (Jaipur: Pinter Publishers, 2007), 62-63.

3

Human Rights Declarations

The First and Second World War had profound influence on the developments related to Human Rights. The horrors of two world wars and the violations of Human Rights made the leaders of the time to create an organ to protect human rights all-over the world. Especially, the allied powers took the initiative in this regard. The UNO was created and the UN charter made promotions of Human Rights as one of its main functions. The International Bill of Human Rights defines the contents of Human Rights, and it was adopted by the General Assembly of the UNO in Paris on December 10, 1948. The UN Commission of Human Rights is an organisation created for the purpose of safeguarding Human Rights. Besides, NGO organisations such as Amnesty International protect Human Rights. It systematically observes the violations and reports them regularly. In countries like India several NGO organisations like Peoples Union for Civil Liberties (PUCL) plays a crucial role in this regard. The UN Charter stressed its faith in fundamental Human Rights and in the dignity and the worth of a human person.

In order to promote Human Rights everywhere, a systematic effort was made to create a body of documents dealing with various aspects of Human Rights. The Universal Declaration of Human Rights was an important milestone in this regard. It was adopted in the UN General Assembly on 10th December, 1948. It was one of a very important fundamental documents discussed in detail in the earlier chapter. It was followed by International Covenant on Economic, Social and Cultural life. Later another important document, the International Covenant on Civil and Political Rights was also adopted by the UNO. These three documents along with two protocols—the Optional Protocol to the International Covenant on Civil and Political Rights, and the Second Optional Protocol to the International Covenant on Civil and Political Rights, aiming at the Abolition of the Death Penalty—constitute the International Bill of Human Rights.[1] These documents formed the basis for the protection and promotion of Human Rights everywhere.

The various International declarations and covenants were mainly concerned with the rights of the individuals. But in course of time due to various developments new concerns and issues led to the emergence of a new set of human rights. It was felt that International recognition should be given to these rights. In this direction, the declaration on the rights to development is also very important development. It was adopted in the UNO on 4th December, 1986. This declaration is particularly relevant to the developing countries. Unfortunately, the necessary means for enforcing the right to development is lacking. Development is a complex process involving economic, social, cultural and political issues.

The UNO aims at the constant improvement through the meaningful participation of people in the development process. The benefits of development should also reach them. It stressed the elimination of human rights violation that exists through colonialism, neo-colonialism, apartheid, foreign domination, occupation and aggression. These issues hamper the progress of development. The declaration also highlighted the necessity to protect civil, political, economic, social and cultural rights for the enjoyment of fundamental freedoms. The international peace and security are considered as the essential elements for achieving the right to development. In the developing countries disarmament measures should be particularly devoted for the economic and social development and for the well-being of all people. The human beings should be the main participant and beneficiary of development. The states must create a favourable condition for the development of its people. A new international economic order should be created through the efforts of international community. The declaration also stressed that right to development, right to self-determination and equality of opportunity as necessary condition for the nations and the individuals who make up these nations. It highlighted the need to provide active role for women in the process of development.

The declaration contains ten articles and its essence is given below.

Article 1

For the realisation of human rights and fundamental freedoms the right to development is very important. The people can participate, contribute and enjoy economic, social, cultural and political development through this right. The right to self-determination to the people should include their right to all their natural wealth and resources.

Article 2

The right to development should include the human person as the central subject of development. The individuals must actively participate and benefited from the process of development. All human beings should protect the necessary political, social and economic order for development. The human being should realize their duties to the community. The states have the duty to formulate necessary policies on national development. It should aim at the improvement of the entire population. The people must actively participate in development and receive a fair distribution of the benefit.

Article 3

The states have the primary responsibilities for the creation of conditions favourable to achieve the right to development. The principle of International law should be respected through friendly relations and cooperation among the states. The states must cooperate with each other to ensure development. They must also promote a new international economic order on the basis of equality, mutual interest and cooperation among all states.

Article 4

To realize the right to development, the states must formulate international development policies for the rapid development of developing countries in addition to sustained action and effective international cooperation.

Article 5

The state should take necessary steps to eliminate the violation of human rights through racial discrimination, colonialism, foreign domination and occupation, aggression, threat against national unity and integrity and the refusal to recognize the right to self-determination.

Article 6

All states should cooperate for the observance of human rights and fundamental freedoms without any distinction to race, sex or religion. The states should also take steps to eliminate obstacle to the development due to the failure to observe the human rights.

Article 7

By achieving complete disarmament and releasing the resources from disarmament for the effective use of comprehensive development.

Article 8

The state should take steps for giving equality of opportunity for all in education, health services, food, housing, employment and the fair distribution of income. Reform should be carried out to eradicate all social injustices. The women must have an active role in the process of development. Popular participation for development should be encouraged.

Article 9

The rights related to development set forth in this declaration are indivisible and interdependent. Nothing in the present declaration shall be construed as being contrary to the principles of UNO.

Article 10

Step should be taken to ensure the exercise and enhancement of the right to development. It should include formulation, adoption and implementation of policy at all level.

These rights are considered as essential for the all-round development of individuals and nations together. While stressing the importance of right to development to people all-over the world this declaration gives special emphasis on the developing countries which faces several problems related to development.

The Vienna Declaration and Programme of Action

The World Conference on Human Rights was held at Vienna from 14th to 25th June, 1993. The main objective of the conference was to revive the progress of Human Rights since the adaptation of Universal Declaration of Human Rights in 1948. It also examines the connection between development and the enjoyment of various human rights and also finds ways to overcome any obstacles. It was presided by three regional conferences held in Tunis, San Jose, and Bangkok. This declaration was later endorsed by the UNO. This declaration recognizes the interdependence between democracy, development and Human Rights. It recommends to the UNO for the establishment of a High Commissioner for Human Rights. It was accepted in December 1993.[2]

UN High Commission for Human Rights

The main purpose of creating a UN High Commissioner's office for Human Rights was to look after the various activities related to the protection of human rights. The duty of United Nations High Commissioner for Human Rights (UNHCHR) is "to protect and promote human rights for all".

Appointment and Responsibilities

The High Commissioner is appointed by the Secretary-General of UNO with the approval of General Assembly. He is selected for a fixed term of four years. A possibility exists also for renewal for another term of office. As discussed earlier, the Vienna Declaration and programme of action and the General Assembly resolution of 20th December, 1993, the Assembly established the post of UN High Commissioner for Human Rights. Later this office is consolidated with the Centre for Human Rights. The single office of the UN High Commissioner for Human Rights was created from 15th September, 1997.

The General Assembly of the UNO gives a detailed list of responsibilities. They are as follows:

I. to promote and protect the effective enjoyment of civil, cultural, economic and social rights including the right to development by all;
II. to provide advisory services, technical and financial assistances in the field of human rights to states that request them;
III. to coordinate UNO's education and public information programme in the field of Human Rights;
IV. to play an active role in removing the obstacles to the full realization of human rights and in preventing the continuation of human rights violations throughout the world;
V. to engage in a dialogue with Governments in order to secure respect for human rights;
VI. to enhance international cooperation for the promotion and protection of human rights;
VII. to coordinate human rights promotion and protection activities throughout the United Nations system;
VIII. to rationalize, adapt, strengthen and streamline the United Nations machinery in the field of human rights in order to improve its efficiency and effectiveness.

The UN High Commissioner for human rights is handling the following important functions:

1. Promotes universal enjoyment of all human rights by giving practical effect to the will and resolve of the world community as expressed by the United Nations;
2. Plays the leading role on human rights issues and emphasizes the importance of human rights at the international and national levels;
3. Promotes international cooperation for human rights;
4. Stimulates and coordinates action for human rights throughout the United Nations system;
5. Promotes universal ratification and implementation of international standards;
6. Assists in the development of new norms;
7. Supports human rights organs and treaty monitoring bodies;
8. Responds to serious violations of human rights;
9. Undertakes preventive human rights action;

10. promotes the establishment of national human rights infrastructures;
11. Undertakes human rights field activities and operations;
12. Provides education, information, advisory services and technical assistance in the field of human rights.

The UN High Commissioner is responsible for the activities and administration of his office. He carries his functions assigned by the UN General Assembly. The High Commissioner advises the Secretary-General of UNO on the policies on human rights. He provides administrative support to the programmes on human rights and related activities. He also carries out special assignments on the advice of Secretary-General and he represents him at the meetings on human rights. His office is headed by a High Commissioner with the rank of Under Secretary-General.

The UN High Commissioner for Human Rights is assisted by a Deputy in the rank of Assistant Secretary-General. During the absence of High Commissioner the Deputy acts as Officer In Charge. He carries out various administrative works decided by the High Commissioner. The Staff office of UNHCHR is headed by a chief who looks after the various duties related to the office. He assists the High Commissioner in supervising the human rights programme to protect and promote it. He assists in the formulation, communication, implementation and evaluation of policies. He also assists the High Commissioner in the maintenance of relations with governments, and other UN agencies, NGOs and academic circle. He is the spokes person of the Secretary-General at New York and Geneva and the media. He carries out fund rasing function and special projects on human rights. He assists the High Commissioner in preparing annual management reports on human rights activities and achievements.

In addition to these offices, the administrative section of UNHCHR is headed by a chief who advices the High Commissioner on the budgetary, financial and personnel matters related to human rights. He looks after the general administrative responsibilities of the office. Further, the New York office is headed by the Director who is accountable to the High Commissioner. He is representing the High Commissioner at headquarters and at meetings of various bodies and NGO groups. He also provides policy advice to the High Commissioner and provides support on human rights issue to the General Assembly. He also undertakes other specific assignments as desired by the High Commissioner. In addition to the above offices, there are Research and Right to Development Branch and a support service branch that also functions under the control of High Commissioner and managed by chiefs for these sections. They look after the strategy for the right to development and carrying out research projects on human rights. It also provides policy analysis, advice and guidance on the procedures. It also prepares documents, reports and materials for publication.

NOTES

1. United Nations Department of Public Information, The International Bill of Human Rights (New York: U.N. Department of Public Information, 1993), 1.
2. Arjun Dev, 110.

Questions

1. What is meant by the International Bill of Human Rights?
2. Examine the importance of the Right to development.
3. Examine the responsibilities of the UN High Commissioner for Human Rights.
4. Write a note on the Vienna Declaration and Programme of Action.

Objective Type Model Questions

1. The Peoples Unions for Civil Liberties is protecting human rights in ....
   (a) Pakistan (b) India
   (c) Sri Lanka (d) Nepal
2. To achieve the Right to development and international peace .... is essential.
   (a) prosperity (b) happiness
   (c) security (d) none of the above.
3. The .... declaration recommends to the UNO for the creation of High Commissioner for Human Rights.
   (a) Tunis (b) San Jose
   (c) Bangkok (d) Vienna.

4. The term of office of the UN High Commissioner for human rights is ....
   (a) two years (b) three years
   (c) four years (d) five years.

Key to Objective Type Questions

1: b. 2. c. 3. d. 4. c.

4

Amnesty International: Regional Human Rights System

Introduction

At the global level, one of a very important Non-Governmental Organisations (NGOs) protecting Human Rights is the Amnesty International. It was founded by a London Lawyer, Peter Benson. With membership strength of over a million spread over 162 countries, Amnesty International plays a very crucial role in protecting the rights of political prisoners or others who are imprisoned because of their faith in certain ideology. It also spread the awareness of human rights. It systematically oversees human right violations all-over the world and exposes it. It also reports human rights violations and the steps taken by the organisation to prevent such violations in its annual reports. Since it projected the failures of the Governments and other agencies regarding the protection of human rights, it refuses to receive any donations and grants from the governments. Among the key NGOs working for the protection of human rights, Amnesty International occupies a very important position and is respected for its almost unbiased reports.

At Helsinki, Finland a conference was organised on 3rd July, 1973 and later during July-August 1975. Besides other issues on European Security and cooperation in several fields including environment, this conference also affirmed its respect for human rights and fundamental freedoms. 35 countries signed the Helsinki charter.

During Second World War the European continent suffered much devastation and experienced the horrors of human rights violation beyond any one's imagination. Hence, after the end of war, the leaders of Europe wanted to take efforts on peace keeping and cooperation. For this purpose, the Council of Europe was founded. It survived the cold war politics and the fall of Communism and till date serves as a forum for dialogue and exchange of ideas within Europe. The Council of Europe promotes the rule of law, human rights and democratic institutions.

The African Human Rights System is regarded as the youngest regional system which recognizes the importance of collective rights and the Right to development. The African Charter on Human and Peoples' Rights was ratified by an absolute majority of states. The charter contains a list of obligations and prerogatives and also the institutional arrangements for the protection of the same value.

Those who are seeking remedies for human rights violations in the International realm, several enforcement mechanisms are available. Likewise, it is necessary to protect International Human Rights in Domestic courts also. Otherwise the people living in various parts of the world may not get proper protection using the principle of universal jurisdiction. But this protection is not available in all cases in several countries. Due to some practical difficulties and interpretation of local laws sometimes the victims may not get justice. The interpretation of national sovereignty also prevented the application of international human rights norms in domestic courts.

Amnesty International

Amnesty International is an independent Non-Governmental Organisation, protecting human rights at the global level. It concentrates mostly on helping those who were arrested and imprisoned because of their religion, race, sex, faith and language. These prisoners do not indulge in violence or preach it. Amnesty International totally opposes the capital punishment. Its founder Peter Benson organized a letter writing campaign seeking amnesty for 'prisoners of conscience'. Amnesty International aimed at informing the public on violations of Human Rights. It focuses its attention on the curtailment of freedom of speech and religion and the imprisonment and torture of political dissidents. It supports the effort for the release of political prisoners. It has membership strength of more than one million in 162 countries. Its first director, S. Mac Bride got Nobel Prize in 1974. In 1977, the Amnesty International itself won the same award.[1]

The Amnesty International undertakes research and action, focused on preventing the grave abuses of the rights of individuals and groups. It opposes torture and killings of prisoners, hostage taking, and arbitrary killings. It assists asylum seekers who are at risk at their motherland. It organizes human rights education and awareness programmes. It cooperates with UN and other organisations like Interpol related to the protection of Human Rights.[2] It ensures proper control of international military, security and police organisations within the parameters of legal framework.

Organisations and Its Duties

The International Secretariat of Amnesty International is located in London. Nearly 350 members of the staff and 100 volunteers look after its administration. In several countries they have organized sections to look after its functioning. This self-governed impartial movement is handled by a nine member International Executive Committee. The day to day affairs of this organisation is handled by the Secretary General. With the consent of International Executive Committee, a wing of Amnesty International may be created in any country.

Protecting the rights of prisoners is a priority area for Amnesty International. It exposes the torture of prisoners in several countries. Amnesty International brought to light the flagrant violation of human rights everywhere. This independent organisation presented its viewpoints on the violation of human rights in all the countries without bothering about the hostile reaction.

It intervened on behalf of individuals and groups that face human right violations in India also. In 1975, during emergency, it advocated the release of political leaders who were imprisoned. In 1978, its representatives visited various important prisons in Delhi, Calcutta and Hyderabad and suggested the necessity of following some rules on the handling of prisoners. It strongly condemned the killing of Sikhs during the riots following the assassination of Indira Gandhi in 1984. It opposes the employment of draconian laws like MISA, TADA and POTA to imprison political opponents and unwanted persons without proper trial. This organisation is urging all governments to observe the rule of law and to implement human rights standards.

How It Operates

Amnesty International gives priority to the projection of accurate truth. It sincerely and honestly collects information on the alleged violation of human rights. The research team at the headquarters in London deploys various novel methods to collect data on human rights violations. Hundreds of Newspapers, journals and government reports besides radio and TV reports are utilized for its unbiased analysis. The letters of the relatives of prisoners are used to evaluate the situation. It deputes fact finding missions to interview the government officials. It takes full responsibility for its report. It corrects its own report whenever any fault of its reporting is proved.

International principles of human rights are the guiding light for the functioning of Amnesty International. All-over the world thousands of people were in prison because of their particular faith. They were imprisoned without any trial. Men, women and children disappeared after taken for interrogation by police and other law enforcing agencies. Several political killings were not at all brought to the court of justice. Cutting across national boundaries, the Amnesty International diligently protects the human rights, which is a challenging task.

Amnesty International doesn't have any political affiliation. It never supports or opposes any government or political organisation. Even though it is fighting for the rights of prisoners, it never supports or opposes their viewpoints. It concentrates its attention on the protection of human rights in each and every case in which it is involved. It publishes annual report in which it lists the struggles in several countries and gives details of political prisoners and the torture employed. Its unbiased reports receive popular reading in several countries. Nearly one million members of this organisation operate all-over the world. They join together as small group and help this organisation in the collection of materials and reports on human right violation. Its unbiased reporting and yeomen service for the benefit of affected individual received encomium. It raised the necessary fund through its membership fees and the contributions of donors. Since it mostly projects the shortcomings of the governments on human rights violation, it never receives any monetary assistance from any government. It thoroughly verifies the credential of the donor before accepting their contributions.

Each year its members campaign on one country or on a particular human rights issue. It concentrates its attention on reporting on human rights issues, and giving pressure on the governments for effective steps for the protection of rights. During 2001, its action groups worked on behalf of people in 81 countries, where they suffered human rights violations including torture, disappearance, death penalty, or forcible return to countries where they would be in danger of encountering human rights violations. In 117 urgent actions, the Amnesty International received good news of positive results. In India the Maoists, abducted four police men in Bihar in September 2010. They killed one police man and demanded the release of some arrested Maoist cadre in prison. It threatened to kill the remaining police men if their demand was not met in time. The Amnesty appealed to the Maoists to release the hostages. It argued that hostage-taking is prohibited by international law. Amnesty stressed that "It is contrary to fundamental principles of humanity, as reflected in international humanitarian law, to seize or detain anyone and threaten to kill or harm them if the government does not comply with the hostage-taker's demands."[3] The Maoists released the hostages shortly afterwards even though the government refused to release the Maoist prisoners. The specialized network of this organisation consists of Lawyers Network, the Military and Police Network, Children's network and the Medical network. This network supports the activities of the Amnesty International in its respective fields.

Amnesty International is a worldwide campaigning movement working for the promotion of human rights. It campaigned against the torture and ill-treatment of women, children, ethnic minorities, lesbians, gays, bisexuals and transgender people. Due to its continued efforts, several governments brought legislation against torture and other human rights violations. This Non-Governmental Organisation is doing a great service to the people in dire need of support.

The European Convention on Human Rights (1950) and Helsinki Charter

The European Union took the first step for the collective enforcement of several rights enshrined in the Universal Declaration of Human Rights (UDHR). We must remember that the European political thought was deeply rooted on human rights. From its inception in May 1949, the Council of Europe makes it as a major policy to respect human rights. The importance of human rights was stressed in the statute of the Council of Europe. The European Convention was signed on November 4, 1950 in Rome. After the deposit of ten instrument of ratification, it entered into force on September 3, 1953.[4] Twenty-two European states ratified this convention.

Provisions of the Convention

The European Convention gives specific legal content to human rights. To enforce these rights, machinery for supervision is established. The contracting parties of the convention should respect and secure the rights and freedom of everyone within their jurisdiction. Section I contained Articles 2 to 18 with details of rights and freedoms that had to be protected. The right to life was protected by Article 2 and Article 3 prohibited any form of torture. While the Article 4 prohibited slavery and forced labour, Article 5 covers the right to liberty and security. Right to a fair trial, no punishment without the sanctity of law, right to respect for private and family life, freedom of thought, conscience and religion, freedom of expression were also enshrined in the subsequent articles.

The right to marry, the right to remedy and prohibition of discrimination on any grounds were also part of succeeding articles of the convention. It also contained limitation of these rights, since public order, economic well-being of the country and protection of the rights of the others were also involved. Like the practice in many other countries, some of the rights can be curtailed during war or emergency, except the right to life which should not be restricted.

To oversee the enforcement of the rights, the Convention established the necessary structures in Article 19. The European Commission of Human Rights ("the Commission") and the European Court of Human Rights ("the Court") will oversee the enforcement of these rights. Section III of the convention entirely covers the commission. The members of the commission were elected for the period of six years. If any contracting party breach the provisions of convention or any person, NGO, or group of individuals affected by violation they can petition the Commission. The conditions for the acceptances of petition were also clearly laid down. It must be investigated by a sub-commission consisting of seven members of the Commission. In case a settlement was not reached the matter should be reported to the committee of ministers. If the case was not referred to the court within three months by the committee, the case would be decided by two-thirds of the members of the committee. The contracting party should accept the decision as binding.

The European Court of Human Rights was established on 3rd September, 1953 at Strasbourg. This court has jurisdiction over Council of Europe member states that have opted to accept its jurisdiction. The judges were elected for a period of nine years. They must possess necessary qualification with high moral standing. The court can deal with all cases concerning the interpretation and application of the convention. When a friendly settlement failed then only the court handles the case. The judgment of the court was final and binding on the contracting parties. Section V of the Convention deals with the national laws of the contracting parties and contains provisions related to the effective implementation. Territorial jurisdiction of the Convention is also covered. The contracting parties could denounce the Convention only after the expiry of five years from the date in which it becomes a party to it.

Following the enforcement of the Convention, a number of protocols are brought in either to add or amend the existing rights. Some of these protocols gave protection of property, the right to education, and prohibited the expulsion of national and aliens' en masse. It also gave the freedom of movement and abolished death penalty except in time of war. Protocol 7 gives safeguards relating to expulsion of aliens and gives the right of appeal in criminal matters. One can claim compensation for wrongful conviction under this protocol. It also affirmed equality between spouses. The state should not interfere in the freedom of assembly and association and on matter related to right to form trade unions. But under some circumstances, the state should intervene on matters related to trade union to protect the rights of any individual from abuse by the trade unions. The European Convention on Human Rights granted basic rights and also provided an instrument of effective mechanism to implement these rights.

Helsinki Charter

At Helsinki, Finland, the conference on security and cooperation in Europe was held on 3rd July, 1973. The conference continued its work at Geneva from 18th September, 1973 to 21st July, 1975. Third and final stage of conference was held in Helsinki between 30th July and 1st August, 1975. 35 countries participated and signed the Final Act. The Final Act formally approved the move for greater economic, scientific, military and social cooperation between the East and the West.

The major issues involved in the conference were related to questions on the security of Europe, cooperation in economy, science and technology and environment. It also covers cooperation in the field of humanitarian issues. It affirmed respect for human rights and fundamental freedoms, including the freedom of thought, conscience, religion and belief. It stressed the principle of sovereign equality, territorial integrity of states, peaceful settlement of disputes and the non-intervention on the internal affairs of other member nations. The Helsinki Charter also adopted the principles of equal rights and self-determination of peoples. The importance of human rights and fundamental freedom is recognized by the participating states.

The international conferences on human rights were organized since 1990 to highlight the most important problems in this regard. These conferences reaffirm the commitment of all states to protect human rights and fundamental freedom. The world conference on human rights recommends increased coordination in this regard within the UN systems. The world conference on human rights evaluated the most important issues related to racial discrimination, intolerance, problems of minorities and indigenous people and that of the migrant workers. It also recommended the necessity of training and education through the curriculum of education. The international conference also takes note of the far reaching changes in world economy and its impact on the social development in all the countries. The Copenhagen declaration highlighted the ten commitments of world leaders in this regard. In its session of 1997, the ECOSOC also followed up these details and passed resolutions for eradication of poverty.

Importance of Vienna and Copenhagen Conferences

At Vienna the conference on Human Rights was held from 14th to 25th June, 1993. Nearly 7000 delegates representing 171 states and several national and international bodies and NGOs participated in this largest ever gathering of this kind. The main aim of the conference was to revive the progress made in the field of human rights since

1948 and to examine the link between development and the enjoyment of economic, social, cultural, civil and political rights. It also aimed at identifying the ways and means to solve the problems concerning the above rights. This Vienna Conference was preceded by three regional conferences in Tunis, San Jose and Bangkok. The conference adopted the Vienna Declaration and Programme of Action. It was endorsed by the UNO. The significance of Vienna Declaration is the recognition of interdependence between democracy, development and human rights. It recommended the establishment of a High Commissioner for Human Rights. It was accepted in December 1993.

Salient Features of Vienna Declaration (1993)

One of the salient features of the Vienna declaration was that it recognized the importance of individual's rights and fundamental freedom. The conference expressed deep concern towards the condition of women and the various forms of discrimination and violence directed against them. With increased international cooperation, the conference was determined to achieve substantial progress in human rights. It stressed the importance of the right to self-determination.[5] This conference considers the denial of the right to self-determination as violation of human rights. The people under foreign occupation should be legally protected and their rights should be respected. Normally, people under foreign occupation experience all sorts of humiliation and faces the denial of fundamental rights and freedom.

The interdependent nature of democracy, development, fundamental freedoms and respect for human rights were indicated in the Vienna declaration. It must be strengthened with the support of international community. The less developed countries of Africa and other continents should be helped to realize democracy and economic development. The right to development is a universal and inalienable right. Concerned about the environmental threat, the conference recognizes the people's right against the illicit dumping of toxic and dangerous waste that threatens the life and health of everyone. It underlines rights of everyone to enjoy the benefits of scientific progress. The development of biomedical and life sciences as well as information technology should not affect the dignity and integrity and human rights of the individual. International cooperation is stressed in this area. The need for cooperation between international organisations and NGOs for the full and effective enjoyment of Human Rights was highlighted in the deliberations of the conference.

The Vienna Conference underlined the need for the eradication of extreme poverty that prevents the effective enjoyment of human rights. It suggested the need for speedy elimination of all forms of racial discrimination and intolerance. The need to combat terrorism and drug trafficking with the cooperation of international community is reiterated.

The rights of women and girl child as an integral part of universal human rights were stressed in the declaration. The women must be allowed to fully participate in the political, civil, economic, social and cultural life at all level. The need for the protection of minority's right in practicing their own culture, religion and language was highlighted in this declaration. It also recognizes the dignity and contribution of indigenous people for the development of pluralistic society. They must be freely allowed by the states to participate in all aspects of society and their rights must be protected. It underlined the need for the survival, protection and development of children. National and international mechanism should be strengthened to protect the girl child, street children, as well as economically and sexually exploited children. Besides, children victims of diseases, refugee and displaced children, children in armed conflict as well as the children victim of famine and other emergencies should also be protected.

Since the global refugee crisis is a very complex problem, the conference recognizes the need for suitable action for the protection and assistance of refugees. Likewise, the internally displaced persons should be rehabilitated and arrangement should be made for their safe return. Humanitarian assistance should be given to the victims of all natural and man-made disasters. The vulnerable group of migrant workers should be protected from discrimination and the states must create suitable conditions for their education and public health. Every state should provide effective arrangements for the redressal of human rights violation. An independent judiciary is necessary for the progress of democracy and sustainable development.

The conference strongly expresses its displeasure on "ethnic cleansing" and all forms of genocide and the systematic rape of women during war. It would lead to mass exodus of the refugees. Such crime should be stopped and suitably punished. It encourages the establishment of national institutions to protect human rights. The conference stressed the need to avoid torture, other inhuman treatments or punishment under any circumstances. It calls upon the states to take all legal and suitable measures to prevent and punish the acts of enforced disappearances. Regarding the disabled persons, the Vienna Conference urged the states to provide equal opportunity to make them fully participate in the affairs of society with dignity.

Human Rights Education

The necessity of human rights education, training and public information for understanding, tolerance and peace was stressed by this Vienna Conference. The state should strive to eradicate illiteracy and education should be used for the full development of personality. It recommends the states to develop programmes and strategies for giving human rights education to its people. Awareness of human rights and mutual tolerance should be cultivated. In this effort, the assistance of UNO should be given to the states. The implementation and monitoring methods for the effective realization of human rights was suggested by this august body.

The Copenhagen Declaration

The world's leaders agreed for ten commitments through the Copenhagen Declaration:

1. Recognizing the importance of social development and human well-being;
2. Eradicate absolute poverty by a target date to be set by each country;
3. Support full employment as basic policy goal;
4. Promote social integration based on the enhancement and protection of all human rights;
5. Achieve equality and equity between women and men;
6. Accelerate the development of Africa and the least developed countries;
7. Ensure that structural adjustment programmes include social development goals;
8. Increase resources allocated to social development;
9. Create economic, political, social, cultural and legal environment that will enable people to achieve social development;

10. Attain universal and equitable access to education throughout the UN.

Mexico Declarations on Human Rights

In Mexico City the regional conference on Human Rights Education was held from November 28 to December 1, 2001. It was jointly organized by the UNESCO, the office of the UN High Commissioner for Human Rights and the Mexican Government. The conference was attended by the representatives of the Government, NGOs, UNESCO chairs in Human Rights and academic institutions. The main aim of the conference was to examine the status of human rights education in Latin America and the Caribbean. It also aims at formulating specific recommendations in this regard.

The conference noted the limited advancement in human rights with regret. It outlined the importance of human rights education for empowering the democratic culture and peace and to strengthen the rule of law. Even before this conference, efforts were made earlier in this region for strengthening human rights education. The Mexico Conference adopted an action programme for immediate implementation. It included general recommendations regarding human rights education and professional training. Human rights education from the point of non-formal education is also included in the action programme.

The Declaration

Transitions to democracy, pluralism and other changes within the global society have created new challenges and expectations for human rights and the rule of law. Human rights education must therefore identify ways and means of addressing such efforts in a comprehensive manner.

Human rights education is an essential component of democratic citizenship. In the past decade, there has been growing awareness that the worldwide struggle against human rights violations can be strengthened. If it is combined with more vigorous preventive human rights work such as human rights education it may be possible.

Human rights education is defined as a programme, which provides knowledge and understanding about human rights. It seeks to develop attitudes and behaviour respectful of those rights. It includes the development of basic skills such as critical thinking, communication skills, problem-solving and negotiation. These are essential for effective human rights activism and participation in decision-making process. A closer look at human rights education shows that it is all about helping people to understand the importance of human rights and provide them with the knowledge, attitudes and skills necessary to promote and protect them. To be successful, such an educational programme must be sustained over a period and involve interaction between two parties—trainer/trainee, teacher/pupil.

Action Programmes and Monitoring

In their National Educational plans, the states were asked to include the issues of human rights, peace and democracy. The process must inculcate the knowledge on human rights so that the awareness must help those who study it. The people of the region must be taught on the cultural plurality of their region and must be aware of the obstacles that prevent the enjoyment of human rights. While imparting education on human rights, encouragement should be given to the use of computer technology.

The states were urged to cooperate with International Organisations, Universities, Research centres and Human Rights organisations in preparing the evaluation instruments. In it, the UNESCO played a crucial role on monitoring and evaluation.

Twenty five states were asked to create a national committee for human rights education. That committee should draw up a national plan of action on Human Rights education. The states were asked to help the NGOs with financial assistances to facilitate the work of human rights education. The Mexico Declaration paved the way for specific recommendations on the inclusion of human rights in formal education, basic education and higher education. It stressed the rights of vulnerable groups such as national ethnic groups, linguistic and religious minorities, migrants, women, girls and boys, people with disabilities and those infected with HIV/AIDS. Inclusion of human rights education in the curricula was strongly recommended.

The state and university authorities were urged to guarantee academic freedom. The Universities must include the components of human rights in all courses. Besides, through non-formal education publicity campaigns should be organized to propagate the idea of human rights. In this attempt audio-visual and mass media such as

TV and Radio can be effectively utilized through artistic mode of expression. Special attentions should be paid on the migrant population, so that the awareness should help this vulnerable group.

The declaration on the rights of indigenous and Afro-descendent people projected the need for human rights education. It would link the process of development with their identity. The human right education must include the geographical, historical and cultural criteria which transcend national political borders.

As a follow-up, the states were asked to publicize the results of the regional conference to public officials, Universities, NGOs and the public. UNESCO and OUNHCHR (Office of the UN High Commissioner for Human Rights) were invited to establish a mechanism to supervise the execution of the recommendation of the conference. The declaration and the follow-up action by the national and international organisations created awareness among the people of this region on the importance of human rights education.

African Human Rights System

As discussed earlier, the African Human Rights system is the youngest regional system. The African Charter on Human and Peoples' Rights specifically recognizes the importance of collective rights. From its standpoint, the rights of the individual and those of the peoples are interlinked and cannot be separated. This instrument also recognized peoples' right to development. Due to the efforts of Organisation of African Union (OAU) and some NGOs, this charter was ratified by an absolute majority of states. Part I of this charter includes rights and duties applying to individuals and groups alike. It places special emphasis on the right and duties of the community, society and nation. The charter also projected the importance of the third generation rights that includes the right to peace, a healthy environment and development. Article 18 (IV) stressed that the disabled have the right to special protection. The African Charter on the rights and welfare of the child was ratified in 1999. It also gives special importance to the rights of persons with disabilities. While dealing with the handicapped children in Article 13, it emphasized on the special measures of protection accorded to them.

The African Charter on Human and Peoples' Right provides for the creation of an African Commission on Human Rights within OAU. In order to promote Human Rights, this commission collects documents and undertakes studies and research on African problems related to human rights. It organizes seminars, conferences and spreads knowledge on human rights. It also makes recommendations to governments and encourages institutions dealing with human and peoples' rights. Normally, the commission accepts complaints after making sure that all local remedies have been exhausted before approaching it. When one state party violates the provisions of the charter, the commission also receives communications from another state in this regard. The commission follows the principles of international organisations like UNO and OAU besides adopting the spirit of instruments adopted by UNO and African countries on human rights. The advocates can also bring issues relating to human rights violations to the African Commission.

In order to assist the people with disabilities, the decade 2000-2009 has been proclaimed as the Africa Decade of Disabled People. This step was taken due to the initiative of NGO community in Africa. The goals of the decades are to promote awareness and the commitment of all concerned for the equality and empowerment of persons with disabilities in the African region. In comparison to other regional human rights systems like the European and Inter-American ones, the African human rights monitoring system is less effective. Several causes like the political climate in Africa and the weakness in the language used in the charter and the limitations on the monitoring of human rights violations had its impact on the effectiveness.

International Human Rights in Domestic Courts

In the International arena there are several enforcement mechanisms available to remedy human rights violations faced by individuals. If women are a victim of human rights violation, they may submit their complaints to any of the six United Nations treaty bodies. Besides these remedies, it is also possible to litigate violations of International law in domestic courts using the principle of universal jurisdiction.

When criminal prosecution would not be possible under ordinary rules of jurisdiction, universal jurisdiction is an important means to ensure justice. The principle of universal jurisdiction allows a court to prosecute the violators of human rights even when no direct link between the country and alleged violation exists. It gives the court jurisdiction regardless of where the crime was committed or what nationality the victim or perpetrator holds. It must be noted here that normally universal jurisdiction applies to violations of international humanitarian law that include genocide, slavery and crime against humanity, piracy and torture. The scope and availability of universal jurisdiction varies from country to country. But several principles on fundamental standards were published by Amnesty International and Princeton Project on Universal Jurisdiction. It addresses the following key areas:

1. Defining the crimes covered by universal jurisdiction
2. Eliminating statutes of limitation
3. Eliminating retrospective immunity
4. Eliminating official immunities
5. Eliminating requiring victim complaints for prosecution
6. Effective training of judges, prosecutors, defence lawyers, and investigators
7. Ensuring the right to a fair trial
8. Facilitating international cooperation
9. Extradition
10. Double jeopardy
11. Barring certain defenses such as duress, orders, and necessity
12. Providing for public trials and international monitoring
13. Protecting the interests of victims, witnesses, and families
14. Strengthening accountability and universal jurisdiction
15. Encouraging national and international legal reform
16. Settling disputes
17. Abolishing capital punishment or other cruel, inhuman punishment
18. Resolving conflicts between competing national jurisdictions
19. Ensuring jurisdiction over suspects shielded by other national laws, and
20. Removing political interference.

When a state has ratified a treaty conferring jurisdiction on States Parties, the universal jurisdiction is available for everyone including a common man. For specific crimes, the Geneva Conventions and Convention against Torture and Other Cruel, Inhuman or Degrading Treatment or Punishment confer universal jurisdiction on State Parties. It grants the States jurisdiction over acts of torture, regardless wherever it occurred. Whenever, the alleged perpetrator of the crime is a national of a particular country or he is present in its territory and the State Party does not extradite, the state parties should take necessary steps to establish jurisdiction in the case. Whenever, the Universal jurisdiction is applied by a state it must adopt its own traditional methods of criminal investigation in the international context.

Despite the existence of several practical difficulties, several states have successfully modified their criminal procedure to accept claims, try cases and convict those who commit extra-territorial human rights violations. In practice an immigration based complaint is very common when asylum or visa seeker is suspected of committing an international crime. The cooperation of immigration authorities is a basic necessity while prosecuting international crimes. In some countries like UK, Spain and France the victims can submit their complaints directly to a judge. It will open the door to international crime investigations when domestic prosecutors may be reluctant to intervene. In two classic cases on universal jurisdiction involving the complaints of private parties, for the extradition of Chile's former dictator Augusto Pinochet and Chad's former dictator Hissene Habre steps were taken. In several countries like Denmark, the Netherlands, Norway, Canada and Ethiopia special units were created to help the prosecution of alleged international criminals in complex cases. But the USA does not currently have a unit to handle such matters. Even without the availability of units specialized in international investigations, conducting much of the research locally is possible. Normally, the evidence mostly based on witnesses' accounts is taken into consideration in the investigation of these types of cases.

In some countries due to slow arrest procedures, the perpetrators of human rights violations escaped despite successful investigation. Before taking action some countries require proof that the suspect is present in their countries. It increases the risk of escape. In order to investigate international crimes, a newly developed international cooperation network involving agencies like Interpol and European Union has emerged. Despite these networks at an early stage of development they are providing limited information on national legislation as well as advice on conducting extra-territorial investigation. Amnesty International's report recommended that the Interpol could improve the effectiveness of state cooperation in universal jurisdiction cases.

The universal jurisdiction may be available in states which adopted them within their domestic legal systems. In the prosecution of Hissene Habre, the former dictator of Chad, who was accused of crimes against humanity, a Belgium judge, indicted him and issued an International warrant served in Senegal. The Senegalese court argued that it did not have the authority on his extradition. Following UN committee against tortures ultimatum to try or extradite him within 90 days necessary legislation was enacted to try Habre domestically based on universal jurisdiction. It was followed by the trial of several cases involving African warlords and Afghan former generals etc. The entry into force of Rome Statute of the International Criminal Court (ICC) may bring positive changes in other states jurisdiction laws. When National courts are unable or unwilling to prosecute suspects, the ICC may act since it has complementary jurisdiction on domestic legal systems. But jurisdiction as well as the cases accepted by ICC is limited.

At present several states have either adopted or adopting legislation to implement the Rome statute and provide jurisdiction over ICC crimes. The crimes included in the list are Genocide, war crimes, crime against humanity including rape, sexual slavery, enforced prostitution, forced pregnancy, enforced sterilization and sexual violence. Countries like Spain implemented ICC legislation in its Organic Law 6/2000 which breaks the principle of territoriality based on the idea of national sovereignty. Some countries allow the victims to file civil claims in criminal proceedings to recover remedies for violation for international human rights. Several recent International Laws recognize the victims' right to recover compensation under civil universal jurisdiction. France provides jurisdiction whenever French Law is applicable to crimes committed outside France or within France.

From the above discussion, it is clear that despite the early stage of development in universal criminal and civil jurisdiction these principles are gaining importance in domestic legislation and in international courts. In several landmark cases involving the prosecution of Dictators and Presidents, the victims were given a great hope. But at the same time those who believe in narrowly interpreting national sovereignty criticized such trials. This issue raised several challenges and problems to international courts, and individual states working on the implementation of international law governing human rights, cutting across national boundaries. But developing a workable universal jurisdiction laws, applicable everywhere is essential for protecting the victims of human rights violation.

International Commission of Jurists

The primary work of International Commission of Jurists (ICJ) is the implementation of international law that advances human rights. The ICJ is an impartial and authoritative legal body that protects human rights through the rule of law. It provides legal assistance at national and international level. In legal field, the Commission also works with national partners to provide training and expertise.

The Commission was founded in 1952 in Berlin. From all-over the world, sixty eminent jurists are selected as its members. They represent various legal systems. The term "jurist" includes judges, attorneys, law professors and legal advisors. The Commission consists of 97 autonomous national sections and legal organisations in 70 countries. It is the backbone of ICJ's network. The Commission works closely with Governments and NGOs. It holds consultative status with UNESCO, UNICEF, the Council of Europe and the African Union.

The Secretary, General directs the functioning of the Commission. The International Secretariat of the ICJ is responsible for the achievement of aims and objectives of the Commission. The governance of the ICJ resides with the commissioners. They assist the secretariat in formulation of policies and the activities of the Commission. The commissioners meet once in every two years at the ICJ's Biennial conference. Between the Biennial conferences, an executive committee looks after the affairs. The commissioners are elected for a period of two years and may be re-elected. The executive committee is composed of between seven and nine commissioners and meets at least twice a year. To assist the commission, a President and two Vice-Presidents are also elected.

Functioning of ICJ

At the national and international level the ICJ covers a wide range of programmes. It strives to maintain human rights values and implementation of programmes related to human rights. It provides legal expertise and assistance whenever its support is needed. It updates international human rights standards and encourages enforcement mechanisms all-over the world. It ensures that at the national level, the human rights law is actually implemented. It looks after the issues involving the proper administration of justice and stressing the independence of judges and lawyers. It also combats gender discrimination at all levels. Legal assistance is provided to governments, as well as to UNO and other international human rights bodies.

The work of training the judges and lawyers is also handled by ICJ. In addition, it looks after fact finding missions, trial observations, research and publications. Whenever the judges and attorneys are persecuted and harassed, it objects to the government and alerts those who could put pressure on the government to stop such abuse. To give additional pressure, it also issue press releases. Depending on the necessity of the situation it also conducts fact finding missions.

Normally, the dictators and powerful criminal groups take the law into their hands whenever the democratic system fails. Naturally violation of human rights became inevitable. In such a situation, it is necessary to protect the judges and lawyers from harassment or persecution. They should not become corrupt or act like a puppet in the hands of government machinery. Only independent courts could provide support to fair trial and the administration of justice. But nowadays in several places judges are threatened with dire consequences if they interpret law honestly and does not please the power centres. Whenever the lawyers try to protect human rights and help political dissidents they are often persecuted and tortured. Those fighting for the establishment of rule of law like the judges and lawyers need protection.

Application for the membership of ICJ is normally admitted from organisations that have a strong legal focus to work for the promotion of human rights. Whenever individuals wanted to create a new organisation, it encourages the creation of an ICJ national section in their home country. Pre-existing organisations can also apply for affiliation with the ICJ. It assists the defenders of human rights with specialized training. It provides analytical studies and reports on international human rights law. It also provides training on the proper use of international norms and procedures and advice for effective lobbying. It protects those involved in this type of activities from the violation of their rights. To protect them, the Human Rights Defenders Office was created in October 2000. This office covers a wide range of issues in support of human rights protection. A number of leading international human rights awards are won by ICJ, for its meritorious service. It includes European Human Rights Prize, Wateler Peace Prize and UN award for Human Rights.

The International Human Rights Conferences play a constructive role in the protection of Human Rights. The conferences in Vienna and Copenhagen concentrate on the complex issues of human rights. It addressed the regional and multinational concerns on a variety of issues. These conferences were used to bring the international community to come together to agree on shared values and goals and on strategies to achieve them. Each conference marked the culmination of many months of intense consultation among member states. The issues covered are ranging from child welfare, protection of environment and human rights, the advancement of women development and support to marginalized groups. The individual and development takes the centre stage. NGOs like Amnesty International are playing a very constructive role in supporting the people in distress. Especially, it protects the rights of those who are suffering behind the prisons. For those who wanted to defend human rights, the International Commission of Jurists provides a support system through its legal expertise.

Questions

1. Briefly evaluate the works of Amnesty International.
2. Examine the importance of the European Convention on Human Rights.
3. What is the significance of Helsinki Charter?
4. Bring out the essence of Mexico Declaration on Human Rights.
5. Is it possible to litigate violations of International Law in domestic courts?
6. Write a note on International Commission of Jurists.

Objective Type Model Questions

1. The Amnesty International was founded by ....
   (a) James Monroe (b) Peter Benson
   (c) Robert Clive (d) Mac Bride.
2. The Helsinki Charter was signed by .... countries.
   (a) 10 (b) 18
   (c) 24 (d) 35.
3. The Headquarters of Amnesty International is located at ....

(a) New York (b) Vienna
(c) Paris (d) London.

4. The European Court of Human Rights was established at ....
(a) Strasbourg (b) Washington DC.
(c) Berlin (d) Stockholm

5. The salient feature of Vienna Declaration (1993) was the recognition to fundamental freedom and .... rights.
(a) human (b) individual's
(c) prisoner's (d) group

6. The main aim of the Mexico Declaration on Human Rights was to examine the status of ....
(a) human rights education (b) women
(c) children (d) bonded labour.

Key to Objective Type Model Questions

1. b 2. d. 3. d 4. a. 5. b. 6. a

NOTES

1. S. Subramanian, Human Rights: International Challenges Vol. 2 (New Delhi: Manas Publications, 2004), 583.
2. Amnesty International, Universal Jurisdiction: The Challenges for police and prosecuting authorities, AI Index: IOR 53/007/2007 June 2007, 1 July, 2008 and Amnesty International, Universal Jurisdiction: Improving the effectiveness of state cooperation, AI Index: IOR 53/006/2007 June 2007, 1 July, 2008.
3. The Hindu, 5 September, 2010.
4. The European Human Rights System, http://www.hrea.org/index.php?base_id =14 (accessed January 29, 2009).
5. Arjun Dev, 110.

5

Contemporary Issues on Human Rights

Children's Rights

In any society children are the assets of nation and the future depends on the quality of life, the children enjoy. Even though human rights violations were experienced by all groups of people including the adults, children's are more vulnerable. Like women they were also exploited in all possible manners. They also don't know the methods of protection from those who exploit them. The UNO is taking all steps to protect the rights of children. A convention on the rights of the child was adopted in the UN General Assembly on 20th November, 1989.[1] Subsequently, the Government of India acceded to this convention on 11th December, 1992. It gives particular attention to civil, political, social, economic and cultural rights of every child.

The Right to Survival

It includes the right to live, the high standard of health, nutrition, and adequate standards of living. This also includes the right to a name and nationality.

The Right to Protection

It includes protection from all forms of exploitations, abuse, inhuman or degrading treatment, and neglect including the right to special protection in situation of emergency and armed conflicts.

The Right to Development

It includes the Right to Education, support for early childhood and care, social security and the right to leisure, recreation and cultural activities.

The Right to Participation

The Right to participation includes respect for the views of the child, freedom of expression, access to appropriate information and freedom of thought, conscience and religion.

Exploitation of child is very common in almost all parts of the world. It is particularly very high in the developing countries. A rough estimate puts the number of child labour around 220 million in which south Asia alone accounts for 90 million. In fact, the actual figure may be much higher since it is not easy to identify child labour in certain sectors like agriculture, plantations, brick kilns and mines. The bonded children are trapped in a variety of industries. It is estimated that 20 million children are working in hazardous and non-hazardous industries in India.[2] In the glass industry of Ferozabad in Uttar Pradesh, the children are exposed to furnace temperatures above 1400 degree Celsius. The children carry the molten glass to be poured into different moulds. In the match and fireworks in Sivakasi, the children played an active role in its manufacture. Every year several children die in blasts and others were crippled for their entire life.

Child Labour

The problem of child labour is one of an important human rights issue at stake. Knowledge of human rights and its exposure in the society is the first and surest defence against the danger that these rights will be plucked away or trampled on. Learning about one's own right builds respect for the rights of others. A working child is defined as a child in the age group of 5 to 14 years who is doing labour, either paid or unpaid, and is busy within or outside the family. It creates a situation in which the child is deprived of proper growth to become a worthy adult. The children work full-time at too young age. At times they have to work for more than eight hours against the stipulated norm of four to five hours per day. Normally, the type of work they are doing gives a lot of physical, social and psychological stress. In most places, they are forced to work under unhygienic and unsafe working condition. Their pay is inadequate and in the name of apprenticeship they may not get any pay. This work prevents their chance to have education and undermines their dignity and self-respect. Child labour is against the proper psychological development of the children. The child labour affects their overall health, vision and hearing.

Causes of Child Labour

1. Poverty is the primary reason that forces the children to work. Since their income is essential to supplement the meagre income of their families they are working.
2. Employers prefer children since they are cheaper, unorganized and more flexible.
3. Parent's perception on the advantages in the child taking up a job early, in view of widespread unemployment even among educated youth.
4. Child labour ensures maximum profits to the employer.
5. They can be easily controlled and tamed by their employer.
6. They do not form unions and create problems for the employer.
7. In industries like carpet making the tender hands of children are more suitable for the work.
8. It is also observed that in some families they at least make one child to continue their traditional occupation. These children were given only minimum education and practically follow the parents' footsteps in learning and practicing their traditional occupation. In professions like goldsmith, potters, barbers, dhobis and farmers regards the continuity of their profession as an essential one. It may be due to societal pressure and sometimes due to the choice of parents who prefer to continue their traditional occupation through succeeding generations.[3]

Nature of Child Labour

Children work in different situations due to a number of factors:

I. Children engaged in domestic work: children doing non-productive, unpaid work for maintenance of the household.

It helps their parents to go out and work as wage labourers. Many young girls handle this kind of work.

II. Non-domestic, non-monetary work performed within the household: It includes children's engagement in agriculture and a variety of cottage industries including handloom and other works.

III. Wage labour: This type of work includes involvement in both organized and unorganized sector like auto workshop, tea stalls, eateries and domestic help.

IV. Bonded labour: Acute poverty and indebtedness are mainly responsible for the emergence of child labour in the field of agriculture and in unorganized sectors in urban areas. Bonded labour in the *beedi* industry in Vellore district, the match and fireworks industry in Sivakasi and knitwear industry in Thiruppur in Tamil Nadu are some examples in this section.

According to Census estimate more than 80 per cent of working children are in the rural areas and are engaged in the second category of work which is non-monetary. Further, a large number of children in both rural and urban areas work in the informal unorganized sector which includes small workshops, restaurants and cottage and small industries. This sector is unregulated and it is difficult to obtain a correct estimate of working children.

Types of Child Labour

Normally, there are three categories of children involved in child labour. They are broadly classified under the categories of street children, bonded children and working children. The street children are living in the streets without the protection of permanent shelter, love and affection. They work as shoe-polish boys, newspaper-vendors, rag-pickers and at times do begging. The problem of this group is more acute in comparison to that of children working in factories and workshops.[4] At least those children can have home to go back in the evening. But the street children are completely alone and are at the mercy of their employers night and day. They live on the pavements, in the bus stands, railway platforms and in small eating places. They are being exposed to the anti-social elements. Due to their complex problems normally they are on the run and are deprived of education and normal childhood.

The children work either as a bonded labour or work without any bondage. The bonded children are those who have been either pledged by their parents for small sums of money. They are working mainly in the rural areas to pay the inherited debts of their parents. Due to the inaccessible nature of these groups of children, it is difficult to assist them. If they are bought by the owners of small eateries or by the middle class housewife or by the landlord in the village they may not allow them to escape from the bondage. Hence, the children must spend their life in servitude till they get married and can sell their children to minimize their debt burden. There are even reported cases in which even a Magistrate in Delhi kept a boy as a bonded labour and only with great difficulty and due to the intervention of higher court he was released from the bondage.

The third category is the working children who are working as part of family labour in agriculture and in home based work. If they are working 10-12 hours a day along with their parents, without any scope for education, their position is more or less similar to that of children working for employers. Even within the child labour, girls have additional responsibility due to the social customs and beliefs. They are supposed to handle the work burden of their parents in complete disproportion to their strength and abilities.

All the above three categories of children face different types of problems. Those who work in the hazardous industries like match factories and other related works which exposes them to the toxic elements that affect their health also. The children working full-time are at greater risk. It is observed that different categories of child labour require different kind of intervention and assistance. In India, children represent nearly 42 per cent of the total population and nearly half of them are girls. Within this group, 40 per cent of all girls are in the age group of 10-14 years. Besides helping their parents with sowing, transplanting, weeding, harvesting, cattle rearing, a large number of these girl children worked in the unorganized sector industries such as match, coir, glass bangles, carpet, and lock and *beedi* industries.[5]

In India children work at all ages. A three year old assists her eight year old sister in arranging the match boxes in Sivakasi, known for litho printing, fireworks and match industries. In the tea plantations too, the young children work alongside their parents in picking the tea leaves. It is unfortunate that government legally permits the small scale industries to use child labour directly or through sub-contract.

Most of the children who work do not have the power of free choice. The vast majority are pushed into labour. It damages their chances of education, and allow the others to exploit their poverty.

In Tamil Nadu one can come across the existence of all the three categories of children discussed above. But in comparison to the major cities like Mumbai and Chennai, the number of street children is less in villages. Death of parents or their neglect due to variety of factors exposed the children to the difficulties of adult world in which they have nobody to care for them. The street children are wandering in the street without any aim and direction. They work as rag-pickers and do any manual work as and when available. The pressure of survival forced them at times to petty thefts and other related crime. Hence, the police regarded them as nuisance and menace to the city. In cities like Rio de Janeiro these street children were eliminated physically by the law enforcing agencies.[6] Since government involvement in India to eradicate child labour was limited due to financial constraint and other factors, there are several non-governmental agencies that are working for their help. These children must be guided to have basic education and support.

Child labour is affecting the very core of the society. Among the child labour considerable segment enters into bonded labour. Unfortunately, the government statistics shed only partial light on their problem. In most cases the state governments refuse to accept the existence of child labour. Non-enforcement of law protecting the children is guaranteed as long as the government is wilfully denying the existence of bonded child labour in large number. The children work in restaurants, mechanic shops, and match factories and in any type of menial work. In the *beedi* making work also considerable numbers of children are engaged. More than any other factor, it is due to economic compulsion parents engage them in this work. Girls even as young as 6 and 7 years work up to 8-10 hours a day. One researcher found that girls start making *beedi* at a very tender age. Nearly half of the *beedi* workers started working when they were between 5 and 10 years and the other half were introduced to *beedi* making between 11 and 15 years.[7] Due to toxic exposure the health is affected. Full-time employment also shut down the avenue for education and the emancipation of the children.

Contrary to popular belief that child labour brings down production cost for the management, the studies conducted by the International Labour Organisation (ILO) pointed out that productivity goes down when more number of children are employed thereby affecting the productivity of the management. The studies pointed out that lack of education has reduced the creativity and self-confidence of children. The spirit of inquiry is lost when the children are forced to a job. It puts them under psychological disorderliness and makes them economically weak. It is also observed that child labour is the prime cause of adult unemployment as well as for the drop in the economic status of poor families.[8] It also perpetuate poverty as a working child grows into an adult trapped in unskilled and poorly paid jobs.[9] If the adults were given reasonable salary that may help the poor families and reduce the incidence of child labour.

Efforts of Government

Regarding child labour the Government of India is taking some legal measures which are inadequate to address the problem. Over the years, a plethora of laws and specific policies to address the child labour emerges. But these laws have been singularly ineffective. Due to lack of proper monitoring, enforcing these laws become impossible. Corruption and generalized apathy of the society on this issue is one important factor contributed for its unchecked growth. Most of the state governments are reluctant to accept even the existence of child labour.[10] Several studies highlights the important role of district collectors in minimizing the child labour. But except in some individual cases where some collectors, pay some attention to eradicate child labour. But in most of the cases, they are not paying enough attention to it. Child labour is not in the priority list of the government and naturally the personnel in the revenue department treat the matter with apathy. Since child labour is linked with the economic and social issues they may view that mere legal solution cannot solve the problem. At the national level 537 inspections were carried out under the Child Labour (Prohibition and Regulation) Act from 1990 to 1993. These inspections traced 1203 violations out of which only seven prosecutions were launched. Even when convictions are obtained under the Child Labour Act, the fines are light.[11]

In Tamil Nadu, the Act was not enforced until 1994. Only eight years after its passage a case was filed in the Vellore district in Tamil Nadu. Regarding Bonded Labour (Abolition) Act, the first prosecution under the twenty-year-old Act occurred in 1995, when eight *beedi* employees were arrested by the Vellore District Collector, M.P.

Vijayakumar. Though they were kept in jail overnight and fined 500 rupees each, it was nevertheless regarded as a bold step considering the official apathy towards the problem. Due to the wide coverage given to this incident in the press, it creates some awareness on child labour in Vellore district in Tamil Nadu. At present at least in some major towns the government conducts surprise check and punishes those who employ children. The district collector is imposing a hefty fine also. To some extent it has its effect on the employer. One can see even boards making announcement that there is no child labour in their establishment. It is a positive development. In 2007, Dharmendra Pratap Yadav was the Collector of Vellore district and he initiated several steps to eradicate the menace. Both the government agencies and the NGOs are geared up to end the child labour through non-formal education.

Since poverty is the main factor in sending children to work parents are encouraged to send their children in non-formal schools where free education is given. The parents are warned that the district administration would not spare the parents who forcibly send their children for work. In states like Tamil Nadu, recent statistics indicates a big drop in the number of out-of-school children in the last few years. The Times of India (Chennai) reports on November 5, 2010, that according to the review reports of Sarva Shiksha Abhiyan, the number of out of school children was dropped from 5,74,069 in 2002-2003 to a mere 56,130 in May 2010. The number of children brought back to school is also increased over the years from 18.81 per cent to 83 per cent in the corresponding period. Through volunteers, summer courses and bridge courses were conducted to make the children catch up with their peers that enable them to enter again in the mainstream schools. Such efforts should be given encouragement to minimize the drop-out rates in the school. When the children are going to schools regularly, their chances of entering into child labour market also would be reduced.

Universalisation of primary education and child labour are no doubt twin issues that have to be tackled on war-footing. Little has been done to involve the local leaders of local Panchayats in the fight against child labour. The Public Report on Basic Education (PROBE), 1998 conclusively proved that poor parents, even in the most educationally backward states of Madhya Pradesh, Rajasthan, Bihar and U.P. were overwhelmingly found to be eager to educate their children. In fact, poverty is not a stumbling block. But mostly the problems associated with the school system prevented the education of these poor children. The problem of child labour was complex and many questions needed to be answered like the alternatives available for working children, the ways to keep them in the state educational system and the changing perceptions of the parents on the importance of education in comparison to wage earning in the long run.

Child Labour and Legislation

In the past, Government policy towards child labour has wavered between the intention to ban it and the desire to regulate it. Some of the earliest Acts like Factories Act, 1948, Mines Act, 1952, Plantations Labour Act, 1951 etc., laid down the minimum age for employment of children (varies between 12-16 years) in some sectors and regulated their hours of work. However, these Acts had limited coverage and applied only to large and organized sector units, while it is the unorganized sector which is the largest employer of child labour in the country. Further, enforcement of these laws remains poor.

In recent years, the concept of regulation of child labour by a comprehensive legislation has found greater acceptance. The Higher Power Committee (Gurupadaswamy Committee) constituted by the Government of India (1979) has held that in the present socio-economic conditions of the country, a ban on employment of children is not possible. However, employment of children in hazardous occupations should be banned and their working conditions should be regulated. Thus, Child Labour (Prohibition and Regulation) Act, 1986 prohibits working of children below 14 years in hazardous industries such as *beedi* making, manufacture of matches, explosives and fireworks, carpet weaving, printing, dyeing and weaving and cement manufacturing. It also prohibits working of children in more than one shift or engaging them in night shifts.

It is clear that the legislation has been drafted on the premise, that since the root cause of child labour is poverty, it cannot be eliminated overnight. The best solution is to regulate the practice of child labour. Accordingly, employment of children above 12 years has been allowed in selected areas of the organized sector, with suitable safeguards against exploitation and provision for educational and recreational facilities. Apart from stipulating the minimum wages, weekly rest days and hygienic working conditions, the Act also takes care of the health need of child workers. The ratification of the ILO convention of 1973, abolishing labour by children still remains a distant dream for India.

Child Soldiers

One another area of great concern today is the use of children in war zones and conflict situations as soldiers. It is estimated that around 3,00,000 children are serving in the current armed conflicts all- over the world. They carry AK-47s and M-16s and involve in all sorts of frontline combat duties. They serve as human mine detectors, and act as spies and carryout suicide missions. Child soldiers are used in more than 30 countries including Sri Lanka[12] and Lebanon. At times they were given drugs to overcome fear or reluctance to fight. The position of girl soldier is really painful and pathetic since they are also subjected to sexual abuse in places like Angola and Uganda. The issue of child soldiers is another problem involving human rights abuse.

The UN conducted a study on the impact of armed conflict on children. It stressed the urgent need to stop this dangerous practice. The use of children under the age of 15 in war as a soldier is termed as war crime by the international criminal court. ILO also prohibits the recruitment and use of children in the armed conflicts. But unfortunately monitoring and enforcement of these laws became very difficult in practical terms.

Some Positive Steps

The availability of free, compulsory and quality education is widely viewed as a key factor in the fight against child labour. The relationship between illiteracy and child labour is very strong. The Indian Council on Child Welfare is working for providing at least minimum education to the children of India. It is aiming at providing non-formal education to the working children. It provides modest financial assistance to attract children including cash stipends and grain allowance. Children on the verge of adulthood are given skills, training to support themselves in future. In the long run such efforts with the active support of NGOs will make considerable impact on the problem of child labour in India. A novel project "transit school for working children" was launched in the Virudhunagar district covering Sivakasi,

Sattur and other cottage industrial centres known for child labour practice. It was funded by the ILO, involving the trade unions; employers and the district administration.[13] There are 80 transit schools with 25 children each will come up in areas known for children not attending the schools. When the children are adapted to the transit school system they will be integrated into the mainstream of regular education. Such efforts should also be taken in other areas of the country where lack of schools pushed the children to child labour. The experience of some developing countries like Brazil and South Korea can be of some help in this regard. In Brazil, a special school programme—the Bolsa Escola—provides education grants or school stipends based on household monthly wages. It enables poor families to send their children to schools. In addition a greatly enhanced programme of labour inspections to discover and punish cases of child labour also exists. In recent years following highly publicized reports of the death of children in work places, the Chinese Government has also introduced stringent laws that includes hefty fine on the employer cumulative over the month of employment. With some regional difference over its implementation, such steps slowly yield desired results.

In Karnataka also a novel scheme of providing education at the door step of the slum dwellers has been experimented. A bus with all the facilities of a class room is used to collect the children and classes were conducted in the bus.[14] The UNICEF appreciated this novel scheme. Such efforts can also be tested in other states. Reasonably raising the wages of the adult, creation of awareness against the child labour, availability of free education, active support of the government—both States and Central—besides the effective contribution of Non-Governmental Organisations will certainly minimize the severity of child labour. The Child Labour is neither socially desirable, nor it necessarily grow out of a particular stage of development. A greater degree of public outrage and social action is needed and for which all of us are collectively responsible.

Women's Rights

All-over the world women encounter many difficulties just because they are women. One way or the other, the women are discriminated in a variety of issues. In India, the status and position of women is not uniform over the periods of history. According to Rekha Roy, they face different types of problem due to their different socio-cultural settings.[15] In the Vedic period they have almost equal status with men folk.[16] They were respected and were not discriminated in the society. Variety of factors led to the decline of women to an inferior position in the later period. In the Sangam Tamil Society also one can see the secondary position given to women.[17] Their education was different from the education given to men. They were trained mostly to look after the family and to be in the good books of their husbands. The Sangam literature gives a lot of information on the dependent position of women. *Sati* was also practiced that end the life of a widow in the funeral pyre of her husband. The cruelty of widowhood is described in Sangam literature. The women were not permitted to participate in the war. Chastity was stressed as an important quality of respected women. But in the Tamil society a separate group of women were assigned the task of satisfying the carnal pleasures of men in separate villages. Latter, they became street prostitutes due to their deteriorated social status.

The Devadasi system also exploited the women over the centuries and due to the efforts of Dr. Muthulakshmi Reddy it was abolished. In Independent India, the Constitution provides several safeguards to women. But still a vast gap exists between theory and practice. Despite the development of education and employment opportunities for women, they still enjoy only a secondary position. Except in some tribal societies, the position of women in India and in other parts of the world is mostly subordinate to men. Basically, the Indian society is a male dominated society. In this system, the birth of male child is preferred over the birth of a female child. In politics, governance and in the decision-making process the men occupies primary position. It seriously affected the position of women and to address this handicap several progressive legislations protecting human rights were passed and implemented. But unfortunately several women are unaware about their own rights guaranteed in the Constitution.

In India, several great reformers[18] like Raja Ram Mohan Rai, Ishwara Chandra Vidyasagar, Jyotiba Phule, E.V.R. Periyar, and Dr. Muthulakshmi Reddy fought for the emancipation of women. But still women are subject to variety of disabilities because of their gender. Due to the efforts of UNO, several steps were taken to protect the rights of women. A special emphasis was given for the protection of women and children due to their vulnerable position. Countries all-over the world incorporated the provisions of human rights in their respective Constitutions. There is variety of rights that gives women special protection against exploitation. But the real problem is in its implementation and the mindset of the society against its implementation. Starting from birth women is normally regarded as a burden and major responsibility to the family. Starting from mother's milk, the girl child is discriminated from its due share in comparison to the male child. Even the quantity and quality of food is restricted to a female child due to the belief system in the society that women must always be physically weak in comparison to a male child. Normally, the lions share is given to the husband and to the male child. Changing the attitude of the society in respect of women will take a long time. Proper awareness and empowerment of women with suitable legislative support may help them to overcome the centuries old bias against women.

Following the efforts of UNO to trace the condition of women and to suggest remedial measures to improve their position, several steps were taken in the right direction. In 1976, the UNO brought special efforts against the discrimination of women. In 1975, the International Women's Conference was organised in Mexico followed by another one in Denmark in 1980. Later in 1985, the third conference was organised in Nairobi and in Beijing in 1995.[19] There are varieties of a right that gives equal opportunity for women and protect them against discrimination due to their gender.[20]

Right to Equality

This right maintains that all human beings are born free and are equal in their rights. All are equal before law. Articles 14 to 16 of the Indian Constitution as well as the International Covenant on Civil and Political Rights stressed that no discrimination is permitted on gender basis. Both men and women can equally enjoy the right to speech, the right to protection and right to religion and family and the right to get social protection and property rights. Like men, women also were protected against exploitation. Various International instruments on human rights as well as the Indian Constitution guarantee the independence and protection of women.

Right to Education

In India, right to equal education was denied to women from its early history. The duty of women is primarily to look after their husband and children and the domestic work. Since the women would go to their husband's house after marriage, the investment on their education is not considered as useful to her parent's family. Even now millions of girl child are deprived of good education despite the Articles 15 and 29 of the Indian Constitution stressed the need for giving equal educational opportunity to women. After considerable delay, now compulsory education up to the age of 14 years became a fundamental right after the 93rd Constitutional Amendment. The Government is trying to implement this in the letter and spirit despite a variety of practical difficulties.

In India, the girl child is mostly given only primary education. In many villages and in hilly regions the education of girl child is not considered as essential. Due to social pressure and practices a girl child is not permitted to continue her education after reaching puberty. The girl child is forced to look after several household works including fetching water, cooking, looking after the younger siblings while her parents are away at work. She has little choice over her education and determining her future. The social reformers and great leaders of the 19th and 20th centuries India tried their level best to destroy the age old custom and convention against the emancipation of women. They laid a strong foundation for the future of Indian women. Mahatma Gandhi stressed the importance of women's education and E.V.R. Periyar made it his life mission to educate the women folk and to uplift their position. Dr. Muthulakshmi Reddy was the first women doctor in South India and faced all sorts of gender-biases in her life. But she successfully completed her medical education and became a torch bearer for the upliftment of women. In independent India, one can see a remarkable change in the attainment of education by women. The Nehru years witnessed the rapid expansion of girl's education. In 1964, the number of girl students increased sixfold and constituted 22 per cent of the total student strength. Except in some courses like Ph.D. they dominate the educational scenario today in securing good percentage of pass as well as marks in comparison to their male counterparts. But in remote areas and in villages where the awareness on education and availability of schools are less, the girl child has little chance for education. Besides, one major concern at the national level was the drop-out rate of girls higher than boys.

The women's organisations which participated actively in the national movement demanded revision of laws regarding women's right. Pandit Nehru who was in the helm of affairs for 17 years was a firm supporter of this demand. He quoted the French philosopher Charles Fourier: "One could judge the degree of civilization of a country by the social and political position of its women". Nehru was instrumental in bringing the Hindu Code Bill despite opposition from conservative Hindu communal organisations.[21] The Bill was later passed in the form of four separate Acts which introduced monogamy and the right of divorce to both men and women, raised the age of marriage and more than anything gave women the right to maintenance and to inherit family property. It was a revolutionary step in the direction of women's liberation. But its acceptance and practice took several decades.

Economical Rights

It is one of the most important rights necessary for the survival of human beings. In 1966, the UNO recognized the International Covenant on Economic, Social and Cultural Rights. It stressed the need for giving various economic rights that are essential for economic equality. It maintains the importance of giving equal economic rights to men and women. They can choose their own work and the government must provide suitable atmosphere for healthy working conditions. The working women should be supported during the time of child birth. Articles 41 and 42 of Indian Constitution stipulated this point. It also incorporates several other rights that are necessary for happy living.

Equal Pay for Equal Work

In unorganized sectors and at times, in organised sectors also, women are not given equal wages for equal work like men. In agriculture, women are paid sometimes 75 to 100 per cent less wages than men. In areas of Bihar and Uttar Pradesh women workers are paid between one and-a half to 2 kg of food grains for a 10 hour work a day. There are cases in India where women are savagely beaten and raped because they refuse to work for poor wages. Even in established private companies sometimes the women has to go to the court for equal pay for equal work. The Indian Government tried to set right this anomaly by incorporating the principle of equal pay for equal work. In 1976, the Equal Remuneration Act was passed to handle the issues related to the disparity in payment of wages. Article 39 D of the Directive Principles of State Policy also stipulated equal pay equal work. Article 39 of the Constitution envisages the need for equal pay for equal work for both men and women.

Women throughout the world are denied human rights in the labour force. On several occasions the Governments turn a blind eye to illegal practices that discriminate working women. In some countries like Mexico, the female applicants for a job must undergo pregnancy test as a condition of work. Normally, these companies deny job opportunities to pregnant women. In South Africa the white farm owners deny legal contracts to black women workers and pay them less than men for same type of work. They also deny maternity benefits to them. Sexual harassment and violence are very common in work places in several countries.

In India Section 4 of the Equal Remuneration Act spells out the duty of the employer to pay equal remuneration to men and women workers for the same work.[22] Likewise, Section 5 prohibits discrimination in the recruitment of men and women workers. In several cases the court directed that equal pay for equal work should be respected and implemented. Women must also work only for reasonable hours and they also need rest after some time. It was stipulated in the Article 24 of the Universal Declaration of Human Rights. The Equal Remuneration Amendment Act, 1987 stipulated that no discriminatory treatment should be met out to women in promotion, training and transfer. They must also have separate rest room and toilet facilities. Women are also entitled for reservation in education as well as in employment. In some cases the Supreme Court also upheld the right of women in this regard.[23] In India, pay equity was debated seriously in the 1980s, but appears dormant in the free market political climate.[24] The forces of globalization had its impact on the pay equity as well.

Rights on Maternity Benefits

According to Article 42 of the Directive Principles of State Policy women must be provided with assistance at the time of childbirth. On the bases of it, an Act was passed in 1961 which provides help during the delivery of women. Those who are working in the Government offices or in private institutions where the workers exceed ten in numbers the women are entitled for 12 weeks holiday during their child birth. They are entitled for their regular pay during this maternity leave. After delivery they are entitled for two times permission in every working day till the baby reaches the age of 15 months.

Social Laws and Women's Rights

The major issues related to social laws covers marriage, adoption, guardianship, abortion, the welfare of the children and other related issues. Regarding marriage several issues are involved. It includes mate selection, age at marriage, polygamy, invalid marriage, restitution of conjugal rights, dowry, maintenance, abortion and custody of child as well as adaptation of children. According to the Special Marriage Act of 1954, girls can select their life partners when they attain the age of 18 years. They can also select their spouses from outside their caste, community and religion. Through civil marriage those who marry outside their religion can bypass the customary ceremonies of their respective religion. But neither of the life partners should have a spouse living at the time of marriage and they should not be close relatives within the degrees of prohibited relationship, unless their community permits such marriages. The Special Marriage Act, 1954 also stipulated various rules and regulations.

Age at Marriage

Before independence, child marriage was very common and normally the marriage of a girl should be arranged before she attained puberty. Several social reformers played an important role in changing this practice. Under the British, the Special (Civil) Marriage Act, 1872 had fixed the minimum age of marriage for girls at 14. But this condition was applied to the girls who married through courts outside their caste. Later the Child Marriage Restraint Act, 1929 fixed the minimum age of marriage for boys at 18 and for girls 14, which was later amended to 15.

After independence the outlook on child marriage underwent radical change. Hence, the Special Marriage Act, 1954 fixed the minimum marriage age at 21 and 18 for boys and girls respectively. The Hindu Marriage Act, 1955 prescribed the minimum age for girls as 15 years and 18 years for boys at the time of marriage. If the 1929 Act is violated it prescribes penalty but the marriage is allowed to remain valid. But in the 1955 Act, the violation would lead to make the marriage legally void. In reality child marriage is a very common practice in several parts of India. In states like Rajasthan and Madhya Pradesh children below five years are forced into marriage and the society is ignorant of the problems involved in such marriages. In Karnataka in a recent survey, in some villages several women respondents agreed that most of them marry at the age of thirteen. Girls from poor background are married off immediately after they attained puberty. Their parents regarded them as a responsibility and burden and arrange their marriage at the earliest. Child marriage and child birth at tender age would ruin the physical and mental ability of a girl child. If the husband dies at a young age they have to lead a solitary life with all the difficulties of the widowhood.

In India, the Muslim marriages are governed by the Muslim personal law. If the girl established that she was given in marriage by her father or guardian before she attained the age of 15 and the marriage is not consummated, she can repudiate her marriage. A Muslim marriage would be treated as invalid if the marriage partners are within the prohibited relationship defined by the Muslim Law. Their children are treated as illegitimate children. Likewise, the Christians as well as the Parsi marriages are also governed by their respective marriage Acts.

Invalid Marriage

Normally, a Hindu marriage would be invalid if it is bigamy; either partner suffers from mental disorder, or impotent; either of them has not completed the minimum age; the life partners are closely related within the degrees of prohibited relationship. The Christian marriage would be invalid for the same reasons attributed for the Hindu marriage that is invalid. Under some circumstances some defective marriages are liable to be declared invalid by law. But if the spouses like to continue their marriage they are permitted. At the same time there are some defects which can make a marriage invalid. If one party refuses to consummate the marriage, wife being pregnant at the time, of marriage by another person and the consent to marriage was obtained by force or fraud the marriage become invalid. On four conditions, the Hindu Marriage Act, 1955 makes a marriage void. The conditions included impotency, unsound mind, pre-marriage pregnancy by other person and consent obtained by force or fraud.

Rules Governing Divorce

A Hindu marriage is considered to be *sanskara* or sacrament and not a contract as it is understood among Muslims. Hence, the Hindu custom never permitted the marriage to be dissolved under any circumstances. Advancement of education and changes in attitude had its impact on Hindu marriages also. Today the Hindu marriage is no longer regarded as in-dissolvable. Hence, both the Special Marriage Act, 1954 and the Hindu Marriage Act, 1955 permits divorce and judicial separation. The grounds are almost the same for divorce and judicial separation excepting that a decree for judicial separation can be converted into a decree of divorce after one year. But the couple should not resume their relationship during the period. Adultery, cruelty, bigamy, imprisonment, insanity, communicable diseases like leprosy and venereal diseases, renunciation, desertion for two years, the spouse not heard about seven years, arranging marriage by force or fraud, impotency, wife pregnant at the time of marriage from another person and failure of any party to comply with a decree for restitution of conjugal rights are the grounds for divorcé. In 1976, an amendment was made in this Act that permits divorce by mutual consent after proving that they are living apart for one year and still prefer divorce.

In 2009, the Law Commission has recommended to the centre that 'irretrievable breakdown of the marriage' be incorporated as an additional ground for divorce under the Hindu Marriage Act, 1955 and the Special Marriage Act. The Commission headed by A.R. Lakshmanan observes that the foundation of the sound marriage is tolerance, adjustment and respecting each other. Tolerance of each other's fault to a certain level has to be inherent in every marriage. Once the marriage has brokendown beyond repair it would be unrealistic for the law not to take notice of this fact.

The report of the Commission said that whenever a marriage has been wrecked beyond the hope of salvage, it must be recognized. Nothing is gained by trying to keep the parties tied forever to a marriage that in fact has ceased to exist. In the case of *Navin Kohli* vs. *Neelu Kohli*, the Supreme Court had recommended to the centre to seriously consider the amendment of law to include the irretrievable breakdown of marriage as a ground for the grant of divorce. Consequently, the Union Cabinet cleared the amendments for 'irretrievable breakdown of marriage' as an additional ground for divorce in June 2010.[25] It is observed that the parties who have filed petition for divorce on mutual consent suffer in case one if the parties abstain from court proceedings and keep the divorce process inconclusive, he or she can cause considerable hardship to the other person in dire need of divorce. To mitigate the suffering in such cases, this amendment was incorporated.

It must be noted here that the right to divorce given to a Hindu is not for attacking the sacramental nature of the marriage. Divorce is introduced to enable the Hindu women to get rid of husbands who humiliate them besides failing in his duty to fulfil their marital obligations. The husband is expected to support to his wife economically during the judicial separation period. After the divorce, depending upon their income and social status, the wife or the husband are entitled to claim maintenance and support from the other partners. But the wife looses this right if she leads an immoral life. Depending upon the status and income of the parties and the reasonable needs of the claimant the amount of maintenance is determined by the court.

Divorce in Muslim community is governed by Muslim Personal Law.[26] The Muslim husband has better place in many ways. The Surah of Quran implies that since man is the supporter and protector of woman in the family[27] he is placed above the women. In the presence of two witnesses he can repudiate the marriage at his will after pronouncing 'talaq' (revocable and irrevocable talaq) three times. Normally, a Muslim wife can seek divorce only by mutual consent. However, the Dissolution of Muslim Marriage Act, 1939 has given a right to a Muslim wife to divorce her husband by filing a petition in the court on the following grounds: Disappearance of her husband for two or more years, neglect and non-maintenance for two years, husband selling the property of his wife and depriving her of her personal wealth, his imprisonment for seven or more years, failure to perform marital obligation for three years, impotency, insanity, leprosy, venereal disease and cruel treatment of his wife. If the girl was given in marriage before she reached 15 years or if she is forced to lead an immoral life she is entitled for divorce.

Islam permits a man to marry more than once and he can marry up to a maximum of four wives. But those who have more than one wife must treat their wives equally in accordance with the guidelines of Quran. Otherwise, the wife can file for divorce. In Muslim law, the divorced wife has no right to maintenance beyond three months or a period of *'Iddat'*. She only gets the *'mahar'* amount fixed at the time of marriage. A divorced Muslim woman is entitled to and can claim maintenance only under the provisions of and in accordance with the procedure covered under sections 3 and 4 of the Muslim Women's (Protection of Rights on Divorce) Act, 1986. In India there is a demand for uniform civil code for all the religious communities by some sections of the society following *Mohammad Ahamed Khan* vs. *Shah Bano Begum* case. It is a sensitive issue and the political leadership at the national level handled it with utmost caution. In 1986, the Muslim Women (Protection of Rights on Divorce) Act was passed. The Act stipulated that the Muslim husband's liability to pay maintenance is only up to *'Iddat'* period. The religious sentiments of the Muslim community were respected in this regard. Being a secular country, it was felt that the Indian Muslims should be allowed to have their own customs and conventions and their individual identity.

In comparison to other communities in India, the rules governing divorce in Christian community is very difficult. According to the Indian Divorce Act, 1869 there is only one ground for divorce. By this Act, Adultery is a valid ground for the dissolution of marriage. The law is discriminatory against the women. If the woman wants to sue her husband for divorce, she must prove the adultery of her husband in addition to his cruelty or desertion. In other words, mere adultery of her husband is not sufficient ground for divorce. It must be coupled with either cruelty or desertion. Then only women can seek divorce. The grounds which are sufficient for divorce in Hindu community are only allowing the Christians for a judicial separation. But the judicial separation among Christians would not get converted into divorce after one year. It remains a judicial separation and both men and women can never marry again. Generally, getting divorce and opting for remarriage is very difficult among Indian Christians.

After suitable amendments the Parsi Marriage Act has been brought on the lines of Hindu Marriage Act and the Special Marriage Act, 1954 as far as the divorce is concerned. Due to the changing needs of time family courts were established in various parts of India. It handles the family dispute that includes issues pertaining to divorce, maintenance issue and the custody of children. The 21st century India witnessed several changes due to the advancement in education and in other fields. Consequently, the role and status of women is redefined. Women's education and career opportunity gives them considerable freedom of choice. As long as they depend on their men folk for sustenance they cannot lead an independent life and make their own decisions on to their life.

The emerging trend indicates considerable increase in the number of women opt for divorce. The changing attitude of the society on gender relations and the status of women and their free choice opt them for divorce. But at the same time there are reports that suggest that both men and women seek divorce on flimsy grounds. Mostly ego problems and the work pressure on employed couple devastate their marriage. Especially in the IT related professions, the shift system, work pressure, lack of rest and affluence affects family life when both of them are earning members. In the family courts normally counselling was given to make them understand reason. They need not separate themselves from the bonds of marriage if the causes are not worth that pain. More than anything the children are the ultimate victims of their parent's choice to divorce. In India, unfortunately the issue of maintenance is proved to be a very uncertain one due to the practical difficulties of women to access court. Getting maintenance order from the court is also a time consuming procedure. Often the amount awarded is also very low. Hence, the Delhi High Court ordered that the maintenance amount should reflect the status of her husband and her practical needs.[28]

Restitution of Conjugal Rights

Due to unfortunate circumstances sometimes a women may be forced to walk out of her husband's home. It may be due to the cruelty of husband, harassment for dowry related issue, ill-treatment by in-laws, obligation to her parents and her dislike for joint family system. In such circumstances, if the husband is unable to persuade his wife to return to his house he may go to the court. He can appeal for the restitution of the conjugal rights from his wife. In some cases, the wife may change her mind after few years and wish to return back to her husband's house. If he refuses to take her back she can approach the court demanding the company of her husband. But if the husband disobeys the court order for giving his company to his wife, his property may be attached. The Civil Procedure Code stipulated this punishment. If the court grants the husband request for his wife's company and she refuses to oblige, she cannot be penalized for disobeying the decree of restitution of conjugal rights. However, after one year of separation either party would be entitled to divorce.

Alimony and Maintenance

The words alimony and maintenance are considered to be the same. But in reality there is a slight difference between the two concepts. Alimony is the amount ordered by the court for the husband to pay his wife after their divorce. On the other hand, maintenance has a broader meaning that includes the money that the husbands pay to whoever he is legally responsible for. It may include his wife, children as well as his elderly parents. The Hindu wife and her children are entitled to be maintained by her husband under the Hindu Adoption and Maintenance Act, 1956. If the husband is suffering from leprosy or AIDS in today's context or known for cruelty, bigamy, desertion or converted to another religion, the wife can live separately. She can also claim maintenance. At the same time, a husband can also claim maintenance from his wife if he needs support from the earning/well to do wife.

According to the Christian and Parsi laws, the husband is not entitled to this benefit of maintenance. One can seek temporary maintenance or permanent maintenance depending upon the circumstances. After enquiry the court decides the maintenance amount. The income status, standard of living of spouses, their property, their age and dependent persons are taken into account while deciding the maintenance amount. Even though there is no specific limit to the maintenance amount, the court usually grants one-fifth to one-third of the income from one party to the other. Through Civil Procedure Code also an order of maintenance can be enforced. The wives as well as the children are eligible for maintenance. The children's maintenance amount varies according to the actual cost involving their educational expenses, clothing and other necessary expenses. Even a working woman can get alimony and maintenance for their children by proving the insufficient nature of her income. The maintenance amount can be revised from time to time due to the circumstances and escalation of costs. The right of maintenance can be enforced by the wife not only during the lifetime of her husband but after his death too against the property of her husband. In the case of *Shantaram Tukaram Patil* v/s. *Dagu Bai Tukaram Patil* this verdict was given. According to the Section 19 of the Hindu Adoptions and maintenance Act, a widowed-daughter-in-law is also eligible for maintenance from her father-in-law in case if she has no means to support her.[29]

Custody of Child

One of the most painful issues involved in any divorce is deciding the custody of the child. Normally, both parents would like to keep the child with them. It creates a lot of heart burn when the opposite party is able to keep the child under its custody. While applying for divorce the spouses can also apply for the custody of the child. The custody of the child can be determined on the basis of Guardians and Wards Act, 1890, The Personal Law, The Hindu Marriage Act, 1955 for Hindus, and the Indian Act, 1869 for Christians and the Parsi Marriage and Divorce Act, 1936 and through The special Marriage Act, 1954.

The welfare of the child is the most important factor that determines the custody of child even though different grounds for custody is practiced in different religions. If the child is above five years of age, the court will elicit the opinion of the child before deciding its future. For children below five years of age the custody of child is normally given to the mother. But under the Hindu Minority and Guardianship Act, 1956, the father is considered as the natural guardian of the child. After the child reaches five years the father may claim custody but the court may decide in his favour or reject it due to variety of factors. When custody is granted to one party the other party may visit the child periodically. If such visit is proved to be detrimental to the welfare of the child the husband might have loose his visiting right.

The Law Commission recommended several changes on the custody issue. At present a preferential position is given to the father against the interest of the minor child's mother. The Law Commission stressed that the minor child should be permitted to be with its mother unless she has remarried and the father remains single. Under no circumstances, a girl child is forced to live with a step father. If both parents remarry the court may entrust the custody of the child to either of the grandparents.

Regarding the Muslims, a child is considered as a minor till he/ she reaches the age of 15 years. In matters related to marriage and divorce they regard the age of puberty as 15 years. The Muslim Law maintains a clear distinction between the guardian and those who are entitled to custody of the child. Accordingly, the father alone, or if he is dead, his executor is the legal guardian of a minor. The mother can have the custody of her male child till he completes the age of seven years and of her female child until she has attained puberty.

Adoption of Children

The First Law which legally recognized adoption in India is the Hindu Adoption and Maintenance Act, 1956. For the first time the Hindu woman is given certain rights of adoption. An unmarried woman, a widow and a divorcee are also given the right to adopt a child. But a married Hindu woman can adopt a child only if her husband has become insane or converted to some other religion or renounced the world. Once the child is adopted the adopted parents cannot cancel the adoption. Likewise, the adopted child cannot renounce his/her status as an adopted child and return to the family of original parents.

Crimes and Violence

The women of succeeding generation are facing variety of crimes and violence that led to insecurity. We have ample evidence from historical and literary sources on the humiliation, torture and exploitation faced by women. Due to various developments in the past six decades women are being gradually recognized as important, meaningful, and powerful contributors to the life of men. Existing ideologies, institutional practices and norms in the society contributes much to the harassment of women. Despite positive legislative measures in favour of women as well as the spread of their education and gradual economic independence, countless women still experience different types of violence. Being victims of violence they are beaten, kidnapped, raped, burnt and murdered. *The Hindu* dated 15th November, 2010 reported that the Supreme Court observed that the crimes against women should be firmly dealt with and no leniency must be shown to the offender. When a life convict Sukhdev Singh challenged the life sentence awarded to him in the trial court, Justice Markandey Katju and Gyan Sudha Misra asked him to show cause why the sentence should not be enhanced into one of death penalty for killing his wife. Justice Katju while writing the order observed that "Crimes against women are not ordinary crimes committed in a fit of anger or for property. They disrupt the entire social fabric. Hence, they call for harsh punishment." The Supreme Court is playing a pro-active role in protecting the rights of women.

Normally, crime against women can be classified into two types. The crimes under Indian Penal Code and Crimes under local and special laws are normally reported in India. The crimes under IPC are rape, homicide for dowry, kidnapping and abduction, physical and mental torture, molestation, eve-teasing, and importation of girls up to 21years of age. The following crimes like *sati*, dowry prohibition, indecent representation of women and immoral traffic comes under local and special laws in India.

Ram Ahuja categorizes violence against women as criminal violence, domestic violence and social violence. Crimes like rape, abduction and murder falls within the category of criminal violence whereas dowry deaths, wife beating, sexual abuse, ill-treatment of widows and elderly women is regarded as domestic violence. The social violence includes the forcing of wife/daughter-in-law to go for female foeticide, eve-teasing, refusal of giving share to women in property, harassing the daughter-in-law for dowry etc. The data related to criminal violence against women from the Ministry of Home Affairs and Police Research Bureau reveals that these crimes have been steadily increasing every year. The data obtained some ten years back indicate that the total crimes against women under the IPC every year cross the mark of one lakh cases. Out of which 25 per cent cases involve torture, and 27 per cent are molestation cases, 13 per cent are eve-teasing cases, 15 per cent cases involving kidnapping and abducting, 14 per cent are rape cases and 6 per cent are dowry death cases.[30] It is reported that a rape takes places once in every 47 minutes and molestation occurs once in every 25 minutes.

Nowadays, due to increase the awareness about gender-parity and women's rights, the victims are able to report the matter to the police. The Mahila courts, Family courts and NGOs working for women gave support and confidence to these victims. Contrary to popular belief that only poor girls are the victims of rape, employees from middle class are also sexually humiliated by their employers. Women inmates face rape in the jail and women daily wage earners were sexually exploited by contractors and middle man. Even the women beggars and lunatic women are not spared from the act of rape. When a woman is the bread winner in the middle class family she bears sexual abuse quietly without protest due to the compelling situation in the family.

Kidnapping mostly involves a minor girl by enticing her without the consent of the lawful guardian. The purpose of abduction may be due to desire to have illicit sex with her or compelling her to marry a person against her will. In kidnapping, the victim's consent is immaterial whereas in abduction the victim's voluntary consent minimizes the crime. The statistics revealed that among the total victims abducted or kidnapped every year 87 per cent are females and 13 per cent are males. In these kidnappings the male involvement is 96 per cent. Sex and marriage are two important factors leading to kidnapping and abduction even though 10 per cent of cases involves economic motive.

When we analyse the types of violence it involves money oriented issue, desire of seeking power over the weak, violence motivated by pleasure seeking, and violence as an outcome of family situations, violence due to the mindset of those who commits it and sometimes violence which is precipitated by the victim herself. Mostly intoxication, provocation of the victim, hatred towards women and situational factors led to violence against women.

In the Indian social system women are always depend upon another male member of the family. The societal norm creates an unseen barrier that prevents a woman to freely act according to her own decision. From the period of Manu, the young girl depends upon her father and after marriage she depends on the shoulders of her husband and after his death she depends upon the mercy of her son and she is never independent is the popular saying on the position of women in India. Even though today's woman comes out of this restricted space to some extent due to their education and economic independence, millions of women follow the age old dictum.

From early childhood she is restricted from moving freely in the physical and mental space. Her dependence on a male member of the family before and after marriage constantly makes her vulnerable to several fears. They were haunted by the fear of physical violence, threat to their modesty, which makes them insecure and restless. This sense of insecurity is created due to the prevalence of gender gap and male domination. Naturally, a woman seeks to gain protection from her family members, especially from her husband after marriage. But when they create problems for her and subject her to violence, her sense of insecurity increases. Due to economic reasons involving property disputes they have to face the ire of their brothers. Likewise, the dowry related issues, domination and ill-treatment of in-laws complicate her sense of security after marriage.

However, the last few decades promised some positive change to womenfolk. The positive attitude of legislature in passing laws protecting women and the role played by national and International Women's Organisations and NGOs dealing with human rights issue instil a sense of protection to women in India. But still millions of uneducated, poor women are beyond the reach of these new developments. They are both unaware of their rights or the changing nature of women's status in recent years and continued to toil under the yoke of male domination and insecurity.

Immoral Trafficking

The term 'traffic' was used to refer the movement of persons for immoral purpose, like prostitution. In contemporary literature, trafficking is variously referred to as modern slavery in the global economy. In 1949, the U.N. brought out the convention for the suppression of the Traffic in persons.

Worldwide both women and children are trafficked for variety of immoral purpose. This organised crime is happening everywhere. In developing countries like India, poverty and ignorance paved the way for large scale trafficking. Pleasure seekers from ancient times use girls of different age. Prostitution is regarded as one of the oldest profession in the world. In different names prostitution was employed as a commercial enterprise all-over the world. By and large women are the victims of this illicit trade that destroys the girl physically, mentally and ruin her future. During early times, the rulers bring women slaves from the place of their conquest. Likewise, slave trade also existed in which young girls are sold like cattle.

In ancient Tamil Nadu, especially from the Sangam Age and later, certain areas and villages are earmarked for prostitution. The women in this area are termed as Kanigaiyar, Vilaymadhar or Porutpendir in Tamil. The Devadasi system also encourages prostitution of a different kind which was eradicated due to the efforts of Dr. Muthulakshmi Reddy. Even now in cities like Mumbai, the Kamatipura area is regarded as the red light area of the city. Those who earn their income through the flesh trade are not willingly entered into it. Due to variety of reasons they were cheated by male members and entered into the brothels. Sometimes, they were lured by agents and middle men who promised them job and sell them to brothel agents. They cannot escape the vicious system of prostitution that ruins them completely. Even if they have children out of this illicit trade they also become victims of prostitution.

People migrate to different places without their family members. In cities and bigger towns millions of men lead a solitary life away from the warmth of their family. Such people used to visit prostitutes and it is one of a most lucrative business today. Due to the expanding nature of this illicit trade and constant demand for fresh young girls they were either lured or abducted, kidnapped by middlemen. Sometimes in the disguise of love, they are cheated by their lovers who dump them after taking away money, jewels and their honour. Organized groups and pimps lure young girls into prostitution. In the rural areas these agents approach poor families and promise rewarding employment for their girls, as domestic helps in faraway cities. They give some advance and the girl ultimately ended up in prostitution. For instance large numbers of Nepali girls were lured into prostitution due to the prevalence of poverty and lack of employment opportunities in their motherland.[31]

In some cases, the parents themselves know that their daughter would enter into prostitution. Economic compulsions led to such painful choice. Some unconfirmed reports suggest that large number of Nepali women and young girls ended up in the brothels of major cities in India. In addition, girls and children are kidnapped forcibly for this illegal trade. The police record speaks on thousands of children and minor girls missing and never traced back.

Despite India's efforts in prevention of human trafficking, no conviction rates remain a cause for concern. The US Department of state released the Trafficking in Persons Report-2012 that suggests the need for India to develop a comprehensive anti-trafficking law to be in line with the U.N. protocol to Prevent, Suppress and Punish Trafficking in persons, Especially Women and Children, 2000 with adequate penalties. The report found fault with the corrupt law enforcement officers, who reportedly continue to facilitate the movement of sex trafficking victims, protect suspected traffickers and brothel keepers. The reports alleged complicity of public officials in assigning the trafficking which is mostly inferred and related to the disadvantaged social strata.

Some nations legalized prostitution and those enter into the profession know the pros and cons of the trade. Periodic medical check-up and legal support is extended to them. In India, prostitution is illegal and those who involve in it face punishment. Hence, secretly agents procure women and minor girls for this trade. Even young boys are kidnapped or abducted for this purpose. Paedophilia is a crime in which an adult has sexual desire for children. Despite the efforts of police agency this crime is committed in Indian soil.

Especially in tourist centres like Goa, Mahabalipuram, this crime is committed mostly by foreign tourists. In countries like Sri Lanka child sexual exploitation by tourists became a major issue of concern. Children are abducted, kidnapped for other purpose also. For the purpose of begging their organs are mutilated and they evoke pity and get alms from the public. In cities like Mumbai, it is a lucrative profession in which some agents maintain large number of children and physically handicapped persons for begging. Even they were sold to other agents like cattle. Sometimes, they ended up in child bonded labour where they are not paid for their hard labour.

The minor girls, women and children are abducted or kidnapped for variety of exploitation. It is a recurring phenomenon despite some efforts by police and NGOs. In order to curb the immoral traffic in women and girls, the Indian Government passed a law in 1956 under the title 'The Suppression of Immoral Traffic in Women and Girls Act'. Later, it was converted into Prevention of Immoral Traffic Act. This Act brought uniformity in the law by repealing all previous enactments in this regard. This Act mainly aimed at the suppression of commercialize vice and not aiming at the punishment of individual prostitutes.

The works on sex trafficking reveals two diametrically opposite standpoint in which one views the prostitution as equal to trafficking that should be eliminated. The other stand is that sex work is a legitimate and willing form and labour that should be decriminalized. At the international level, the adoption of U.N. Convention against Transnational organised Crime in 2000 with supplementing protocols aimed at the prevention, suppression and punishing those involved in trafficking problems, especially women and children.[32] It is termed as the Palermo Protocol which came into force in 2004. In South Asia, the SAARC Convention on Prevention of Trafficking in women and children for Prostitution in 2002 indicate the growing awareness on the seriousness of this issue by countries of SAARC region.

In India, there are practical problems in curbing prostitution. If a prostitute carries her work within a distance of 200 yards of any public place, place of religious worship, educational institution, hostel, hospital etc. she may be penalized. This provision according to the police official seriously restricted their powers to suppress this traffic. Because, nowadays prostitution is shifted to posh colonies and the police find it difficult to prosecute such women or girls soliciting their bodies for immoral purpose. The difficulties associated with the provision for witness in Section 15 (2) of this Act stress that police officers conducting raid should have at least two or more respectable inhabitants including women of the locality and witness the search by police. It is natural that due to existing social condition no respectable people in any locality will assist the police in arresting the sex offenders. Even if someone comes forward he will face the wrath of criminal gangs associated with prostitution.

The Indian law and the punishment awarded for the crimes related to prostitution is inadequate. In comparison to the volume of traffic, the number of prosecution under this Act is very small. The lesser punishment of fine and admonition would not prevent the recurrence of the crime. It is necessary to rehabilitate women caught under this Act. Instead of put those women behind bars they may be send to protective homes. These homes should also have some programmes to help the prostitutes. B. Goswami argues that an aspect of Indian Law on prostitution is that it simply prohibits public prostitution and does not touch private prostitution. Private prostitution is prohibited if it is carried within a distance of 200 yards from a public place. Again a person who uses a prostitute normally goes scot-free while the women are punished by law. These are some of the weaknesses within the clauses of law that needs immediate attention. Some scholars argued that whether criminalizing prostitution prevents traffickers or it endangers the trafficking victims. Does legalizing sex work protect the right of women or led to increase in the sex trade? There is no answer to these complex questions.

Classification of Offences

Under the Indian Penal Code different crimes against women are classified with punishment for such crime. The Criminal Procedure Code (CrPC) elaborates the details related to the procedures of the police and court. The Indian Evidence Act gives details on how evidence can be used to prove a crime in the court. The following sections deal with various crimes against women.

Section 498 A deals with the cruelty of husband or his relative to his wife. The punishment for cruelty is up to three years imprisonment and also fine. Here, cruelty is defined as any wilful conduct likely to drive the women to suicide or causes grave injury to life, limb or mental or physical health or harassment with a view to get a property. Section 498 A of CrPC allows a court to take cognizance if women or her relative make complaint of cruelty. Section 306 of IPC deals with suicide committed by a woman. The presumption of abetment is provided by amendment section 113 A in Indian Evidence Act. If the suicide is committed by women within a period of particular years of marriage and there has been cruelty, there is presumption of abetment. Normally, the present practice is that if a woman commits suicide within seven years of marriage an enquiry is conducted by the local government official before closing the case. Section 304 B deals with cases involving death possibly due to dowry issue. If a women's death is caused by burns or bodily injury or even it appears as normal but there was harassment for dowry such death will be termed as dowry death. Under the circumstances, her husband and his relatives shall be deemed to have caused her death. The CrPC provides that post-mortem is compulsory, when the case involves suicide of women within seven years of her marriage and if her relatives made request in this regard due to suspicion on the cause of death. In rural areas of India, there is a practice of destroying all evidences related to suicide. Normally, if someone commits suicide the village elders or community elders help the family to burn the dead body secretly and destroy all possible evidences thereby hampering the legal process to take its due course. In the name of protecting the honour of the family, they commit this crime where at times even the murderers can escape from the clutches of law.

Section 493 deals with the deceit by a man on women that she is the wife and he has sex with her. It is punishable with fine and jail up to ten years. Section 494 deals with bigamy. Normally, both marriages have to go through necessary ceremonies associated with wedlock. The second marriage is void besides it is also bigamous in nature. Here the law of bigamy applies not only to men but also to women. Concealment of first marriage to second wife by husband aggravates the crime. Section 496 deals with fraudulent marriage ceremonies and its punishment. Adultery is also a problem affecting the family and the society. Section 497 deals with this crime which is defined as sexual intercourse with married women without her husband's consent. Peculiarly, the law holds the view that if the husband agrees to this act it is not adultery. The wife is never punishable. This stand seems to be a step in favour of women. In reality it means that adultery is an offence against the husband, not the wife. The law does not allow the wife of the adulterer to prosecute him or the adulteress. The Indian law punishes adultery with a fine and jail up to five years. Section 498 deals with enticing away, concealing or detaining married women for illicit sex. It may be with or without her consent thereby protecting the husband's right to custody over his wife.

Crimes related to rape are covered under Section 375 of IPC. The following context of sex is defined as rape by the Indian Penal Code. If sex is forced against the will of the girl or with her consent under fear of physical injury/death it may be considered as rape. Sometimes, physical intercourse with her consent under the impression that she believes she is married to that person or with a minor under 16 years of age is a crime. In cases of custodial rape, the onus of proof is with the accused.

Sections 361-371 of Indian Penal Code deal with kidnapping, abduction, and slavery. Especially Section 361 deals with anyone enticing/taking a minor female under 18 out of the custody of the lawful guardian without the consent of the guardian. The accused can face imprisonment up to seven years and fine. Section 363 deals with crimes associated with the custody of a minor to use her/him for begging. The accused is liable for imprisonment for 10 years and fine. Section 363 A maintains that anyone injuring a minor for begging is liable for imprisonment and fine. It is not uncommon to damage the body parts like eyes, hands and legs to earn the sympathy and alms from the public while employing the minors for begging. Even babies are hired/abducted for begging purpose and some sedatives are given to the baby to make it docile.

Section 366 A maintains that anyone procuring a minor girl is liable for imprisonment for 10 years with fine. The same punishment is given under Section 366 B if anyone is importing a girl four foreign country. The same punishment is given to anyone selling, buying or letting to hire a minor for prostitution under Sections 369, 372 and 373. In addition, the use of force to injure, annoy or frighten a woman is a crime that can be punishable with jail for three months. Pulling the veil, touching her body come under this provision.

Insulting the modesty of a woman is covered under Section 509 by uttering any word, making a sound or gesture showing any object, intending to include upon the privacy of a woman is punishable. In a particular case in this context in *State of Punjab* v/s. *Major Singh* (AIR 1967 SC 63) a question arise whether the female child of seven and a half months could be said to be possessed with modesty which could be outraged. The learned judge J. Bachawat observed that the core of a women's modesty is her sex and from her very birth she possess the modesty, which is the attribute of her sex.

Section 294 deals with obscenity in public, singing, reciting obscene songs or act is punishable for three months jail and fine. The CrPC Section 51 (2) gives special protection to woman searched by a police officer in connection with a crime. The search shall be handled decently by another woman. Under Section 160 a male below 15 years or women shall not be interrogated at a police station. Normally, such enquiry can be conducted in their place of residence. Any examination can be done only by a lady medical practitioner.

In addition to the above protection, several other laws were passed for protecting the human rights of women such as Indecent Representation of Women Act, the Immoral Traffic (Prevention) Act, 1956 etc. Some protective welfare legislations for women are also passed over the years. The Dowry Prohibition Act, 1961 bans the giving or receiving of dowry as a consideration for a marriage. Various sections of this particular Act deals with dowry related crimes and punishment. Under Section 8 A of this Act, the burden of proof rests on the accused. In order to implement this Act dowry prohibition officers can be appointed by the state.

Domestic Violence and Women's Rights

One of a major problem confronted by women of all the countries is domestic violence. In countries like India the wife faces physical and mental abuse not only from their husband but also from their in-laws. In the recent years, the husband addicted to drink became a major source of problem to his wife and the family. Physical torture is a routine affair in many cases which made the condition of women miserable.[33] The women after marriage are expected to tolerate all the problems in her house. She is not encouraged to return to her parents even though her condition becomes miserable. It would lead to suicide of the affected woman in some cases.

The demand for dowry is a major social problem confronted by married woman. She is expected to bring money and other comforts of life whenever the in-laws are demanding it. Killing the married woman for dowry or for other reason is a recurring phenomenon. A number of cases on dowry related problems reached the courts in India even though several cases were not reported.[34] In 1961, the Dowry Prohibition Act was passed. It prohibits both the act of giving and receipt of dowry. Under Section 3 of this Act giving, taking or abetting dowry can lead to imprisonment of not less than five years and fine not less than Rs. 15,000. Under Section 4, penalty for demanding dowry can lead to imprisonment for six months to two years and fine up to Rs. 10,000. But there are several loopholes in this Act that were remedied in the Dowry Prohibition Act (Amendment) in 1984. To protect the woman from domestic violence, the Protection of Woman from Domestic Violence Act, 2005 was passed. It was pointed out that Domestic Violence is undoubtedly a human rights issue and serious deterrent to development. Several international accords and declarations acknowledged this fact. This Act provides more effective protection of the rights of woman guaranteed in the Constitution. Domestic violence has been exhaustively defined in Section 3 of the Act.

Sexual Harassment and Rape in Workplaces

Besides domestic violence women also undergo sexual harassment at workplaces. The term sexual harassment refers to any unwelcome sexually determined conduct whether physical, verbal including sexual advances, demands for sexual favours, molestation, sexual gesture, comments, and remarks or jokes verbal, textual, graphic or electronic. It was an invisible problem till recently but now it became a major social problem. Even senior woman IAS officers go to court that they were sexually harassed by their superiors and in some cases the Ministers of the department concerned. A Minister from Kerala allagedly misbehaved with an air-hostess on duty. The issues were taken to the court. In *Rupan Deol Bajaj* v/s. *K.P.S. Gill* (AIR 1996 SC 309), the court observes whoever uses criminal force upon any woman, intending to outrage her modesty shall be punished with imprisonment up to two years, or with fine or with both. In this case K.P.S. Gill is charged for slapping Mrs. Bajaj on her posterior and thereby outrages her modesty. But in the final decision of the court, the compensation amount for Rupan Deol Bajaj has been increased. But the accused K.P.S. Gill was exempted from undergoing imprisonment which shocked the civil society.

The inability of Section 354 of Indian Penal Code to address adequately on issues of sexual harassment led to filing of a petition in the Supreme Court in 1997. The petition was aiming at the prevention of sexual harassment of women in all work places through judicial process. The Supreme Court in the *Visakha* v/s. *State of Rajasthan* case stressed that the sexual harassment is a clear violation of the rights under Article 14, 15 and 21of the Indian Constitution. It also involves the fundamental rights of the victim under Article 19 (1) (g). The Supreme Court directed those who are in charge of the workplaces to take appropriate steps to prevent sexual harassment. They must also create a mechanism for the settlement of the complaints. The court framed 12 guidelines in this regard. It was followed by the NCW which prepared a draft Bill on sexual harassment in 2001.

Since large number of women have entered into the labour force, the issue became a major social problem nowadays. This problem was portrayed very well in a Tamil cinema *'Magalir Mattum'*(Women only). Today the working women are vulnerable to this problem irrespective of their status and type of their employment. The sexual harassment at the place of work results in the violations of fundamental right of gender equality and the right to life and liberty. Several legislations were passed to protect women's rights including the cabinet approval given for a Bill that specifically seeks to protect women from sexual harassment at workplace. But the "Workplace Sexual Harassment Survey", carried out by the Centre for Transforming India, an NGO, in the Information Technology and BPO/KPO companies reported that 88 per cent of the female workforce reportedly suffer some form of sexual harassment in their work environment. While analyzing the report of the survey in *The Hindu* dated November 15, 2010, Arti Dhar listed out the type of harassment faced by women that includes abusive language, physical contact or seeking sexual favours from them. The survey covered all major IT destinations and 600 female employees, who continued with this ordeal due to fear of professional victimization. It also revealed the fact that around 72 per cent of the incidents, the perpetrator was a superior. Considerable numbers of the respondents are not aware of the workplace sexual harassment policies of their organisation and thought that it was not a part of hiring process. It is observed that sexual harassment is emerging as an important issue in service sectors like the IT industries that involves 24 × 7 working that includes odd-hours. The IT enabled service industries have to develop some sort of policy framework in such issues.

According to Section 375 of Indian Penal Code, rape is defined as sex against her will or with her consent under fear of injury or death, or without her consent and with a minor less than 16 years. If a husband has sex with his wife who is above 15 years, it is not a rape. The minimum punishment for rape is 7 years and if it is custodial rape the minimum punishment is 10 years. The punishment for rape in custody invited stringent punishment following popular upheaval against a number of rape cases like the *Rameeza Bi* case in 1978 and *Maya Tyagi* case in western Uttar Pradesh in 1980, and the gang rape of a girl named Mathura in the police station in Chandrapur District of Maharashtra. Mathura a sixteen year old girl was gang raped in the local police station. The Supreme Court acquitted the policemen, stating that the victim had not raised an alarm. Since there was no injury marks that suggests the consent of the girl for that act. Due to the increasing incidence of rape, woman's groups and organisations along with mainstream political parties are taking the issue of rape in a big way. Because of their pressure and follow-up efforts, the sentence of former Haryana DGP, S.P.S. Rathore was enhanced from just six months to one and a half years for molesting 14 year old Ruchika Talwar, who committed suicide later. It is one of a sensational case in which the media played a major role in highlighting the crime in a big way.

In order to meet the increasing demand for the amendment of law, a Bill was introduced in 1980 to amend the existing law on rape. It was passed latter in 1983. By this amendment, if a victim said that she had not consented, the court would presume that rape had occurred. It also shifted the burden of proof from the victim to accused in custodial rape and increased the possibility of bringing convictions to the offenders. In cases involving gang rape and rape of a pregnant woman the amendments provides for in camera trials. The name of the victims should not be published without their permission. Disclosure of the identity of the rape victim is a punishable offense with imprisonment for two years.[35] The cross-examination in the court is normally a very painful process in which the victim is forced to explain the act in presence of the general public. Hence, in order to relieve this mental suffering, the court orders in-camera proceedings, in which the lawyers of the victim and the accused as well as their parents are permitted.

In some cases women were raped by their dear and near who suppose to protect their honour. In March, 2009, Joseph Fritzl in Austria was convicted for homicide, enslavement, incest, rape and for other charges. He was sentenced to life in psychiatric prison. In this horrific case, the accused kept his daughter captive for 24 years in an underground cellar and fathering her seven children. The heart wrenching account of the victim shocked the entire world. In Tamil Nadu also in March, 2009, the police arrested a father, mother and a sorcerer for a crime of rape. The sorcerer made the father to believe that if he rapes his daughters he could get immense wealth hidden somewhere in the earth. The mother too assisted her husband to commit this heinous crime on their own daughters. The sorcerer also raped the girls. There are some cases in which the drunken fathers raped their helpless daughters. *The Hindu* dated 16th June, 2012 reported on the incidence of a French diplomat, Pascal Mazurier held on charge of raping his three and half year, old daughter. The complaint was lodged by his wife Suja Jones Mazurier in Bangalore, who stated that she respects the repetition of this crime for some time. She presented her complaint with the medical report that confirms sexual abuse. If fathers are behaving like this what sort of protection a girl would expect from the society?

The draft Criminal Law (Amendment) Bill 2010, now seeks to tighten laws dealing with rape and sexual assault. Due to the sustained campaign by women and civil society groups for the past three decades, the government is working for tightening the existing laws in this regard. They argued that the provisions of IPC dealing with rape are based on 19th century law that needs amendment.[36]

Political Rights of Women

If we trace the history of women's political rights, even in England women were granted voting rights only after the passage of Peoples Act, 1918. But this right was extended only to married women, women householders and graduates. Only in 1928, all women above the age of 21 years got the right to vote. The Nordic countries provided highest political representation to women in the world.[37] The Indian Constitution provides voting right as well as eligibility for the legislature. In India, few provincial legislatures, like Rajkot and Travancoor and Cochin enfranchised women in 1923 and 1924 respectively. Gradually, this right was extended to other provincial governments. In Independent India, women enjoy equal voting right with men and they can also contest for elections.

The Panchayati Raj Institutions provide one-third reservation for women. It lead to a situation in which India can boost that there are more elected women representatives in India alone than in the rest of the world put together.[38] It was a silent revolution at the gross roots level. Reservation for women in Panchayati Raj Institutions has yielded excellent result despite some setbacks. The 73rd and 74th Amendment of the Constitution provided this opportunity. In Kerala, the process of providing political leadership to women at the grass roots level following[39] this amendment led to the gradual empowerment of women at the local level. It ensures conditions for gender equality in the political sphere. In certain states like Maharashtra and Karnataka women's representation is far greater in 33 per cent. But in certain states like Kerala male domination is a major problem despite some advancement in women's empowerment. This reservation provides excellent opportunity for empowering woman. They can also act as a catalyst in social change and development in rural India. At the same time, the Woman's Reservation Bill providing for reservation in Parliament and State Legislature is pending for over a decade. The women Self-Help Groups in several states including Tamil Nadu also play a key role in bringing women to decision making process as well as in organised wealth generating schemes at the grass roots level.[40] It gives confidence, self-esteem and training to women to handle local socio-economic and political issues.

Laws Protecting Rights of Women

In addition to the above laws and legislation passed by the Parliament, there are some other rights which also protect women. The Sati Prevention Act declared it as an offence and prohibited the glorification of *sati*. By Section 498 A of the Indian Penal Code, it is punishable with imprisonment up to three years. In case if any wilful conduct that drive a woman to commit suicide or do cause grave injury or danger to life or health it is punishable by imprisonment. The Suppression of Immoral Traffic in Women and Girls Act, 1956 is aiming at protecting helpless women and girls from exploitation. Selling a minor girl for the purpose of prostitution is punishable under Section 372 of the Indian Penal Code. Section 376 of the Indian Penal Code covers rape and other related crimes. The Tamil Nadu Government passed an additional legislation in this regard to protect them.

In 1971, the Medical Termination of Pregnancy Act was passed. This Act maintained that a pregnancy may be terminated where it does not exceed 20 weeks. Two medical practitioners should also give certificate that such termination would not involve a risk to the life and health of pregnant woman. The Indecent Representation of Woman Act is passed to prevent the usage of woman indecently in films, newspapers, magazines and posters etc. Presenting woman in an objectionable manner is punishable under law. Despite the passage of several effective legislations against the violation of the rights of woman, many problems still persist. The failure cannot be traced to the ineffectiveness of legislation alone. In several cases, the law has been unable to reach the barrier behind the closed doors of family. In the Supreme Court, it was observed that the legislation cannot by itself normally solve deep-rooted social problems. Even though legislations are necessary, the other factors such as education and awareness can also create public opinion in favour of women's rights.

Female Infanticide

Despite development in education and awareness, some crimes against the girl child are continuing even today. One such inhuman crime is the female infanticide. In India the girl child is not always a welcome addition to many families. It is partly due to the social status accorded to women. Starting from the days of Manu, woman is considered as a burden and responsibility to the family. The investment on her education and upbringing is considered as a waste since she is going to live in her in-laws house. The birth of male child is always welcomed in the Indian context. The dowry issue became a major problem to the girl's family at the time of her marriage and after. Hence, to avoid these difficulties new born female babies are killed silently. This practice is prevalent all-over India. In Tamil Nadu, Usilampatti area in Madurai district, Dharmapui, Salem and Krishnagiri Districts are known for the practice of female infanticide.

Following reports on the occurrence of this grave crime, the Government as well as NGOs are taking suitable measures against this practice. But at times, the volunteers were threatened with dire consequences if they preach against female infanticide. The Government of Tamil Nadu through its medical network at the grass roots level records pregnancy and child birth. The Government is trying to ensure the safety of new born female babies through monitoring. The 'Cradle Baby Scheme' was introduced to assist the helpless parents who are unable to raise their female babies. The Government is looking after the maintenance of the girl child as well as its future. The civil society activists, argues that it only encourages the parents to abandon female child. It is not a substitute for minimizing the crime of sex selection and female foeticide.[41] However, the scheme is necessary, still the child would be accepted in their families naturally. But it is a long drawn process that involves lot of social change and mental make-up on girl child. The scheme so far protected several girl children who would otherwise be eliminated in their birth. Bharathi Raja, a veteran Tamil cinema director handled the issue of female infanticide effectively in his film '*Karuthamma*'. But still the practice continues in a limited scale in Tamil Nadu, despite some parents are convicted for this crime.

The Department of Social Welfare in Tamil Nadu introduced several schemes to lessen the burden of the parents of girl child. It provides support to widows, destitute and women willing to continue their regular education starting from VI standard up to plus two levels. Tailoring, computer courses and other vocational trainings were also given to make them self-dependent in future. If they wish to pursue degree courses, they were also given assistance to meet the expenditure. The women can also keep two of her children with her in the hostel and their educational expenditures in other schools were met by the government. All these schemes were carried out through Government Service Home Higher Secondary Schools located in different district headquarters in the state. The State Government provides four grams of free gold for making 'mangal sutra' for poor girls entering into wedlock. Certainly, such schemes would reduce the incidence of female infanticide when poor, illiterate parents are aware of such schemes to support the girl child.

Female Foeticide

In India, the birth of a female child is not a happy moment for the family members always. Due to age old bias against female child that includes problems associated with marriage and dowry, parents preferred a male child. Through prenatal diagnostic techniques it is possible to diagnose the sex of the foetuses. The ultrasound machine is used for these diagnoses and the female foetuses are normally aborted. The ultrasound machine is actually introduced to detect genetic, metabolic disorders, chromosomal abnormalities or certain congenital malformation and sex linked disorders. But it is reported that this modern scientific tool is effectively used for the elimination of female foetuses before its birth. Hence, the government brought out the Pre-Natal Diagnostic Techniques (Regulation and Prevention of Misuse) Act of 1994. The Act was amended in 2003 to make it more stringent to control sex selection not only at foetal stage but also at conception stage.

The Act provides for imprisonment for a term of five years and a fine of Rupees one lakh besides cancellation of the offending doctor's registration and license. But it is reported that the doctors are not writing anything about the sex of the foetus but through oral or sign language indicate the sex of the foetus. In Punjab, Haryana, Rajasthan and several north Indian states thousands of female foetuses were destroyed even in educated and higher income groups. It led to the decline of female child ratio to an alarming level. Hence, in certain states there is a major problem of finding brides for their grooms. It lead to a situation where the people are buying brides from other states for some moderate amount from poor families. These brides are forced to live their life in a totally new surrounding were she is not even able to speak the local language. Only awareness and collective action at the grass roots level can eliminate the practice of female foeticide. The girl child should be allowed to see the light of the day and given a chance to live.

Inheritance and Succession Rights

One of the major area of discrimination still persists in our society is the property of woman. Starting from her early childhood, the woman is conditioned by a situation in which she has to depend upon either her father or her brother or her husband and finally on her son. She has never been allowed to independently live a life with dignity and self-esteem. Earlier, property right was highly discriminatory. Even the *sati* was forced upon the wife after the death of her husband mostly to share the property of the deceased. In several societies the widow is not permitted to enjoy the property of her husband or her father. The property normally goes to the male child. She has to depend upon her male child. '*Sridhan or Manchakani*' refers to the property pass on from mother to her daughter hereditarily. In some states like Kerala where matriarchal system is mostly followed by several communities, the property right goes to woman. After marriage the son normally goes to the bride's house and lives there with his wife.

In independent India several legislations were passed to change the property related injustice to women. The Hindu Succession Act,

1956 has conferred extensive rights to women in the matter of acquiring and holding property. Section 23 of this Act debars a female heir from independently raising a suit for partisan in respect of her share in dwelling house. Since it was regarded as discriminatory this section was omitted in the Hindu Succession (Amendment) Act, 2004. By this Act, a daughter whether married or unmarried is entitled to raise a suit for partisan or for her separate share in property. She need not wait for partisan to be raised by other coparceners.

The Supreme Court also emphasized time and again, that the Hindu Succession Act should be construed as an instrument, in removing gender based discrimination and effecting empowerment of Hindu females. After amendments the daughter gets the same share as the son from the property acquired by the father. Likewise, section 14 of the Hindu Succession Act initiated drastic changes in the nature of women's rights to property. As such the mother and daughter as well as the widow not only inherit the property along with his son but also have an equal share with him. The Government of Tamil Nadu took special efforts in protecting the property rights of woman. Accordingly, the Hindu Succession Tamil Nadu Amendment Bill was passed in 1989. Section 29 of this Act stipulated that a daughter shall by birth become a coparcener like a son. The woman can also enjoy the property she received from her parents as well as from her husband and father-in-laws side. She can also enjoy the property earned by her independently. She can sell her property, pledge or gift it to somebody else. Earlier, the agricultural land was exempted from inheritance by daughter on the ground of preventing the fragmentation of land.[42]

The Muslim personal law provides certain rights to woman in inheritance. She is entitled for certain shares in the property depending upon the number of heirs that are left behind. A widow is entitled to receive one-eighth share of her husband's property when there are children. If there are no children she is entitled for one-fourth share. A daughter is given half of the share when she has no brother. In case of the existence of a brother she gets only half of whatever share her brother gets.

The succession rights of a Christian woman are determined by the Indian Succession Act, 1925. The Christian widow is entitled to one-third of her husband's property if there are children. The children have the right to enjoy the remaining two-third of the property. The property can be divided equally between sons and daughters. The

Christian daughter has an equal right in her father's property like that of his brother. If there are close relatives and widow alone were left behind after the death of a person the widow is entitled for half of the property and the remaining property goes to the relatives. If the widow is the only person left behind after the death of her husband she is entitled for the whole property.

In India, the Constitution became the first document that in spirit brought men and women on equal footing. In 1975 after the release of the report titled '*Status of Women in India*' the feminist movement gained momentum. Several Marriage Acts passed in 1954-55 and the Abolition of Dowry Act, 1961 sought to give women an equal space in society. The collective voice of women through several forums including the All India Democratic Women's Association (AIDWA) had its effect on the legislations passed to help women. But there has been an escalation of all forms of violence against women in India for the past two decades. Especially, the economically vulnerable woman takes the brunt of this trend.

The annual Global Gender Gap Report of the World Economic Forum (WEF) ranks India 114 in a list of 128 countries.[43] Smaller states like Cuba and Sri Lanka has done better than India. The data projected the magnitude of the gap between men and women in four critical areas, namely economic participation and opportunity, political empowerment, educational attainment and health and survival. The sex ratio at birth in India is 0.89 that dragged India down to its 128th rank. Despite great straits in Economic growth and achievements, the status of women indicated alarming decline. The Central Statistical Organisation (CSO) brought out a publication entitled '*Women and Men in India, 2006*'. According to its report, there has been a steady rise in the total incidents of crimes committed against women over the years. Especially, cruelty by the husband and in-laws accounted for the highest number of the crimes against women. In 2007 in Uttar Pradesh alone between January and July 11,453 crimes against women were reported. The statistics revealed attacks on minors and adolescent children besides increase in child rape and trafficking of girls. From poorer states young girls are trafficked regularly to 'women deficit' states of Punjab and Haryana. In most cases, they live the life of sex slaves.

The presence of dowry inevitably makes most of the Indian marriages as an arrangement for economic transaction between families. If we analyse why the Dowry Prohibition Act is not working properly, we come to the conclusion that the society accepts dowry as an inevitable part of marriage. The emergence of educated middle class and the prosperity of the society only worsened the situation. In crimes against woman, instead of booking the case and initiate action against the culprit, the police mostly acted as a broker for compromise between the parties concerned. They dissuade the women from filing a complaint. In Tamil Nadu this process is popularly termed as *'Kattapanchyat'* where money and influence determines the outcome of such 'out of court' settlement. The lengthy legal battle and its attendant problems are cited to dissuade women from pursuing the case further.

The Women's Rights Initiative of Lawyer's Collective brought out an evaluation report on the implementation of Protection of Women from Domestic Violence Act, 2005. Up to 2007 July 7,913 cases had been filed and most of the proceedings were pending in court. In Kerala, high degree of awareness among women led to the declining number of cases affecting them. In states like Rajasthan, lawyers in civil society organisations help the victim to register cases. In several states, protection officers are not even appointed to look into the issues related to violence on women.

According to the National Crime Records Bureau (NCRB), the number of dowry deaths in 2006 was 7,618. Statistics also revealed the increase in dowry linked suicides by women. Among the states, Madhya Pradesh alone accounted for 45.9 per cent of the cases of rape of tribal women, the highest among the states. Police officials agreed that cases involving violence on women are not given much importance. To the police, terrorism and riots gets first priority and women's issues are always handled casually. Even the women constables in night duty at Delhi have felt insecure, a survey lamented. In Tamil Nadu, a women constable who attended bandobust duty in a remote area was sexually assaulted and murdered. Given the Constitutional framework, things would have changed in favour of women. But that has not happened. India's legal response to violence against women has by and large been marked by the absence of sympathy for the victims. The laws aimed at limiting violence against women often reflected male-centric attitudes in their interpretation.

The independent India witnessed several changes in relation to the protection of women's right. In 1988, the Government came up with a National Perspective Plan for Women. It covers plans for women's health, education and political participation. Later, the

Panchayati Raj Bill was passed in 1993 that provided scope for women to occupy one-third of the seats in the Panchayats through reservation.

Today 33 per cent reservation for women in State Legislature and Parliament is a possibility since it was passed in the Rajya Sabha.[44] But there is a constant pressure from the male MP's against its passage. According to Ranjana Kumari, women activist and Director of Centre for Social Research, the feminist moment is learning from experience. That has moved from the politics of protest to politics of influence. On the issue of Women's Reservation Bill, the women's groups have demanded its passage and organised several protest meetings in the street. Now the women members of the Parliament try to influence the system from within. From the streets to Parliament, the women movement in India has traversed a long way to restructure the balance of power between the two sexes.

Despite the existence of variety of problems faced by women, certain states like Tamil Nadu scores high on female security index. According to the study conducted by the Tata Strategic Management Group, Tamil Nadu has emerged as one of the 'safe' states in terms of female security and has overall scored high on the well-being index as well.[45] The study also lamented that most well-off states like Punjab, Haryana, Delhi and western U.P. secured worst rating for female security index. There are number of factors that contribute for the well-being and the security of women. Through consistent efforts in creating awareness on the need for the well-being of women their position can improve steadily in other states as well. The role of media, education and society in eradicating the age-old bias against women folk is an urgent necessity.

In Universities and in several research centres women studies became a focal point. It led to considerable research on women related issues that generated lot of data. Several Journals like the *Journal for Gender Studies* are launched exclusively to deal with women issues. Education and employment opportunities for women are increasing steadily.[46] Despite social pressure a women can pursue her goal if she is properly educated and empowered. Awareness and attitudinal change in the society is a very slow process that will bring changes in the lives of millions of women. In a conservative Indian society, the age old customs and myths work against the real liberation of women. The learned Justice Markandey Katju rightly pointed out that:

> In India we live in a transitional age, the transition being from a feudal, agricultural society to a modern, industrial

> society. We are neither totally modern, but somewhere in between. Hence remnants of the feudal culture, for example, casteism and communalism, persist. It is for this reason that our society is still largely male-dominated, and most women do not have real freedom…
>
> What is the remedy? We have to get over the transitional period and become a modern, industrial state. We must spread scientific thinking on a massive scale, and encourage people to give up superstitions and backward, feudal ideas, for example, casteism and communalism. This is only possible by means of a complete revolution in our thinking and attitude towards women. What is needed is a massive cultural struggle involving hundreds of millions of people which will sweep away all remnants of the disgusting feudal and medieval practices and mentality, particularly with respect to women. These should be replaced with scientific thinking and genuine and complete equality between men and women….When and how this will come about is not known. But come it will, and all patriotic people in India, including men must strive and contribute to this goal.[47]

Dalit's Rights

In the Indian context, the society is stratified on the basis of caste rather than class. Though Rig Vedic literature as well as the Tamil Sangam literature never mentioned about untouchablity, these differences emerged later. Manu Smriti divided the society on the basis of four-fold division. The Brahmana occupied the prime position followed by Kshatriya and Vaishya. The Sudras occupied the lowest position in the stratification. Later Panchaman, a fifth class is added to this four-fold division. Among the four divisions mentioned by Manu, the sudras were considered as the low born and has to serve the other three divisions. The Panchaman was even looked down by the sudras as the lowest caste. Even though these divisions were based on professions, they became markers to symbolize the status and position of a community later.

In the Sangam society '*Kadasiyar*' constituted the lowest component of the society and were looking after the agricultural manual labour like sowing, transplanting and reaping etc. In the medieval period most of the labourers hailed from Palla and Paraiya communities which occupied a lower position in the caste hierarchy. They were forced to live in separate quarters known as Cheries located on the outskirts of villages. They were regarded as hereditary slaves and were attached with the land and sold along with the land. Normally, slaves had to work from dawn to dusk. Several Imperial Chola period inscriptions described the slaves as the property of their masters.

After the Sangam period one can witness the steady erosion of the position of people belonging to the lower strata of the caste system. Later, the rigidity of the caste system intensified the difficulties of the people of lower strata. In Tamil Nadu, Kerala and in several states of India, the position of lower caste people became increasingly difficult. Under the British, availability of education and employment opportunities at least to smaller sections of these groups elevated their position to some extent. But untouchability, social ostracism continues to haunt these helpless communities. They were not allowed to enter into the temples, and in several streets as well as into the houses of upper caste Hindus. It was regarded that their entry might pollute the place where they trod.

In the Tamil speaking regions of south India normally the slaves belong to a community rather than to an individual. F.W. Ellis, the Collector of Madras observes that "the Paraiyars and the Pallans most of whom are slaves attached to the land of Vellalars". During the British period some British officials due to their liberal and humanistic upbringing raised their voices against slavery. Even though slavery was abolished later in most of the countries, the prejudices on caste basis continued to haunt Indian communities at the lower level.

Due to the rigid structure of society, the lower caste people were not permitted to hold any land or worthy property. Because of upper caste domination they were not allowed to have education and other avenues that could elevate their position. Only under independent India, the Government takes a lot of measures to improve the position of untouchables. Great leaders and social reformers like Mahatma Phule, Gandhiji, Pandit Ayodhya Dasa and E.V.R. Periyar waged a crusade against the Hindu society, to liberate the untouchables. Ayodhya Dasa repudiated the Manu Dharma that created the caste hierarchy and strongly projected the need for the total emancipation of the Dalits.[48] Dr. B.R. Ambedkar made it as his life mission to emancipate the millions of untouchables toiling under the rigid caste oriented social system. Reservation in education and employment is possible for these communities because of his untiring efforts. He organised the real struggle for Dalits to find a Constitutional position in the society. Through his great attempts Dr. B.R. Ambedkar was able to get seats reserved in Parliamentary elections for the upliftment of Dalits.[49]

E.V.R. Periyar led Vaikom Satyagraha in Kerala for the temple entry of untouchables and courted arrest by the local ruler. Even though these untouchables belong to different caste, they were generally termed as *Harijans* by Gandhiji which means the Children of God. But as years pass on the term Harijan itself became derogatory signifying lower status. Hence, the untouchables detest that identity. In the British Government records they were termed as 'Depressed Class'. The Act of 1935 included them in a schedule containing a list of these classes. They were termed as Scheduled Castes latter. In the last quarters of 20th century the terminology Dalit is used as a most acceptable term for their identity.

Dalit Literature

As such in course of time Dalit literature also emerged to portray the real difficulties and day to day struggle of untouchables. The Gana songs also became popular in local areas of Chennai city that projects the down to earth feelings of these groups. It covers love, infatuation, frustration, economic inequality, problems of inter-caste marriage and other social inability experienced by these groups. It was also felt that a non-Dalit could never realize the pangs of sorrow and insult experienced by the untouchables in everyday life. Hence, they argue that the Dalit literature must emerge from the Dalit community itself. Several non-Dalit writers like Premchand in Hindi; Mulkraj Anand in English; Keshao Deo in Malayalam and Arun Sadhu in Marathi have put their heart and soul while depicting the sufferings of Dalit. To the Dalit writers, Manu, the ancient architect of Hindu social laws, has been crucial in their theme. Manu the prejudiced law giver is still alive in their memory even though the Indian Constitution thrown him away. To them, Manu lives in the hearts of millions of Hindus. Earlier Jyotiba Phule proposed the idea of burning the Brahminical text and later Dr. B.R. Ambedkar set it on fire.

A considerable number of Dalit short story writers have described the pride, humanity and other positive attributes of their fellow Dalits. The Dalit literature actually rebels against the assumptions of Hindu ideology that were obstacles in the path of self-respect and freedom of Dalits. Some writers tried to reject the concept of God and the traditional Hindu culture. In addition, the Dalit literature is also significantly concentrating on self-criticism. These writers never hesitate to attack inferiority and superiority complexes among their fellow Dalits. They also criticize some Dalits who occupy higher position in the Government and their superiority complex in comparison to their brethren. They attempt to imitate the high society and it lead to other problems. It prevents them from freely mixing with their own community and at times they try to conceal their caste and identity thereby alienating from their community. It was regarded as a serious issue strongly criticized by some Dalit writers.

They also attacked the political leaders who have exploited innocent followers for their own advantage. Besides atrocities on Dalit women, the problems faced by uneducated women are the subjects of writings by several progressive writers like Mrs. Aruna Lokhande, Mrs. Asha Thorat etc. Kumud Pawade is teaching Sanskrit, which is regarded as a language of God that is beyond the reach of lower caste women. She also published several works on Dalit women, social education and on culture. Gail Omvedt concentrate her work on the Dalit movement in Maharashtra, Mysore, and Andhra from 1920-1956. It is an excellent analysis on comparative regional history in addition to the focus on Dalit movement.[50]

The Dalit literature aims at speaking for them and not aimed at pleasing the non-Dalits. The writers expressed their ideas without any fear or guilt feeling. It is rather an attempt in search of their cultural identity. The works are based on socio-cultural and economic inequality.[51] However, the Dalits have risen through education and slowly they are coming up in life. The Government of India also passed several laws to protect their interest and honour. But still the stigma continues on the communities in one form or the other and that is the theme of Dalit literature.

In various parts of India Dalit communities are treated in a way that would offend their feelings. The Reports on the National Commission on Scheduled Castes and Scheduled Tribes reveals the increasing violence against these communities, including rape.[52] They were not treated equally in hotels and in small eateries separate tumblers are given for the exclusive use of Dalits. Temple entry on equal footing with the caste Hindus is not a reality in some villages. There are reports on some incidents of temple related confrontation between Dalits and sections of caste Hindus in recent years at Koothirampakkam village near Kanchipuram. The Dalits are waging a prolonged legal battle to assert their rights for free worship in local temple. Likewise, the Dalits of Kandadevi village in Devakottai taluk in Tamil Nadu are fighting for their right to pull the temple car of Sri Swarnamoortheeswarar during the annual festival.[53] When state intervention provided scope for their entry into the temples, the caste Hindus objected it strongly.

Of course, independence brought several progressive changes through legislation. The Constitutional guarantee on equality, and advances made in the field of education and employment, the empowerment through reservation in Panchayat Raj system, and the economic advancement made by at least some sections of the Dalit communities reasonably raised their status. According to the data available in 2007, their literacy rate among them has gone up to 57 per cent and unemployment diminished. Sukhadeo Thorat, who was the Chairman of the UGC, in his book *Dalits in India: Search for a Common Destiny* argued that the practice of untouchability and discrimination have reduced to a certain extent in some public spheres. But at the same time he notes that on an average about 23,000 cases of human rights violations and atrocities are registered with the police annually by the Dalits. Thorat makes a strong plea for a parallel reservation policy for the private sector to address the needs of the STs. Recent studies bring out the need for giving due share to Dalits in education, employment, capital for business, housing, water and other amenities to improve their conditions. But still millions of Dalits in rural areas need education, empowerment and social recognition to make them worthy citizens on equal footing.

Caste imposes enormous obstacles to the full attainment of various rights for the Dalits and other untouchable groups. It is reported that the caste system dominates in housing, marriage and in social interaction among various caste groups. Despite formal protections in law in countries like India, discriminatory treatment remains a major factor in the society. Discrimination exists in the allocation of jobs, land, basic resources and amenities as well as in physical security. Since, the Dalits mostly depend on the other backward communities and upper caste people, they cannot raise their voice against any abuse.

The rape of Dalit woman was also a serious issue in independent India. In 2004, 1,157 cases of rape were reported and the figure was 1,172 in 2005. Madhya Pradesh is accounting for 29 per cent of the rape of Dalit women. It must be also noted that several cases of rape and molestations were not reported due to the existing social structure. The police is also not interested in booking the cases of rape and used to dissuade the victims from filing an F.I.R. They used to make an out-of-court settlement by providing some monetary compensation to the victims.

Dalit Issues

It is estimated that around 240 million people in South Asia live a pathetic life because of their ranks as untouchables. Dalits were discriminated and abused and even killed in the hands of powerful people. It is unfortunate that the law enforcing agencies also discriminate them in the name of caste. The Dalits may not use the same wells, visit the same temples and churches and drink from the same cups used by other communities in tea stalls in certain places. The Dalit children are frequently made to sit in the back benches at the class rooms.

In some places entire villages remain completely divided on caste lines. A case in point is the demolition of the 'caste wall' at Uthapuram in the Madurai district of Tamil Nadu. A 30-meter wall was constructed to segregate the Dalits from the rest of the residents of Uthapuram by caste Hindus in 1989 following caste riots in the village. The issue was brought to the notice of State Government by the Tamil Nadu Untouchability Eradication Front (TNUEF). Political parties like the CPI (M), PMK and VCK supported the idea of demolishing the wall. Following wider public attention the wall was electrified to prevent the Dalits from climbing over it.[54] The issue was raised in the Tamil Nadu State Assembly. The former Chief Minister, M. Karunanidhi consulted the parties concerned and finally made arrangements to demolish the wall. But the caste Hindus left the village in anger. They argued that they may not return to the village till some of their demands were met by the district administration. Following assurance from the District Collector, they returned to the village. This event clearly shows how despite decades of development and education, the independent India cannot come out of its centuries old caste bias. The caste division and a feeling of impurity are associated with the untouchables. Even though the Dalits and other suppressed communities are emerging economically in the post-independent era, they are unable to break the customs that ill-treat them.

A study conducted by TNUEF found that postman has also been practicing untouchability. In two villages in Madurai district the postman did not deliver postal articles to Dalit addresses. Instead, the Dalits were asked to collect their postal articles at the post office.[55] In North India too, a variety of discriminatory practices and atrocities committed against the Dalit community. In the Gohana subdivision of Sonepat district in Haryana, 53 Dalit homes were burnt and looted. The Valmiki community is one of a Dalit group in these houses deserted their homes following the murder of a Jat youth. The reprisal was not aiming at targeting their life but at their property in August 2005. An upper caste mob resentful of Dalit communities' relative prosperity destroyed their homes and looted the valuables like refrigerators, washing machines, TV and computers. The prominent Jat community was irritated over the prosperity as well as the organised nature of Valmikis. The construction of pucca buildings for the Valmikis and their elevation through education and employment earned the wrath of the caste Hindus.[56]

A number of such incidents are reported in various parts of India and the Dalits were at the receiving end. Atrocities against Dalits have been on the rise in Haryana and in number of other states in India. Social boycotts of Dalits are very common due to a number of factors. Consequent on their political awareness, they retaliate in some areas that naturally creates inter-caste tensions and violence.

One another important issue related to Dalit is their responsibility to dispose the night soil as they are regarded as 'polluted castes'. Manual scavenging is a disgusting reality in most states including the outskirts of Delhi despite an Act of Parliament banning this practice. Even after six decades of independence India continues to dehumanize, degrade and shame the most vulnerable section amongst us. Annie Zaidi in her article "India's Shame" in *Frontline* September 22, 2004 argues that it is not the problem of allocating resources or providing alternative to the manual scavenging. But the problem is related to the attitude that is rooted in caste psyche. There are number of works available on the issues related to manual scavenging like the work of Gita Ramasway's "India Stinking" and Mari Marcel's "Endless Filth". Several State Governments even denied in court the existence of manual scavengers. The passage of the Employment of Manual Scavengers and Construction of Dry Latrine (Prohibition) Act, 1993 has not changed the reality. According to rough estimate that even in Mahatma Gandhi's Gujarat, there are about 55,000 scavengers since others have not learnt to clean their own toilets. The Government and municipal authorities tend to ignore sanitation since it is not a big issue like water and power supply. As long as the dry latrines exist manual scavenging will also exist. Even among the scavengers, the women carry the burden of doing the dirtiest jobs. Caste discrimination against the scavengers exists in town and village Panchayats. It is observed that considerable number of the scavengers reported about respiratory and skin diseases. Jaundice also affects them in large number in addition to trachoma, leading to blindness.

The scavengers are living in segregated colonies with little chance to use common facilities like well and drinking water taps. In cities where manual scavenging is eradicated they are engaged in other dreaded works like cleaning underground drainage systems and septic tanks. Many died of carbon monoxide poisoning while cleaning septic tanks and tanks containing industrial waste. The public as well as the local authorities found it convenient to exploit the poor Dalits with poor wages. The authorities continued to maintain that there are no scavengers. In the 13 years up to 2006 after the passage of Manual Scavengers (Prohibition) Act not even a single prosecution is reported. It clearly indicates the implementation of the Act in letter and spirit.

Process of Emancipation

In the Constituent Assembly Dr. B.R. Ambedkar tried his level best to get his men what he wanted in reality. The Indian Constitution provides many securities and protections for Dalits. The Preamble of the Constitution and the Directive Principles of State Policy as well as in the sections dealing with the fundamental duties, one can find a special treatment given to this downtrodden people. Article 14 specifies that every citizen of India is equal in the eyes of law. In the Article 15, the state prohibits the discrimination of its citizens on the grounds of religion, race, caste, sex, or place of birth. This Article also deals with the reservation for SCs and STs. The State can make special provision for elevating the scheduled class people and nothing in the Constitution comes in contradiction to this provision.

Article 16(4) of the Indian Constitution enables the Government to give reservation to the downtrodden in public employment. Article 17 incorporates a key ideology of Gandhiji by abolishing the practice of untouchability in any form. Article 21 provides protection of life and personal liberty to all its citizens without discrimination. Later, the element of dignity has also been added in this Article.

In ancient Indian society, the practice of slavery was very common and this practice continued very well even up to the modern times.[57] The Indian Constitution prohibited slavery in any form. Article 29 prohibits any traffic in human beings as well as forced labour. Article 29 provides the downtrodden people the freedom to conserve their own ways of living. According to Article 38, the State shall make every effort to secure a social order aiming at the realisation of social, economic and political justice. Article 29 (A) is noteworthy and provides equal justice and free legal aid. Article 45 directs the Government to provide free and compulsory education for each and every child up to the age of 14 years. After more than six decades the Government has made necessary legal framework recently, to realize this important concession to the downtrodden.

The Government provides many concessions and scholarship to the children belonging to the scheduled classes. Article 46 gives particular attention to the promotion of education and economic interest of the SCs and STs as well as other weaker sections of the society. In order to give representation for the SCs in the House of People—the Supreme Law making body—Article 330 has been framed. No political party can ignore these representatives of the Dalits while forming the Ministry as well as taking a major political decision. When Indian polity changed from single party dominance to coalition politics, the support of MPs belonging to these suppressed communities counts much. One may recall the words of B.R. Ambedkar on the importance of playing a role in the law-making body in this context. While addressing the Dalits at a Depressed Class Workmen's Conference he declared that:

> You must abolish your slavery yourselves. Do not depend for its abolition upon God or a superhuman. Your salvation lies in political power and not in making pilgrimages and observance of fasts.... It is the duty of the Legislature to provide you food, clothes, shelter, education, medicine and all the means of earning a livelihood. The work of law-making and its execution is to be performed with your consent, help and will. In short, law is the abode of all worldly happiness. You capture the power of law-making.[58]

Regarding the social emancipation of Dalits successive Governments after independence have taken several concrete and positive steps. Especially, the Untouchability Act of 1955 and Protection of Civil Rights Act of 1976 have outlawed untouchability. Besides the Bonded Labour System (Abolition) Act, 1976 abolished forced labour in any form. The employment of children in hazardous occupations was prohibited by the Child Labour Prohibition and Regulation Act, 1976. The 73rd Amendment to the Indian Constitution, gives scope for Scheduled Castes representation in all levels of Panchayat in proportion to their presence in the district population.[59] It provides political leadership and decision-making powers to the Dalit communities. For the upliftment of Scheduled Castes intuitional structure was built by the Government through the National Commission for Scheduled Castes. For the benefit of the SCs the Central and State Governments have invested over 10,000 crores per annum.[60] For the economic development of SCs the Central and State Governments have evolved reservation policies for jobs in public service. Statistics indicated that on an average 1.5 lakh SCs have benefited annually by these steps.

In the liberalized economy the job opportunities are mostly available in private sector. The private sector is not interested in implementing the reservation policy of the Government and hires labour according to their merit and skills. Hence, there is a demand that the Government must pressurize the private enterprises to adhere to some per cent of reservation policy. The reservation policy which was first introduced for 10 years is extended over a period of six decades. Still large sections of the SCs are unable to enjoy the fruits of reservation policy. But in the long run some scholars opined that these communities must prepare themselves to come out of this protection so that they can enhance their real capabilities to get opportunities both in the public and private sphere. Such a step would enhance their ability to play a constructive role in shaping their destiny and that of the nation.

The Dalits in the past were denied property rights. Especially cultivable land ownership was only a dream to them. But since independence, land reform measures ensure their access to ownership of cultivable land. Even though this attempt creates tension, it has a positive impact on the status and confidence level of Dalits. In the recent decades, the Dalit women groups expressed their concern on the impact of state policies, patriarchal bias of Dalit Movements, and the upper caste, middle class leadership of the women movements in India.[61] They are unable to secure justice from the law and the community, in most of the issues affecting their life. Addressing the rights of the rural Dalit women is also a key to building an egalitarian society.

Historically speaking, the Dalits experienced a variety of discrimination and victimization over a long period of time. The Manusmirti and its four-fold division of society segregated the Dalits. The entry of British and modern education had its impact on the Hindu social system. The role of social reformers and great leaders from among the Dalits like Mahatma Phule, Dr. B.R. Ambedkar tried their level best to strike at the roots of untouchability. Their stress on education and capturing political power through Constitutional means uplifted the community. The reservation policy and its utilization for the past six decades slowly yielded results in various avenues. Due to education and awareness, the Dalit community is realizing its potential. In the business venture too, the self-employed Dalits emerging successful in India. Despite caste and social prejudices, a study on Dalit business in two urban centres of Haryana and western Uttar Pradesh, indicate that they are doing well economically and felt they had a dignified existence.[62] They felt proud about their ability to come out of 'slavery' and regarded themselves as role models to other members of their community. Through organised efforts by their associations and political outfits they are trying to protect their community interest.[63] For instance, Dalit Indian Chamber of Commerce and Industry (DICCI) was started to help Delit entrepreneurs and is organising Dalit Trade Fairs. One Ashok Khade, who was a son of a cobbler, started Offshore Enginering in 1990. The Rs. 550 crore firm which has 4500 employers is the biggest company owned by a Dalit. He laid water pipelines to every house in his native village, irrespective of caste. Ashok installed a gold idol in the temple, where he could not inter in his boyhood. The puja is performed by his mother now. Dalits like him are not employment seekers on reservation basis, but provider of employment to thousands of people.

However, the caste prejudices are deep-rooted in the psyche of other caste Hindu man. Concerted efforts by the Government agencies and Dalit groups in addition to the understanding by other communities may change the destiny of Dalits.

One must appreciate the various steps taken by the Centre and State Governments in alleviating the problems of the Dalits. But in certain states the Dalits cannot raise their finger against the dominant caste groups. In sharing of water, cultivable lands, roads, wells and burial grounds one can see a constant struggle between the caste Hindu groups and Dalits. The two tumbler system and the prevention of entry of Dalits into caste Hindu localities and Temples still haunt our conscience. Only when all the Dalit children are able to have their basic education there is no scope for their salvation in future. The recently enacted Right of Children to Free and Compulsory Education Act, 2009 is a positive step in India's journey to fulfil the rights to education. It will provide hope for more than eight million children by giving opportunity to go to school.[64] Still the manual scavenging of the night soil is practiced in several places despite a legal ban on this practice. It is one of very cruel practice in which the Dalits are forced to eke out a living by carrying the excreta of other human beings in baskets in their head. No civilized society with any sense of sanity would allow this horrible practice to follow.

The Transgender Community and Human Rights

We normally thought that the population is basically divided into two genders namely male and female. But in this assumption we left a considerable number of persons, who are neither male nor female but regarded themselves as third gender or transgender. These groups of people were popularly termed as hijra, kothi, aravani, thirunangai and in different names in different parts of India, Pakistan and Bangladesh. The evolution of this particular community is deeply rooted in the South Asian regions history. Surprisingly, there is still not a lot known about this community which is largely ostracized from society. They are often denied basic education and work opportunities and mostly rejected by their kith and kin. Their problem is both physical and psychological.

There are reports about the existence of eunuchs—castrated males—from the 9th century B.C. onwards. There were references on transgender in the epics like *Ramayana* and *Mahabharatha*. *Tholkappiam*, the treatise on Tamil grammar also contains reference on them. They were in popular demand to guard the royal harems. It is believed that this practice started in China, where at the end of Ming dynasty there were nearly 70,000 eunuchs to serve in the grand palace of the Emperor. In India there are about one million of them living in different parts of the country. But no effort was taken to enumerate the Aravani population in India that contain various informations like their number, location of dwelling, education, employment, income and other statistics. After the Mughal dynasty the hijra population faced lot of problem. They no longer got the royal support for their sustenance. By the Criminal Tribes Act, 1871 under the British, the Aravanis were regarded as criminal by birth and could be arrested on mere suspicion. Even though this Act was repealed in 1952, the community continued to suffer the stigma attached to this Act. The transgender persons feel that the section 377 of the Indian Penal Code goes against their interest. This colonial legislation criminalizes 'unnatural sex' and is seen as an outdated law that interferes on the rights of adults to engage in consensual sex, whether heterosexual or otherwise. Since sodomy is a criminal act by this legislation, the third gender faces problems from the police. The Law Commission under Justice Jeevan Reddy recommended that section 377 of the IPC be repealed. But it was felt, that a progressive revision of law is a necessary step to remove the social prejudices against the transgender persons.

The literature on the hijra population is very limited. Sometimes, it is misleading or inadequate or contradictory to explain their life, culture and various facets of this particular community which lives in seclusion. They face several problems including the male chauvinistic social prejudices and draconian laws that criminalized alternative sexuality. Despite the fact that India has 4000 years history of third gender and eunuch culture, they live a pathetic life. One must understand the differences within this group. The hijra is a biological male taking on the gender role of female; a kothi is a feminine homosexual. The major dispute in identification of this group is whether the hijra role includes homosexuality also.[65]

Who is Thirunangai or Aravani?

In Tamil nadu the transgender population is given different names at different periods, such as Nabumsakhi, Ali, Pedi, number nine and aravani. But off late they prefer to identify with the terminology 'thirunangai'. Normally, they 'born as men but not men'. In most cases their identification is known only when they are approaching puberty. Even though biologically they have a male body they usually identify with women. They exhibit inability or lack of desire to engage in sexual act as men with women.

Their behaviour, dressing pattern and gender identification is contradictory to the stereotyped male in the society. Some of them were born with improper, or malfunctioned male reproductive organ. They term themselves as born real aravani. In some cases they born as female but whom never menstruate. They are unfit for normal family life and cannot produce children. Ambiguous male or female genitalia also marks this particular group. Even parents may not know the true identity of their children till they reach puberty. At adolescent stage their behaviour, dressing pattern and walking style shows a significant difference from that of a young boy.

The Aravanis tend to behave like an adolescent girl and it would normally shock their parents and relatives. It leads to scolding and beating so that the boy can behave properly like a boy of his age. Since psychologically they regard themselves as girl, no amount of persuasion or pressure will change them. The neighbours and the society normally ridicule or make derogatory remarks on this abnormal behaviour. Sometimes they may be sexually exploited by his friends and neighbours. Even though such exploitation is painful at first they used to enjoy this new sex role that suits their mental make-up. It will further strengthen their desire to identify with female role. They carve for a female body even though it is not possible since nature endowed them with a male body. This conflict of mind and body will ultimately ruin their normal adolescent life. In most cases the parents are unable to understand the conflict going on in their children's life. Finally, this conflict will have very serious consequences on the future of the boy who is destined to be an aravani. They escape from the safe custody of their parents and go in search of fellow aravanis who can understand their state of mind and would help them to start a new life of their choice.

The Legend

In Tamil Nadu, mostly the persons desirous to become aravani usually goes to Mumbai where a considerable number of the hijra population lives. Some of them may contact the local aravani or thirunangai groups to escape the conflict they are facing within. All-over India, the hijra population worships Bahuchara Matha, one of the Mother Goddess with whom they identify themselves. They believe that Bahuchara Matha gives them special powers to bless or curse others.

We have lot of stories on Bahuchara Matha. According to one legend Bahuchara Matha was once a princess who castrated her husband because he was behaving like a woman instead of consummating their marriage. Another story narrates that a man who attempted to molest Bahuchara Matha was cursed with impotence.[66] The Goddess forgave the man only after he shed his masculinity and dressed himself like a woman before worshipping the Goddess. In Gujarat a temple was dedicated for this Goddess.

The Aravanis who sacrifice their maleness by undergoing castration believe that they can receive the blessings of Bahuchara Matha. But till recently, the act of castration is a crime and cannot be performed legally in a government hospital. Hence, it was performed in a very crude manner without administering local anaesthesia. The aravanis believe that one must have the willpower to withstand this painful process, without any pain killers or anaesthesia. Sometimes this crude operation or the complications arising out of it may kill the Aravani. In practice, such deaths are not reported. According to the medical fraternity, urinary stenosis/stricture following castration is common among those who perform this crude operation. The transgender persons also restore to taking hormonal injections without medical advice. They take this step to feel more feminine. There are some private doctors who do this operation for a considerable fee. Those who have money can opt for this painless process by undergoing castration in a modern clinic. But the availability of such doctors is very limited due to variety of factors. In 2009, there was a media report that a senior doctor in Chennai operated a young boy without the consent of his parents and the boy. The parents alleged that the boy was abducted by some aravani groups which forcibly castrated him with the help of the doctor. The police arrested the doctor and the aravanis involved in this episode. The aravani groups argued that they never indulge in this sort of activities. To them the decision of a person to become an Aravani is purely the individual's choice and they are not forcing this option upon anyone.

Emasculation and Initiation

When a boy wishes to become aravani he will join that group. He would be adopted by a Guru, an elder aravani. Their relationship is equated with mother-daughter as well as Guru-chela (follower/ shishya). They have to pay *dand* (fine) to their Guru to sponsor them before their acceptance into the community. The initiation fine can be compared with the dowry that ensures safety and stability within the new community. The aravani must give her earnings to the Guru who distributes an allowance for her expenses. They have to look after the day to day works like sweeping, cooking and the general maintenance of the aravani house. In exchange for such service, care and protection is offered by the elder aravanis.

The aravanis who performed the removable of male organ (nirvana) argued that it is a necessary process in initiation.[67] For forty days the operated aravani has to take complete rest and the aravani family that adopts her would look after her needs. The aravanis normally call a fellow aravani as mother, sister and use only terms of female relationship. In a way it compensate the family life they have broken earlier from their blood relatives. The new member of the aravani group learns about the clan's customs and tradition at the feet of his Guru. The upbringing of the young aravani is the responsibility of the Guru. Her adopted family of fellow aravanis provides a loving environment and gives her food, shelter and cloth. In course of time she is given the full security and care of a family and naturally she feels part and parcel of this union.

Regarding the crude operation, the aravanis feel that they have no choice as the government regarded it as a crime and never permitted them to do it in the government hospitals. This Sex Reassignment Surgery (SRS) is legally permitted in some South East Asian countries like Malaysia and Thailand. In Thailand those who underwent SRS conducted several entertainment programmes for the sake of tourists and the Government gives active support to them. The Government of Tamil Nadu issued a G.O. legalizing Sex-reconstruction surgery that will be done in the Government hospitals also.[68]

Vidya, a transgender in Chennai narrates her painful experience of facing the operation by paying just Rs. 6,000. In her autobiography '*I am Vidya*', published by Kizhaku Pathipagam, she recalls the fear, anxiety and the excruciating pain she experienced during the operation. During operation she kept calling the name of Bahuchara Matha to withstand the pain.[69]

Myths and Rituals

In Greek mythology reference is made on the aravanis. In Hindu mythology also Lord Vishnu assumed the beautiful woman form

Mohini while a dispute broke out between the Asuras and Devas for sharing Amudham from the ocean of milk. Lord Shiva's desire for this Mohini led to the birth of Hariharasudan or Ayyappan. Ambai a woman character in Mahabharatha, reborn as 'Shigandi' in her next birth to take vengeance on Bhishmacharya. In Mahabharatha, Arjuna, while living in the palace of Keesagan, disguised himself as 'Pedi' (feminized man).

In Christianity, eunuchs are referred in Bible. "Jesus replies not everyone can accept this word but only those to whom it has been given for some are eunuchs because they were born that way; others were made that way by men; and others have renounced marriage because of the Kingdom of Heaven". (Mathew–19-12). In the Muslim community the eunuchs were appointed as servants in the palace. In the Mughal Empire'a large number of eunuchs were employed to guard the harem in the palace. They enjoyed a very respectable position in the army as well as the administration of the government. The aravanis believe that since they have sacrificed the normal sexual life, child birth and blood related family, they are given spiritual powers as compensation. The common man also believes that the aravanis can have the power of blessing and cursing. Goddess Bahuchara Matha's temple is located in Gujarat where this Goddess is sitting atop a cock. The aravanis take a holy dip in the pond in front of the temple. Visiting the temple at least once is an important part of their life. The aravanis irrespective of their religious belief worship Bahuchara Matha as their Goddess. The aravanis represent almost all the religions that exist in India. In Tamil Nadu at Koovagam village in Villupuram district a temple is built for Aravan, the patron god of transsexuals. Every year the Aravanis visit this temple on Chitra Poournami day to participate the festival. In recent years media has focussed lot of attention on this festival. Various health and HIV/AIDS seminars are conducted during the festival season to create awareness to this high risk group. Popular channels like BBC Three and National Geographic channel cover the experience of the third gender in the festival.[70]

Human Rights Issues

The transgender persons are experiencing the brunt of male chauvinistic social prejudices and draconian laws that criminalized alternative sexualities in India. Despite India having more than thousand years of a history of third gender and eunuch culture they are facing ridicule and insult. Till recently, these groups cannot even imagine the possibility of enjoying some civil and political rights. They cannot find mainstream jobs, vote, marry, inherit property or adopt a child legally. They are treated like social outcastes and for survival and sustenance they have to depend upon begging, dancing and involved in sex trade. Since there is no enumeration of the transgender population in India we are in the dark about their socio-economic status. Even in the 2011 census there is no effort to enumerate the transgender. They got voting right in 1994 but the issue of voter identity card created problem on the question of gender identity. The court ruled that a transgender person can register as either male or female depending upon their statement.

The usage of public convenience like toilet and bathrooms also created problem for the third gender. While the women refuse to allow them inside a lady's toilet, they are unwilling to use the men's toilet. Due to lack of awareness and revulsion on third gender identity, the parents and the society would not accept the choice of young men to become an aravani. In some cases the irate parents restored to very crude methods to ensure gender conformity. There are cases in which the parents administer electric shock on the genital of their son to teach him a lesson for his fondness for girl's clothes. They hoped that it would rouse the men in him.[71] In some cases, the honour killing of a transgender person is also practiced and such killings are never reported.

The aravanis feel that discrimination exists in the hospitals. During medical examination some sex coloured words and remarks are passed upon them. They regret that they are not museum pieces to be shown to every medical student as an exhibition item. Dr. C. Venkatesan working with Solitary Action against the HIV Infected in India said that doctors are reluctant to address the needs of third gender. It is partly due to their lack of clarity on transgender issues. Besides, castration is illegal and cannot be performed by a medical practitioner till recently. It led to a choice between costly private hospitals and a crude operation lacking scientific procedure. Since the Tamil Nadu Government issued a G.O. recently legalizing SRS in Government hospitals the long felt demand of Aravani group is fulfilled.

The economic problems of the aravanis are another important human rights issue. They are not accepted in most of the job opportunities available. Their desertion of their family at a young age ruins their chances of school education. It led to an insecure life. The police harassment on charges of enticing clients is a routine problem faced by this group. They complain that the police often demanded sexual favours from them.[72] They are treated like criminals and whenever a crime occurs they will be first target of suspicion. Renate Syeed, a writer familiar with Hijra way of life pointed out that the aravanis have three types of jobs. They collect gifts in the local bazaars or bless bridegrooms and newly born sons. During the night time they earn through prostitution. But some hijras prefer prostitution only as the last resort to earn money.

In north India, they may visit the house where the birth of a male infant occurs. It is customary to invoke the blessings of aravanis to the new born male baby for a prosperous and healthy life. The hijras demand and get suitable monetary gift from the parents for such blessings. They usually inspect the genital of the infant to confirm whether it is normal. It is believed that if the child has defects they would lure the boy to join their group in his adolescence. In south India, they perform poojas in the shops and business establishment to get rid of evil eyes (Thirushti kazhithal). They are not invited to the marriage ceremonies and at the birth of male child to invoke their blessings. Lack of such income, coupled with denial of job opportunities led them to dancing, begging and prostitution as a means of survival.

Welfare Measures

The Aravanis are not welcome in public places like the hotels, parks and theatres. Usually they go out with fellow aravanis. They express their desire to move freely in the public space like men and women. Earlier, they were not eligible for bank loans or any other financial assistance due to their gender identity. Nowadays, it is slowly changing in states like Tamil Nadu, where a separate welfare society is created by the government to look after their problems. The Department of Social Welfare passed an order in December 2006 that contains recommendations to improve the living conditions of the aravanis.

Several issues related to the counselling to families that faces the transgender child are covered in the G.O. The teachers must also be trained to counsel the children with behavioural change. This G.O. clearly pointed out that transgender person can join in any school and college and there should be no discrimination on the basis of their sexual identity. Likewise, various human rights organisations also extend their support for the rights of third gender. The NGOs working with the aravani groups provide financial assistance for the works mostly related to the prevention of HIV/AIDS.

In March 2009 a helpline for members of the transgender community, their families and the public was launched in Chennai. This helpline '*manasu*' is set up by Tamil Nadu Aids Initiative-Voluntary Health Services (TAI-VHS). The number is 044-25990505. It provides information on transgender community. This helpline is primarily useful in finding employment for the transgender. The TAI is doing excellent work with a clear focus on the rights of the transgender throughout India. This help line would help the families to accept their transgender children. It also tries to reduce the stigma associated with this group. Lakshmi Bai, the TAI Director stressed the importance of recognizing the skills of transgender. She opined that a lot of government support to the transgender is there but the community support was lacking. *Manasu,* the helpline would try to fill the gap through its service. In the function organised to open the helpline three members of the public who supported the transgender were felicitated. One of the public accepted the transformation of her son into an aravani, the other woman renting her house to transgender. The third woman, a beautician is organizing occasional training course for the aravani groups.[73]

The Aravanis are able to get recognition for their gender identification through a court order in a case filed in Chennai in 2003. In the ID cards they can choose their gender. But still among aravanis there is a difference of opinion regarding their proper identity. Some of them prefer the identity of transgender (TG) while others prefer Third Sex as their identity. In order to help them three divisions are earmarked to identify the gender of the person (Male/Female/Eunuch) in the Indian passport application. It is a proper recognition to the aravanis in their struggle for equality with other sexes.

In several districts in Tamil Nadu, ration cards are issued to the aravanis. In 2010 alone 315 houses are allotted under the Indira Awas Yojana Scheme for them. The District Collectors have been asked to conduct special grievance redressal meetings. Meaningful interaction between the police and aravanis is another programme initiated in Tamil Nadu. Even though education as a means to elevate their position is not attempted seriously, there are some aravanis with postgraduate and professional qualification occupies better position. There are some educated aravanis like Priya Babu, Vidya and Revathy have written books highlighting their problems[74] and are aware of their rights and the course to be followed for their betterment. They are trying to help the other less fortunate aravanis. Though the government provides chances to join any educational institutions, the aravanis are reluctant to take this route to prosperity and gender equality.

In Tamil Nadu, a number of aravani associations are working for their welfare.[75] Due to awareness a positive change in the attitude of aravanis regarding their earning is noticeable. In Salem city a popular idly shop (steamed rice cake) is successfully run by a group of aravanis who provides varieties of idlies with tasty chutneys and side dishes at an affordable price. It provides employment opportunity and sustenance for several Thirunangai. Likewise, they are also organizing Self Help Groups to earn their living in a legitimate way. Such attempts should be encouraged by the public and the Government. They can erase the negative image of transgender by earning through hard work and innovation.

The aravanis are demanding the repeal of section 377 that deals with sexual intercourse. It recognizes only men-women relationship as natural. It makes physical relationship with the aravani as illegal. It provides scope for the police to take action against the transgender community. Even certain organisations challenged the validity of this Act in Supreme Court. The Law Commission chaired under retired Justice Jeevan Reddy recommended that section 377 of the Indian Penal Code be repealed. The aravanis are awaiting a favourable judgment to their sexual right. Unless this right is recognized they cannot marry and adopt a child. Even though several aravanis are living with male partners as husband and wife, they don't have any legal sanction for their marital life. Regarding the application of international law on the human rights violation on the basis of sexual orientation and gender identity, a group of International Human Rights experts drafted the Yogyakarta principle in Indonesia in November 2006. It recognized that the sexual orientation and the gender identity are integral to every individual's dignity. It must not be the basis for discrimination or abuse.

There are some aravanis who are living alone in their old age. Some of them are addicted to alcohol and drugs. The aravanis expect some sort of protection to them in their old age. If the government is serious about their welfare, basic data on the aravani should be gathered. The aravanis are approached mostly by government and private agencies to prevent the spread of AIDS. To create awareness on the life of aravanis some art troupes are staging dramas in various parts of India. The aravanis sincerely believe that among those who speak about women's right and human right, the existence of third gender is not at all registered properly. They expect that they should be treated as a fellow human being with heart and soul. Even there are suggestions to curb derogatory portrayal of transgender community in movies and TV serials. These are the minimum efforts expected to start a process in which the transgender can integrate into the main-stream of the society.

But one can also ponder over the image created by at least a section the Aravanis in public. In moving trains and in buses they demand money from the youth. If the passenger is unwilling to part with his money sometimes they take liberty by taking money from their pockets. They move in groups and pass lewd remarks and project sexual suggestions. Sometimes, they force the bystander to part with their money by lifting their sari to expose their body. The shocked onlooker would normally obey their demand. He may feel insulted by a totally strange group. In addition to their rude behaviour in public there are newspaper reports that indicate the abduction of boys and forcible castration in the private clinics. The recent case involving a senior doctor in Chennai is one such example. Even though such cases are rare, it reinforces a negative feeling against them. The aravanis must ensure that one's choice to become aravani is purely voluntary without any act of coercion. The general impression that the aravanis are luring youth to unconventional sex also creates revulsion. If it is the voluntary choice of the youth no one would blame the third genders. These are some of the issues that tarnish the image of transgender in society that needs serious introspection from third gender.

Documentaries on Aravanis

Considering the plight of the Aravanis, a sexual minority, attempts were made to project their life and problems to the outside world. In addition to films and literature, documentaries were also taken on the life of transgender groups in India. BBC is covering the aravanis of India and Thailand. In Thai culture and in the tourism industry this transgender population has a significant place. In India, several documentaries were prepared to create awareness on the sexual minorities.[76]

Even though the aravanis exist in our society for over several thousands of years, we are unable to understand their life, culture and beliefs. It is partly because of the image and taboo associated with aravani groups. Their sexual preference is away from other stereo-typed options followed by men and women. They use to complain that in comparison to the position enjoyed by gay groups the aravanis are treated worse.

Religion, social practices and legal norms suggest that the male-female relationship is normal. So the aravani who is imprisoned in a male body with a desire to be a woman poses challenge to the societal norms. Their behaviour in public places and the way in which they force the public to give money creates a negative image. They are treated not as normal but being a centre of ridicule and fun. Due to lack of awareness on the plight of aravanis from their adolescent years to their nirvana, the society only looked down upon them. Since they cannot reproduce children in a male body their choice is very narrow. In a traditional sense no one can raise a family with them as husband even though their sexual desire can be satiated by them in a different way. This ambivalence created lot of problem in the choice of their partners.

Even those who live with aravanis mostly lead a secret life away from their actual family. Sometimes they have a wife and children in some other place and maintain regular contact with a particular aravani. But there are others who openly break the tradition of society and permanently live with aravanis as life partner. But unfortunately this voluntary choice of the individual is not approved in our legal system. Like the gay group and other sexual minority groups in western countries—which got several rights including the right to marriage and property—the aravanis in India should also be given such rights.

The Aravanis must come out boldly to have higher education. Education is a surest means to inculcate courage, awareness and an attitude to challenge the age-old beliefs against them. Despite government encouragement, only a very few aravanis are pursuing their education. They must change their mindset and choose education as a window to better job opportunities and higher status.

The government as well as private agencies should provide training and employment opportunities to the transgender groups. If they are given financial assistance to start any business venture they may gain confidence and come out of their traditional occupation—sex trade. In the old age also they may be given old age pension like the general population that has no support base to protect them. The transgender group's behaviour in the public is also a matter of concern. If these issues are addressed there is scope for their integration into the main-stream of the society. Like any other group the rights of the transgender population is to be respected and implemented in the proper sprit.

Bonded Labour and Wages

Among the various rights enjoyed by human beings, the economic right is an important fundamental right. Every individual should have the choice of his employment depending upon the availability and his capacity to handle the work. They must be given reasonable salary in accordance with the nature of work. But this fundamental right is denied to millions of people in Asia, especially in countries like India. While India is progressing steadily after her independence in various spheres, the stigma of bonded labour still haunts it.

The practice of using bonded labour is not confined to any particular geographical area in Indian sub-continent. Invariably this is practiced in rural areas, semi-urban areas as well as in cities. Both educated and uneducated people use bonded labour even though it is illegal. If we go back to the pages of history, the practice of using bonded labour is a system embedded in the psyche of Indian population. To understand the horrors of bonded labour one must understand how it is practiced and how the labourer suffered permanently. It is vicious circle in which a person once trapped cannot come out and his family members are also pulled into the vortex. The developing countries experience the bonded labour issue more often than the other countries. To understand this human right violation one must know the concept and the causes responsible for this practice that refuse to disappear.

What is Bonded Labour?

Exploitation of labour and paying very poor wages for the hard work, using coercion, threat and written bonds to make the labour submissive are normally associated with bonded labour. Whenever a poor labourer was in need of money he borrows it from a landlord or from some other wealthy person. Since the poor labourer don't have any valuables like gold, land, house, he pledges his services for the money received. In almost all the cases of bonded labour their illiteracy is exploited to keep them in permanent bondage. They have to execute bonds after collecting some advance amount. The bonds are mostly plain papers to collect thumb impressions. Empowered with this document, the landlord asks him to work in his land or house for a very low wage. Sometimes, their wages would be even below 1/4th of what other free labourers receive for the same work. Due to his poor condition he borrows further for his survival and increases his debt with his master. In order to reduce the burden he is forced to bring his wife and children into the bondage. Since he cannot educate his children they also follow his footsteps as an illiterate. Unless the bonded labourer repays his accumulated debt with interest he cannot liberate himself and his family from bondage. His master would never provide such an opportunity for him. The bonded labour system involves indebtedness and forced labour. While 98 per cent of the bonded labour is believed to be due to indebtedness and 2 per cent due to customary social obligations.[77]

Generation after generation their hard work is systematically exploited by the wealthy person. It is a vicious circle in which the labourer cannot come out. He also mortgages the future of his family by totally depending on his master who never allows him to clear his debt. His illiteracy and lack of awareness of his rights make his position more miserable. Though the bond executed by the labourer is used to threaten him, it is not valid in a court of law. Through such bond no one can force a person to work under him permanently and making such bond itself is illegal. Lack of awareness of this fact continues the system of bondage. Not only in agricultural lands, but bonded labour system exists in unskilled hard labour. In brick kilns, stone crushing units, fish and other processing industries, bangle making units, match factories, cracker making units, construction industries, hosieries and in *beedi* factories the bonded labour system exists. The middleman who acts like an agent lures them into bondage. They promise higher wages and bright future and usually encourage the entire kith and kin to migrate to the place of work. They give some advance to trap them. Once inside the workplace, they cannot move out freely and have to work for long hours for a very poor wage. The advance as well as other money they receive from the owner will accumulate with usurions interest. He cannot repay the amount and becomes a bonded labour. He is given only basic amenities for survival. But his spirit and energy would drain away systematically.

Evolution of Bonded Labour

In human history bonded labour existed in one form or another, from the early times. Exploitation of vulnerable group is not new to humanity. In early Indian societies, a variety of labour exploitative systems existed. In the early Tamil societies and later, the labourers are not properly paid and kept in bondage. Slavery also existed and was mostly prominent in the agricultural production. In early Greek and Roman societies slavery existed. During war the victorious ruler made a part of defeated subjects and soldiers as slaves to do hard labour. Women are the worst affected in addition to their hard labour they were also sexually exploited. There was no payment for their labour. Only their basic requirements were met by their captors. Sometimes they were used for amusement purpose in which their life was exposed to the brutalities of their masters. The popular English movie 'Gladiator' portrays the condition of slave soldiers. To amuse the nobles, rich and the public they were forced to fight with lions, tigers and well equipped fighters in Coliseum. They have to kill the beasts and the fighters or they would be brutally eliminated. It is believed that the Pyramids of Egypt were constructed only with the forced labour. The Great Wall of China was also constructed mostly with forced labour. Under modern dictatorship, millions of people were forced to do hard labour without any monetary compensation and ended their life in a pathetic way. The Communist regimes in Russia and China also extracted forced labour from the public with poor wages.

In USA, the Negroes were treated as slaves. Like cattle they were counted and sold in the public markets. As civilization advanced, progressive legislations slowly eradicated this evil practice in several countries. In India, the *Manu Smriti* was instrumental in bringing caste based varnashrama dharma that legitimized the ill-treatment and exploitation of lower caste groups. Under the Imperial Cholas, compulsory labour system existed in which the labourer must work without pay for at least few days in every month. The Tamil word '*pannaiyal*' refers to a permanent farm hand termed as '*Adimai*' meaning slave. Slaves were obtained or purchased for a sum of money. They and their children were the property of the masters. When the land is sold the slaves working in it were also sold along with it to the new master.[78] The British abolished slavery in 1843 but the practice of compulsory labour system continued. Despite subsequent legislations in 1860, work was extracted for a poor wage. The labourer was forced by circumstances to borrow money and enter into debt bondage.

Conditions after Independence

In independent India several protective measures were taken by the Government of India to protect the labour force. Following the guidelines of International Labour Organisation (ILO), several progressive steps were taken to improve the condition of Indian labour. Starting from Minimum Wages Act in 1948 several laws were enacted to improve the condition of bonded labour in India. The Indian Constitution also incorporates several provisions against forced labour or bonded labour. Any such attempt is punishable under law. Especially sections 21, 23, 39 and 49 of the Indian Constitution prohibit bonded labour. The social system, caste hierarchy, illiteracy, and the pathetic condition of millions of underprivileged masses facilitated the growth of this evil system. The nexus between the rich and law enforcing agencies only stifle the cry of helpless bonded labour. Still millions of bonded labourers are suffering in several work-places despite several progressive legislations. One major factor that prevents their escape from this vicious grip is their abject poverty and lack of awareness on their rights.

Efforts of Government

The Government of India is taking several steps to abolish this evil practice. According to article 23 of the Indian Constitution, trafficking, debt bondage and forced labour are specifically prohibited. The Bonded Labour System (Abolition) Act, 1976 was aimed at freeing all bonded labourers and cancel their debts. It also envisages the establishment of rehabilitation measures to the victims and punishing the guilty. The implementation of the Act is the responsibility of respective state Governments. The state must empower the District Magistrates to protect the economic interest of bonded labourers.

The Act paved the way for the creation of vigilance committees to support the rehabilitation of freed bonded labourers. The committee involves various persons including individuals from SC and ST community, social workers and those who work in official and non-official capacity in rural development agencies.

The District Level Vigilance committees are expected to play the crucial role in identifying and rehabilitating the bonded labourers. In reality these committees are largely non-existent. In case such committees are established they are ineffective, corrupt and non-functioning. The Human Rights activists who work for the emancipation of bonded labour face threat and harassment. More than anything there are no records for the prosecution of the guilty. In some states statutory registrars related to bonded labour are not maintained. The details given by state governments and its district units may not corroborate on the number of bonded labour. Sometimes, the data given by the State Governments contain several glaring errors. For instance, in Orissa for a particular year the number of identified bonded labour was 48,657. But the number of rehabilitated were 51,751. Regarding the funds for rehabilitation of the released bonded labour, the State Government and the Central Government share it on 50:50 bases. It was executed through IRDP and Jawahar Rozgar Yojana (JRY).

Much of the money allotted for rehabilitation was unspent and reabsorbed by the government. In 1989-90 only 76.16 per cent fund was utilized. In 1991-92 only 48 per cent was utilized.[79] The Central Government refused further grant since the State Governments fail to send reports on expenditure over their rehabilitation. It also suggests that the failure to report expenditures indicate the failure to enforce the relevant law on bonded labour. Corrupt practices in utilizing the fund minimize the share of the labourers. Official apathy in the eradication of bonded labour is also a major problem. Up to 1988, there were 7,000 prosecution under the Bonded Labour (Abolition) Act. But out of this, only 700 cases resulted in conviction. After 20 years of passage of the Act, in 1995 Vellore Collector, M.P. Vijayakumar arrested 8 *beedi* employers. It got wide publicity in the local newspapers. The agents spent one night in jail and were fined 500 rupees each, even though the Act allows punishment up to three years. The bold step of Collector, M.P. Vijayakumar was very much appreciated by several NGOs working for human rights. Because, up to that time the District Collectors all-over India have not seriously pursued the matter.

The Human Rights Watch observes that profound lack of concern for the plight of bonded labour from the enforcing official is a major concern. The State Governments also failed to frame the necessary follow-up rules to suit the national level Act. Opposition from local leaders against the abolition of this system is another stumbling block. The inordinate delay in court cases pending on bonded labour issue delays conviction. Caste and class bias are also reported while dealing with the persons employing bonded labour. When there is a complaint of this practice the local Thasildar enquires the matter in the presence of those who employ bonded labour. The bonded labour may not accept his bondage in the presence of his master. In some cases, the Vigilance Committee Members themselves or their relatives engage bonded labour. One cannot expect justice from them.

For effective implementation of the Act, the officials can establish direct contact with grass roots level service organisations. One another practical problem is that if the official is not properly protected there is a great risk from ruthless owners. The workers escaped from the clutches of bonded labour are caught by local police or informers. The owner's punishments to such persons were very cruel. No food and water is given for few days after repeated thrashing to instil fear.

Lack of accountability is hampering the progress in solving this problem. There is no machinery existed to verify the veracity of the district level reports. The rehabilitation of the rescued bonded labourer's future hangs in balance. The standard answer given by official is that the labourers released were unavailable for rehabilitation. According to NGO sources, the rate of return to bondage by released labourer was very high due to the delay in the release of money for their rehabilitation. Lack of adequate staff, inadequate training and sensitization of labour inspectors are other problems. The District Magistrates are already overburdened with other works and they cannot show any particular interest in periodic reporting. Till few years back, for entire Tamil Nadu there is only one assistant section officer looking after bonded labour issue in addition to his other responsibilities. These are some practical difficulties from the government side that needs attention.

In certain districts like Vellore in Tamil Nadu, some effective steps are taken. The labour inspectors are making routing check-up on bonded child labour. They fine those who employ children. They also encourage the parents to send their children to schools by giving some assistance. When the owners are fined for a hefty sum, it is a warning to others. But the public awareness on bonded labour is very low despite media reports on the release of bonded labourers from time to time.

A case was reported in *The Hindu* in November 2000 on the plight of a boy who worked as a bonded labour in Andhra Pradesh. The boy was hailing from Madurai area in Tamil Nadu. He was lured by agents and ended as a bonded labour. The working condition was very pathetic and he was forced to work without rest and relaxation. After few months servitude he felt miserable and tried to escape. But he was captured and punished by his masters. Out of frustration he started eating nail and iron pieces that created unbearable stomach ache. When he was taken to hospital he managed to escape since the employer abandoned him. In a very serious condition he was admitted in the government hospital in Madurai. The doctors removed 33 nail and iron pieces from his stomach. Imagine the fate of millions of others kept under bondage.

In another case involving the writ petition from a worker who had escaped from a weaving factory in Erode district, the Madras High Court directed Erode District Collector to enquire the matter. The petitioner said that around 450 persons including children were kept as bonded labourers in the weaving factories for the past two years. They were forced to work for nearly 18 hours a day. No treatment was given to the sick and injured. They were paid very poor remuneration and treated inhumannely. Likewise, the Society for Community Organisation (SOCO) trust has secured the release of couple employed as bonded labourer in a textile godown at Senguttai village in Perunthurai in Erode district. On false promise of a weekly wage of Rs. 250 and other basic amenities including a house for dwelling, the couple Shanmugaraj and Sankari with their child from Sankaran Koil in Tuticorin district were employed in a textile godown. Before hiring him they asked him to work for ten hours daily and paid an advance of Rs. 2000. Once inside the premise he was forced to work from 7 a.m. to 1 a.m. for a very meagre salary. His wife was forced to work as a domestic help in addition to agricultural work without any pay. They were not permitted to return to their native place and were mercilessly beaten. When he escaped and return with some of his relatives to repay the Rs. 2,000 advance and attempted to end the debt bondage he was beaten again. The owner has asked him to pay Rs. 10,000 for releasing his family. His relatives were also detained by him. Some well wishers approached a lawyer in Madurai and with the help of SOCO Trust they moved the court and released them. The officials in the SOCO Trust alleged that the local police was unhelpful in filing FIR which could fetch compensation under the Bonded Labour System (Abolition) Act of 1976.

Reports suggest that several State Governments failed to treat the bonded labour issue as a very serious problem. Till 1993, the total number of bonded labourers identified and released were 2,51,424. Among them 2,27,404 persons were reportedly rehabilitated. The numbers of rehabilitated persons are strangely more than the number of bonded labourers identified and released. [80] The State Governments grossly underreport the existence of bonded labour. In 1994, 13 State Governments including Tamil Nadu, Karnataka, Kerala, Andhra Pradesh, Rajasthan, Haryana, West Bengal, Maharashtra, U.P., Meghalaya, Bihar, Gujarat and Madhya Pradesh presented sworn affidavits to the Supreme Court stating that there were no bonded labourers in their jurisdiction. The Supreme Court appointed a commission to conduct a survey of bonded labour in Tamil Nadu and submit its report. The commission examined some 20 industries and concluded that there were over one million bonded labourers in the state. In addition, a large number of bonded labourers are also migrating to other states. Another survey conducted on behalf of the Supreme Court estimate that at least six lakh bonded labourers are employed in around 130 sugarcane factories alone. In Karnataka, a survey carried out by a non-governmental organisation JEEVIKA identified over 18,000 bonded labourers in 48 sub-districts.[81]

In the absence of reliable official statistics, it is very difficult to estimate the actual number of bonded labourers in India. In 1996, a report—The Small Hands of Slavery—was published by Human Rights Watch Asia, which provided a comprehensive overview of the evidence for child labour in India. It estimated that among the bonded labourers at least 15 million child bonded labourers exist in India.

Child Bonded Labour

Within the bonded labour system, the most pathetic case belongs to the condition of child bonded labour. Sometimes, when parents are in debt bondage and are unable to repay the mounting advance and interest amounts they were forced to pledge their children also. These children despite their tender age are forced to work for several hours beyond their physical endurance.[82] Sometimes, they were sexually abused by their masters or by the supervisors. They never have opportunities to play with others or enjoy the childhood with the usual unhindered joy. Bonded child labour is used almost in all the small and major industries as well as in agriculture. Their working condition is very pitiable. Few years back, a *beedi* agent in Vellore district repeatedly had beaten a boy to death for his slackness in work. The parents who were indebted to the *beedi* agent sent their child to the agent. In 2009, a case was reported in Chennai in which the neighbours, who were unable to bear the crying sounds of a young girl, reported the matter to the child helpline. The owner of the house was employing the girl child who was hardly ten years old. She was not properly fed and constantly beaten by the woman of the house. The child was forced to work from morning till late night. At times, she even branded her with hot iron.

In several small scale industries, hotels and in agriculture millions of such children are suffering under cruelty. Especially in brick kilns, they are employed with their parents.[83] Illiteracy of the parents, poor background, drunken nature of their fathers, and irresponsible family member are fuelling the growth of child bonded labour. The child labour itself is a crime and the child bonded labour is a worst form of crime. Apathy of officials as well as the general public increase the incident of child bonded labour. The child helpline member is a welcome addition. Any public witnessing an act of cruelty on children or child bondage can report the matter. This scheme is paying dividend and several child bonded labour cases are reported and follow-up actions are taken. Yet, the volume of child bonded labour is enormous that requires focused attention. The need of the hour is the implementation of the existing laws in letter and spirit. In reality, there is little accountability for implementation.

Bonded labour system is a bane on the society. As long as greed and demand for cheap labour exists it will continue in one form or the other. Proper education, awareness on the part of the bonded labour group would reduce the burden. But the problem is intricately linked with the economic vulnerability of people suffering below the poverty line. When a welfare Government's measures reach at the grass roots level, the people at the bottom level would think about educating their children. Education is a surest means to get out of the vicious cycle. The general public, NGOs and the Government has a moral responsibility to eliminate the bonded labour system.

Refugees and Human Rights

Refugees' issue is one of the most important issues that haunt many countries across the world. Almost all countries face this problem in one form or another. From early history there are references on the refugee movements. Ethnic issues, war, and natural calamities force millions of people to migrate to unknown places for survival.[84] Refugees leave their homeland because they have no other choice. They flee their country when their Government cannot protect them from serious human rights abuses. In most cases they have to move to a far-away place and their hope of returning to their native place diminishes later. In human history, refugees move out of their countries due to persecution, political violence, and other natural and man-made situations that threaten their life and honour. During war the victorious army might punish the defeated ruler and his subjects. Sometimes, an alien ruler may create unbearable condition for a section of the population that escapes to other country. Ethnic conflict between majority and minority communities like the situation in Sri Lanka may lead to the fleeing of large number of refugees to neighbouring countries.

In the 20th century, during Second World War, Adolf Hitler persecuted millions of Jews for ethnic cleansing even though most of them were the citizens of Germany. The Jewish people fled to other countries where they are safe from the secret police of Hitler. Not only under Hitler in the modern era but the Jewish community has faced persecution in Europe and other places for the past 2000 years. But the irony is that the Jewish authorities are insensitive to the plight of Palestinian refugees after the creation of Israel. In other countries, millions of minority and ethnic groups are facing persecution and are fleeing to other countries. In the African continent ethnic violence against one tribal group or ethnic minority led to the exodus of refugees to neighbouring countries. The refugee problem is not confined to one country or to a particular period but a regular feature of human history.

During the early periods, no specific efforts were taken to redress the human rights issue of refugees. Under the League of Nations, some serious efforts were taken in the 20th century. Following the First World War large number of people were uprooted and fled to other countries. In Russia, the 1917 Communist Revolution forced a large number of people out of Russia. They were either unable to digest the anti-religious attitude of the Communist regime or loyal to the Tsarist regime. They escaped to the neighbouring countries of Europe in the hope of retuning to Russia after the downfall of Communism. But such desire become a reality only after seven decades. It forced the refugees to settle in a country where they have moved earlier. To help these refugees High Commissioner for Refugees was created in June 1921 by the League of Nations.

In the post-World War I period the refugee issue emerged as a major concern affecting millions of people. One of the main problems faced by the refugees was their identity crisis. They don't have any documents to prove their nationality since their escape was forced by circumstances. They may not be in a position to apply and collect their passport and other relevant documents that establish their national identity. Without this document no country can help them at the times of their crises. The League of Nations appointed Dr. Nansen as the High Commissioner for Refugees. He provided refugee passports to millions of uprooted people. This Nansen passport, a travel document gave its owner the right to migrate more freely across the national borders. It helped them to get all temporary assistance till a permanent solution was found. It was a major relief to the refugees in their day to day life of uncertainty. This passport was accepted by more than 50 countries at that time.

The 1967 United Nations Refugee Protocol defined a refugee as "any person who, owing to well founded fear of being persecuted for reasons of race, religion, nationality or membership of a particular social group or political opinion is outside the country of his nationality and is unable, or owing to such fear, is unwilling to avail himself of the protection of that country, or who not having a nationality and being outside the country of his former habitual residence as a result of such events is unable or owing to such fear is unwilling to return to it". From the above definition refugee is a person who fled to another country due to political reasons and not due to economic factors alone. Anyone who moves to another country due to economic reason is regarded as an economic migrant or economic refugee. Normally, they do not come under the purview of refugee who is facing persecution and denial of human rights. But it is argued that continuous denial of economic opportunity to a particular ethnic or minority group should also be considered as political refugees as per the convention.

In addition, asylum seekers are people who submitted their claim for refugee status in another country. Till the acceptance by the host country they have not been formally recognized as refugees. Article 14 (1) of the Universal Declaration of Human Rights stressed that "everyone has the right to seek and enjoy asylum from persecution in other countries."[85] Refugees have the right to international protection. It is roughly estimated that 200 million people live outside the country of their birth. The estimate of refugees varies from 15 million to 40 million in different borders of the world. The majority of refugees and internally displaced people are in Asia and Africa. The Amnesty International is doing systematic work for the rights of the refugees and IDPs. It exposes human rights abuses and failures to protect them.[86] Its activists lobby their Governments for changes in national laws and practices to protect the refugees in more than 50 countries. It focuses its attention on the risks people would face if they were forced to return to their country. Amnesty International is working to end the unlawful detention of asylum seekers from the countries where they seek protection.

International Efforts for Refugees

In order to mitigate the sufferings of refugees who swell in number during Second World War, United Nations Relief and Rehabilitation Administration (UNRRA) was created. Forty four nations signed the agreement for creation of UNRRA. This UN agency provided medicine, camp materials and other assistance to the displaced persons. The Economic and Social Council of the UN (ECOSOC) created a special committee on refugees and displaced persons. It drafted the constitution as well as the new organizational structure to take-over the activities so far handled by UNRRA. It led to the creation of International Refugee Organisation (IRO) in December 1946. It provided support and new homes for over a million displaced persons and refugees and extended assistance to millions of refugees living in camps in different national borders. Vocational training and other assistance is given to the refugees for supporting them in their efforts to resettle in their motherland.

In order to develop a body of international law concerning refugees, several attempts were made and the process was completed in 1951. A special UN conference approved the convention relating to the status of refugees. The 1951 convention with its 1967 Protocol sets the standard for the treatment of refugees as an important legal document. This convention provides broad definition of refugees and allows the freedom to practice religion and other important human rights. Especially, the refugee children are entitled for elementary education, public assistance and access to courts. They should be treated at least like as other nationals of a foreign country in the matters related to housing and job. This convention is signed by 136 nations in June 2000. These contracting nations shall provide the minimum rights to the refugees in areas such as work, education, religion and social security without any discrimination. It also stipulated the condition under which a refugee can lawfully expel from a country of his choice on the grounds of national security. Due to political reasons, sending away the refugee to the country of his origin is prohibited after this convention.

In addition to the above arrangements, the United Nations High Commissioner for Refugees (UNHCR) is created as a subsidiary organ of the General Assembly of UN. The 274 offices of UNHCR spread over various continents assist the refugees in all possible way remarkably. It assisted the refugees who wish to return to their homeland under voluntary repatriation. For its resettlement work and humane approach, this UN Organisation was awarded with the Nobel Peace Prize twice in 1954 and 1981.

In South Asia the refugee problem affects most of the countries like India, Bangladesh, Pakistan, Maldives, Nepal and Sri Lanka. India due to its vast size and resources attracted large number of refugees from neighbouring countries. There are Chakma refugees from Bangladesh, Bhutanese refugees, Tibetan refugees, Ara Kauese refugees from Myanmar, Afghan refugees and other minor refugee groups that entered into India after different points of time since 1947. Dalai Lama, the spiritual leader of Tibet escaped Chinese persecution and entered into India with large number of Tibetan refugees. They have settled in the Dharmashala region and it created lot of tension between India and China. Even though India generously handles its refugees from South Asian countries it has not acceded to the 1951 convention or its 1967 UN Refugee Protocol.

The Second World War and creation of new nations following independence from colonial masters unleashed the refugee problems. In countries like India partisan on the basis of religious identity created communal animosity and violence followed by large scale migration of refugees from both sides of the India-Pakistan border.[87] The Hindus and Sikhs migrated from Pakistan whereas large number of Muslims moved from India. It took several years to settle the issues of refugees on both sides. The settlement of their property claims, tracing the missed persons created lot of heat and animosity that bedevilled the Indo-Pakistan relationship. India had to tackle nearly 6 millions refugees from Pakistan who lost everything. But the exodus of Hindu refugees from East Bengal continued for years. They stayed during the initial years of independence but when communal riots broke out periodically they steadily moved to India till 1971. Providing them work and shelter besides the creation of safer environment for their sustenance is an uphill task.

When Burma was dissected from India and got independence the Indians, especially Tamils faced persecution from the Burmese Government. Those who opted to return to India lost everything and become penniless. Their settlement was also a painful task for India. In Madras they were allowed to start petty shops in and around Paris corner. It later became the Burma Bazaar selling imported and at times smuggled goods.

In 1971, relationship between East and West Pakistan deteriorated due to demand for a separate state. The West Pakistan army's atrocities led to the forcible migration of millions of people to the bordering states of India. It touched 10 million and their rehabilitation including food and shelter drastically affected India's economy. The refugee problem and other related issues led India to the 1971 Indo-Pakistan war. Even though a considerable section of these Bengali refugees returned to Bangladesh after its independence, the remnants stay in Assam and other states. Their stay considerably affected the local population which started agitations against their stay. The presence of vast refugee groups creates lot of problems in social, cultural, political and economic spheres. Due to economic compulsions still illegal migrants cross the border that seriously affects bilateral relations between India and Bangladesh. The Assam Ghana Parishad was started by the students that led to violence and political change in the state.

The problem of Indian Tamil labourers settled in the hilly regions of Sri Lanka became a major issue in Indo-Sri Lanka relations. The Lal Bahadur Shastri-Srimavo Pact of 1964 and subsequent agreement in 1974 forced 5,25,000 Tamils on India. Due to the Governments' political decision, the Indian Tamil labourers were forced to return to India as refugees.[88] The resettlement of these refugees also created lot of humanitarian problems as well as political tension between two countries. Due to improper rehabilitation arrangements and limited scope for employment in Indian plantations, the Tamil refugees suffered a lot. It discouraged the Tamil labourers in Sri Lanka to return to India as a refugee. Only after a long delay, the Sri Lankan Government was forced to grant citizenship to them due to the intensification of ethnic issue and Eelam demand.

After the July 1983 ethnic violence in Sri Lanka the affected Sri Lankan Tamil refugees arrived at the shores of Tamil Nadu. Around 2 lakh to 2.6 lakh refugees were driven out of their homes due to insecurity and violence. They were put up in refugee camps in different parts of Tamil Nadu. In addition to the refugees, there were 60,000 to 70,000 Sri Lankan Tamils stayed outside the camps with their own resources or from support abroad. But they are neither regarded as refugees by the Government of India nor fall under the refugee category of United Nations High Commissioner for Refugees (UNHCR). Following Indo-Sri Lankan accord between Rajiv Gandhi and Jayawardene in July 1987 almost all the 30,000 refugees from the camps in Tamil Nadu were allowed to return to Sri Lanka. But when war broke out again between LTTE and Sri Lankan forces, the next flow of refugees started in June 1990. The arrival of refugees from various countries created a variety of problems to India. When conditions improved India repatriated around 65,000 refugees back to Sri Lanka.

The UNHCR started its office in Madras and helped the rehabilitation efforts. When the Sri Lankan Tamils felt they are forced to return to Sri Lanka by the pressure of Indian Government, the UNHCR represented their case to India. A Indian court ruled that forced repatriation should be stopped. The Tamil Nadu Government agreed for a voluntary repatriation with the involvement of UNHCR. This organisation tries to ensure that families are not split while being repatriated. It screened all those who repatriated above the age of 12 years about their knowledge on the condition of Sri Lanka and their real desire to return to that island nation.[89]

The Government of Tamil Nadu is trying to redress the long pending grievances of the Sri Lankan Tamil refugees living in the camps. The Ministers and Government Officials paid visit to these camps and took some special efforts to provide basic necessities. Even colour TV sets were given for their entertainment. There is a demand from the political parties and public that this refugee population may be allowed to assimilate with the local population by the grant of Indian Citizenship.

In some countries like Afghanistan civil war between different militant groups and the government created a miserable condition for the people. For more than 40 years the people are facing the wrath of different warring groups. Al Qaeda and other terror outfits operate freely in Afghanistan. In the name of punishing them the US planes mercilessly bombarded the country in which the innocent civilians were mostly killed. They fled to neighbouring Pakistan and their resettlement in the refugee camps created humanitarian and political problems. According to a recent statistics Pakistan is the most heavily burdened state in the world with 745 refugees for every $1in per capita GDP. In comparison Europe's richest economy Germany has 17 refugees for every $1 of national income. The UN High Commissioner for Refugees, Antonio Guterres described the problem as an arc of crisis reaching from Pakistan and Afghanistan through the middle east to Yemen, Somalia, Sudan and Chad that produces two-thirds of the world's refugees.[90] He regretted that still there is no true European asylum system existed but a patchwork of different national system that is inadequate to address the mounting refugee crisis. Among the refugees, the 7,00,000 Somali refugees face the worst treatment everywhere.

The UN is also facing a lot of financial difficulties that hampers its relief operations. In Myanmar, Iraq and in number of other countries dictatorial rule, war, sectarian violence and occupation by international troops create a hostile environment to the local people. They move to neighbouring countries as refugees. Despite UN efforts and NGOs, the refugee problem is mounting day by day thanks to changing political equations. Advancement in civilization has no effect on the refugee question that is steadily deteriorating. Lack of concern for fellow beings, greed for natural resources, and hatred towards other religious, ethnic, language groups aggravate it further. The efforts of international organisations like UN are hampered by financial constraint and politics of big powers.

Terrorism and Human Rights

Terrorism became a popular terminology in the 20th century even though its use can be traced from earlier centuries. Terrorism is defined as the systematic use of terror or unpredictable violence against governments, public or individuals to attain a political objective. It also raises the question of the factors responsible for terrorism. S.D. Muni argued that "violence whether social, political or physical perpetrated by the state against other states or its own people is the womb of terrorism, humiliation is its cradle and continued vengeance by the state becomes the mother's milk and nourishment for terrorism."[91] Today we are witnessing one terrorist act followed by another that slowly destroys the foundations of society, that builds on mutual trust and faith. Terrorism also raises several issues for which there is no simple answer. It is a very complex problem that eludes solution due to the availability of difficult choices.

No civil society is insulated against the horrors of terrorism. Almost all the countries of South Asia including India is witnessing several acts of terrorist attack in which large number of innocent people were killed or maimed. The response to the acts of terrorism varies from Government to Government. Experts on terrorism advises that using violence against terrorist in the name of counter-terrorism may not solve the problem since the factors responsible for the emergence of terrorism have not addressed in this way. Some countries swiftly retaliate with brutal force whenever terrorist strike harm their interest. The US attack on Taliban militants, and its drone attack in Pakistan border is an example in this direction. Needless to say, countless innocent civilians are dying as a result of air attack on suspected terrorist hide-outs. The act of violence by the terrorist as well as the counter terrorist measures of the state inevitably leads to human rights violations.

Our question in this context is whether even a legitimate Government has the right to violate human rights flagrantly while taking punitive action for a terrorist attack? Why terrorists use violence as a means to achieve their objectives? How terrorism violates the basic tenets of human rights? Is it possible to tackle terrorism within the existing national and international legal framework? These questions should be addressed to understand the challenges to human rights in the context of terrorism.

Violence and Terrorism

There exist variety of theories on violence and terrorism. While analyzing the source of the human desire for violence, Ted Robert Gurr argued that frustration-aggression mechanism may be one important factor.[92] The frustrated terrorists use violence as means to achieve their goal. They believe in the justness of their cause. They believe that they have exhausted all available options to legitimately change the society they live in. Hence, the terrorists argue that they have no other option except resorting to the violent means. Some of the most common reasons cited by terrorists as justification for their violent action are related to political oppression, economic exclusion and deprivation, marginalization, religious intolerance and even divine revelation.[93] But contrary to popular belief that poverty and unemployment cause terrorism, Walter Laqueur, who is the author of the basic texts on terrorism, pointed out that terrorists operating in Europe and America are usually of middle-class origin.[94] Terrorists tend to argue that due to denial of human rights and denial of chances to participate in the society or in the processes of change, they are forced to take drastic action. They would regard themselves as freedom fighters and are able to make common cause with the people who suffer such violations of their rights. The terrorists will bring a moral basis for their struggle and most people tend to ignore, forgive or justify their action in the name of the justness of the cause. In reality terrorist acts are a clear violation of basic human rights. No motive can excuse or justify terrorism.

Under International Law large scale terrorist acts are crime against humanity. Whether it was the attack at the New York World Trade Centre, or serial bomb blasts and terrorist attack on Taj Hotel and other places that rocked Mumbai and other cities in India, or the Ajmer Dargah Sharif blast, or the bomb blast in the Underground train network of London or the Chechen rebel attack on the Beslan School which killed more than four hundred school children, one can see the cruel hands of terrorist against humanity.[95] When a terrorist organisation is unable to press its point of view in any other manner, it resorts to terror tactics. Noam Chomsky observed that violence is powerful instrument of control[96] and the terrorists never hesitate to use this instrument for their cause. Han Van Ginkel suggests that "terror is the weapon of choice of those who harbour the sense of being wronged, who are too weak to do anything about it through conventional means and who are motivated to seek vengeance by other means."[97] The terrorists have their own logic and justification for their act of terror. Since they believe that terrorism is essential to protect their perceived interest and honour, they normally don't have a guilty conscience on the effects of terror on innocent people.

Violation of Human Rights

The act of terrorism violates human rights. A terrorist act not only affects the physical well-being of an individual and the society but also the psychological balance of the entire society. The terror strike will leave deep scars on the society. Those who are directly affected would develop serious problems like post-traumatic stress disorders or experience numbness, and severe anxiety. It serves the actual aim of the terrorists who wish to create a deep impact on the society by disturbing the collective will through their terror tactics. Since they wish to disturb peace through terror, the terrorists never care about the violation of others' rights. They employ unethical means to achieve unethical ends. Whether it is children, women or aged people they have no hesitation to execute them if it serves their purpose. Even children were used as child soldiers to fight their cause. In Kashmir, the Lashkar-e-Toiba and in Sri Lanka the LTTE recruited child soldiers to fight their cause despite a ban under the UN directive.[98] Both Amnesty International and the United Nations Children's Fund (UNICEF) have been critical of the LTTE for not honouring its commitment to UN on the above issue. The terrorists never hesitate to blackmail their opponents. To serve their political vision they would sacrifice innocent individuals as in the murders of Daniel Pearl, Nicholas Berg, and Margaret Hassan and many others including school children and their teachers.[99] What the terrorists are doing is total destruction of human rights and rejection of justice and morality.

Today, suicide bombing is emerging as a potent weapon in the hands of terrorists. In India, Sri Lanka, and Iraq and in number of countries it is used effectively to eliminate important political leaders and massacre the public. Due to indoctrination, the suicide bombers are subjected to brainwash and do the dastardly act in the name of martyrdom. Such acts were clear case of violation on the individual's right as well as on the rights of the victims. A resolution adopted in the UN General Assembly on Human Rights and Terrorism strongly denounced all acts of terrorism, "as activities aimed at the destruction of human rights, fundamental freedoms and democracy, threatening the territorial integrity and security of states, destabilizing legitimately constituted Governments, undermining pluralistic civil society and having adverse consequences on the economic and social development of states."[100]

Counter-Terrorism and Human Rights

In the aftermath of 9/11attack, there were suggestions that the human rights era had come to an end. It is argued that human rights concern should yield to security concerns.[101] It is obvious that human rights and terrorism cannot be separated as two unrelated compartments. Any logical approach to understanding the dynamics of terrorism should not ignore the human rights angle. As discussed earlier, the terrorists believe and compel others to believe that they are fighting for a just cause. A mere passage of laws and improvement in the prosecution of terrorism will not result in a long term solution. Here the international human rights organisations provide instruments which cover almost all aspects of human existence. When terrorism emerges as major challenge to civil societies, international organisations such as U.N. takes serious note of it. It passes several resolutions and guidelines to combat terrorism within the parameters of human rights. A society that is protecting and advancing human rights reasonably reduces the risk of terrorism. It also minimizes the support base of a terrorist outfit. At times, following an act of terrorism, a state may pursue a harsh path against the terrorists. It will only aggravate the situation further and provide fuel for the propaganda of the terrorist organisation, that the state is unjust in its dealings. It will only strengthen the terrorist outfits. The argument is that the State must act within the parameters of human rights, and at the same time, it can take strong actions suitable to counter-terrorism measures.

In countries like India the law enforcing agencies demand special legislative measures to curb terrorism. But several such Acts like TADA, and POTA mostly complicated the matters further. Nearly half of the cases booked under these anti-terrorist acts were directed against political opponents and innocent people including children.[102] Testimonials presented before a 'people's Tribunal' in New Delhi in 2004, bring out the vast human tragedy resulting from the abuse of POTA in virtually every corner of India.[103] Due to popular opposition to such draconian Acts and its misuse they were withdrawn by the successive governments. When the opposition BJP demanded the reintroduction of POTA in the Parliament on July 25, 2006, the former Union Home Minister, Shivraj Patil argued that POTA is no answer to Terrorism.[104] The judgments in the Parliament House attack and the Red Fort attack cases have contributed to the evolution of a significant aspect of contemporary criminal jurisprudence. These cases show that it is possible to ensure effective trial in cases of terrorism without taking recourse to draconian laws such as POTA. The accused were convicted by the trial court.[105] The authorities should introspect whether such laws are absolutely necessary. In case the existing laws are not sufficient to tackle the menace of terrorism, changes can be introduced after careful consideration. Scholars argued that the existing national and international legal framework is reasonably sufficient to handle the terrorist threat.[106] A proper balance should be maintained between the interest of the state security and individual liberty.

Sometimes, the state actions on terrorism may be counter-productive. In the name of countering terrorism, states such as Israel and US overstretch their reach. The showdown between Israel and the Hezbollah militants in Lebanon is one such example. In the ensuing battle Israel not only bombed civilian targets killing more than four hundred people, but also targeted the UN observer post which killed four UN observers.[107] It was condemned by the former UN Secretary-General, Kofi Annan as a deliberate act. Israel's disproportionate response only increased the resolve of the militant organisation to hit back with vigour.[108] Israel is known for kidnapping non-combatants, including minors, and holding them as hostages[109] earlier. The Israeli-Palestinian conflict has the potential for more violence in the years to come. In his well researched work on Islamist phenomenon and Jihad, Gilles Kepel argued that before embarking on terrorist violence, Islamists should mobilize popular support to seize political power.[110] Otherwise it would only be a death trap for them.

Likewise, the US 'War on Terror' is also emerging as major areas of concern. In response to the attack on the World Trade Centre in New York, the US forces almost decimated the Afghan territory to crush the Taliban regime and its recruits. In this war on terror, countless number of Afghan civilians were killed, wounded or reduced as refugees. The invasion of Iraq, aimed at liquidating Weapons of Mass Destruction (WMD), only led to forced occupation. Everyday, we hear news about suicide bombing against the occupation army. Despite U.S. victory, the invasion appears as a huge setback in the war on terror. An U.S. official conceded that the Iraq war only led to sharp increase in Al Qaeda recruitment.[111] The global domination of America and its efforts to maintain that position at any cost, continues to reinforce terrorist elements. One can also note that the American response to terror strike in U.S.A. is different from such attack on other countries like India.

Terrorism is a vicious cycle and it would devour those who perpetuate it. Whether we like it or not, terrorism is likely to be with us for the years to come. We must evaluate the underlying causes of terrorism and wherever possible corrective measures should be taken to address it. But Walter Laqueur argued that terror groups with global ambitions cannot be appeased by any concessions. The states' response to acts of terror must balance between effective control over terrorism and looking after the existing human rights norms. The U.N. General Assembly resolution stressed that "states must ensure that any measure taken to combat terrorism complies with their obligations under international law."[112] Given the emotions involved, it is certainly a difficult task. But we have very limited options.

There are variety of reasons for the emergence of terrorism. Some are real and some are imagined one. The terrorist outfits always try to justify their cause and use violence as a means to achieve their goal. They propagate the idea that they have a common cause with the general public who experience the violation of their rights. Irrespective of the justness of their struggle, terrorist violence in any form is a violation of basic human rights. There is no political, economic, military, religious or humanitarian motive that can excuse or justify terrorism. Violence will eliminate individual freedom and destroy the cultural history of affected nations. Nations must unite together in their effort towards the elimination of terrorism. In the name of counter-terrorism mighty nations should not overreact and subject other nations to inhuman attack and subjugation. It will be counter-productive and fuel further violence.

Any step to combat terrorism should be within the parameters of national and international legal framework. The past experience to bring draconian anti-terrorism legislation has only added fuel to fire. Its misuse only aggravated individual's grievance against the state and its jurisprudence. The national and international legal framework is sufficient to tackle counter-terrorism measures.[113] Despite provocations, the nations must find ways to combat terrorism within the ambit of human rights norms. Security policies gain strength and credibility only when they are implemented in a manner consistent with international human rights and humanitarian law. It is opined that the present system of international human rights law is flexible enough to respond to acute terrorist threats effectively. Terrorism will be with us at least in the foreseeable future, as the grievances and ambitions of individuals and groups will multiply in the present system. The challenges facing us are so great that we will have to overcome all the barriers to ensure the safety of humanity. As long as the terrorist believe that terrorism will provide them with what they desire, it is difficult to stop the act of terrorism. Religious hatred and blaming one particular community for terrorist act will only alienate the community further.

Julio Ribeiro who was the former Punjab Police Commissioner argues that winning the hearts and minds of the community that has been affected is most important.[114] Unless the people themselves decided that they did not want terrorism any more it is very difficult to stop its occurrence. It is observed that the tourist organisation need the support base of their own community for its sustenance and growth. Sometimes, counter-terrorist tactics followed by the authorities led to harassment and to fake encounters. It only tarnishes the image of the state and hampers its effort to eliminate terrorism. The Sorabuddin fake encounter case as well as the encounter killing of Ishrat Jahan by the police[115] in the name of counter-terrorism discredits the state machinery. Protection of women, minorities and vulnerable groups from this type of human rights violation is important in a composite culture like India.[116] The minorities should have the feeling, that they have every chance to get justice and equal treatment like that of other majority communities in India. Blaming a community for every terrorist act will only alienate it from other communities.

Capital Punishment

Crime and punishment is a natural process evolved from the period the mankind started an organised way of life. The government must punish the persons committing crime to maintain law and order. The nature of punishment also varies due to the gravity of crime. The capital punishment or death penalty is the execution of convicted criminal by the state for committing most serious crimes. These serious crimes are termed as capital crimes. There is lot of difference between the death penalty carried out through due process of law and the murder committed by individuals for personal reasons. Human life is supreme and wasting it for whatsoever reason is not good is the argument forwarded by the human right activists. Several governments freely awards capital punishment for political or religious offences. It violates the most important human right—the right to life.

The tribal societies enforced justice by the principle "an eye for an eye, a life for a life". In their social system the victim's relative have the right to score vengeance on those who commits the crime or a member of his family. When organised religion and proper legal system emerged in course, some changes were effected in the punishment. Still revenge killings are accepted as legal practice in tribally organised societies, especially in countries like Africa. The Code of Hammurabi (C.1800 B.C.) was one of the most ancient written law codes that authorized the death penalty. In the Hebrew Bible, death penalty was awarded for kidnapping, murder, blasphemy and wide range of sexual crimes. In reality, the existing evidences suggest that actual executions of death penalty were rare. With the expansion of state power the use of death penalty increased, to enforce the power of the state.[117] Draco in about 621 B.C. had written the Athenian legal system in which death penalty was awarded for a wide range of crimes. Due to the harshness of these Draco's laws the word 'draconian' was derived for later use. During the 18th century Britain, nearly 222 crimes including cutting down a tree and stealing an animal were punishable by death.

When civilization advances, the modern democratic systems insist on the concepts of natural rights and equal justice for all citizens. Death penalty for minor crimes was regarded as cruel and excessive. During the world wars large number of enemy soldiers and civilians were summarily executed without any formal trial. The authoritarian states like that of Nazi Germany and Soviet Union under Stalin, ruthlessly employed the death penalty as a means to suppress political opposition. In communist China under Mao and in number of military regimes millions of civilians were executed for variety of reasons. These excess alarmed the advocates of human rights and several concerted efforts were taken to prevent death penalty.

Methods Used for Execution

For the execution of death penalty different methods were employed by different regimes. During medieval Europe religious heretics and those who were believed as witches were burnt to death. In addition, crucifixion, beheading, electric chair, gas chamber, hanging, impalement, lethal injection, poisoning and shooting by firing squad are some of the methods normally employed for execution. In the Nazi camps like Auswitz millions of Jewish prisoners were condemned to death in the gas chambers. In India crushing by elephant was a common method of execution adopted by several rulers of early and medieval period. With the advent of British rule hanging till death was commonly practiced. The legal system also moves towards a less painful or a humane method of capital punishment. The use of electric chair and the gas chamber were introduced in the US as a humane alternative to hanging. When lethal injection was introduced in US, it was criticized as a too painful punishment for a convict.

Practice of Capital Punishment

Following the creation of UNO and sustained efforts for human rights protection, the perception on capital punishment also underwent considerable change. Nearly 138 countries have either abolished or stopped the practice of awarding death penalty.[118] Nearly 30 countries retain this punishment but have not used it for at least a decade. In 68 countries the death penalty is retained and used. In countries like China, capital punishment is awarded even to cases of corruption and the convicts were regularly executed. In the year 2004 alone, China executed more than 3,400 persons representing 90 per cent of executions carried out worldwide. In Islamic countries sexual crimes including adultery and sodomy invites death penalty. Generally, stoning to death or beheading at a public place is practiced. With the execution of Troy Davis on September 21, 2011, a total of 1,269 prisoners were executed in the US since the restoration of death penalty in 1976.[119] Singapore is also considered as a country with highest execution rate in comparison to its total population. North Korea, Yemen, Iran and China are considered as few of the countries that regularly execute condemned prisoners.

Bikramjeet Batra, in his article on the practice of capital punishment in India argued that there is a marked decline in the cases of execution in recent years. He evaluated the death sentence carried out from independence and the role of mercy petitions handled by the President of India. Table 5.1 indicates how the Indian Government is moving towards the use of death penalty on rarest cases.

Table 5.1: Mercy Petitions Commuted and Rejected by the President

Period	*Total petitions disposed*	*Commuted*	*Rejected*	*Executions per year*
1948-54	1,430	341	1,069	152.7
1955-64	2,083	601	1,482	148.2
1965-74	1,034	543	491	49.1
1975-84	173	52	121	12.1
1985-94	45	4	41	4.1
1995-2004	8	1	7	0.7
2005-present	2	2	0	0

Source: Rajya Sabha debates and informations obtained from National Archives of India quoted in *Frontline*, June 4, 2010, p. 21.

It is observed by Batra that the Presidents of India, starting from K.R. Narayanan, followed by A.P.J. Abdul Kalam and the present incumbent Pratibha Patil played a significant role in virtually ending executions after 1997.[120] The President Pratibha Patil has commuted to life sentence given to the thirty murder convicts in ninteen separate cases. The decision of President Pratibha Patil is commute the death sentence of highest number of convicts led to fresh debate on death Penalty in India. Since most of the victims were raped, tortured before murder, there was a feeling that pardoning the convicts send wrong message to the society. Even though the power of President is limited on deciding the mercy petitions, nevertheless they have played a significant role by delaying the decision for long time. No time limit is prescribed for deciding on mercy petitions when it reaches the office of the President of India, and this was used as leverage in several cases for delaying execution.

It appears that coalition politics also contributed in some cases where some state governments played a role in convincing the centre to stay the execution. In some cases, the mercy petitions rejected by the President did not resulted in the execution of the convict. In a case pertaining to Govindasamy from Tamil Nadu his death sentence was commuted as life imprisonment following appeal and pressure from several quarters. A.P.J. Abdul Kalam also indicated his dissatisfaction over the existing system of death sentences and lamented that why there were only poor people on the death row. He favoured a detailed discussion on the issues related to capital punishment and all aspects of mercy petitions as well as the need for a comprehensive policy on this matter.[121] In the case pertaining to Nalini, who was convicted for her role in Rajiv Gandhi's assassination, the Congress President Sonia Gandhi is believed to have played a key role in commuting her death sentence to life imprisonment despite her personal loss in the assassination. The other persons like Murugan, Santhan and Perarivalan who face death sentence in the same case were not hanged till date. The rejection of their mercy petition by the President after 11years and four months became an issue in Tamil Nadu politics. Senior advocates like Ram Jethmalani who appeared for this case argued that the delay made the death penalty illegal and unconstitutional.[122] A stay was given for eight weeks in this case since the writ petitions raised the issue of delay in the disposal of the mercy petitions. The Tamil Nadu State Assembly also passed a unanimous resolution on August 30, 2011 urging the President, Pratibha Patil to reconsider the clemency petition.[123] But according to the Home Ministry communication dated March 5, 1991 if a petition for grant of pardon was rejected in case of death sentences by the President of India, it would not be open for the government of a state to seek exercise similar powers under Article 161 in respect of the same case.[124] One can see popular appeal based on ethnic affinity playing a part in such issues. On the other hand, the delay in the execution of some convicts created media and public attention that led to agitation and pressure.

The delay in the execution of Afzal Guru, who was convicted for the Parliament attack case, is an example in this direction. While the parties like BJP demanded his immediate execution for political reason, human rights activists are favouring clemency. At the same time, a prolonged delay in executing a death sentence can make the punishment inhumane and degrading. Afzal Guru, being frustrated with the delay in deciding his mercy petition has said that "I really wish L.K. Advani becomes the next Prime Minister as he is the only one can take a decision and hang me. At least my pain and suffering will ease then."[125] Keeping a person under suspended animation on his execution for several years is an inhuman punishment. Likewise, the expectation on the speedy execution of death sentence to Ajmal Amir Kasab, the lone survivor among the 10 gun men who attacked Mumbai on November 26, 2008 also created media frenzy. At times, these pressures have some impact on the decision makers. However, it is a very complex issue on which human rights and public safety and security hangs on the balance.

On principle, the Indian legal system on capital punishment regards it as an essential element of jurisprudence. In the recent decades the public and media in addition to NGOs dealing with human rights issues projected the need for abolishing death sentence irrespective of the nature of crime. The European Union and the Council of Europe strictly require member states not to practice the death penalty. In the 1980s, following the replacement of authoritarian regimes by democratic governments in Latin America, the popular sentiment was widespread against the abolition of death penalty. In most democracies in Asia, the death penalty is not used by government in excess. Hence, these countries enjoy popular support for death penalty. Likewise, in African and Middle Eastern countries, the support for death penalty remains high. In USA in several states the death penalty has been banned for several years while some states follow it. Always there exists active public discussion on the merits and demerits of capital punishment.

At the international level, there exists a strong debate on the desirability of capital punishment. Those who oppose it argue that life imprisonment is an effective substitute and in case if an innocent person is executed wrongfully it cannot be corrected. It is observed that new forensic methods and DNA testing have brought to light errors committed in earlier convictions. Those who criticize death penalty argue that it is a violation of right to life. It is argued that the right to life is natural right that exists independently of laws made by men. But those who defend death penalty argue that they plucked this natural right from someone whom they murdered. Further when they were in life imprisonment, they have to lose their right to liberty which is another natural right.

Those who argue against the capital punishment point out that when the state carries out the execution on legal ground, it creates justification in the minds of individual to commit murder as they feel their action was correct like that of the state. One another argument against capital punishment is that mostly the poor who cannot defend properly in the court get death sentence. Due to their poverty, they are unable to afford competent legal representation. Racial bias, political influence, public pressure and media attention at times may tinker with the decisions pertaining to death sentence.

The history of capital punishment indicates how it was abused as a tool of oppression over the progress of humanity. Its abolition or usage for only the most serious crimes is definitely a progressive step in the onward march of civilization. The rarity with which this punishment is awarded indicates how the people have given importance to the right to life and its value. Of course, there are situations that warrant capital punishment even though it is an unfortunate option to preserve justice and social order. Our legal system should reflect on the need for creating opportunities for criminals to reform during their prison terms. When we create a social order and system that inculcate a value based society that nurtures conscience and compassion for fellow beings, the situation for capital crime may decline.

Environment and Human Rights

Protection of environment is an important global issue that needs urgent attention from the developed and developing countries alike. The use and abuse of natural resources beyond the sustainable level creates a very dangerous situation on which the future of mankind oscillates. USA, China and India are making enough carbon footprint to create complications on the future of global environment in addition to the contribution of other countries. Reckless use of resources and destruction of forest and other natural wealth gradually impacted upon environment in alarming way. Growing population and other issues seriously affected the environment and ecological balance.[126]

The threat to environment invariably affects the present and future generation. Unless all-round attention is paid to the causes disturbing global environment, far-reaching consequences awaits humanity. Already the deterioration of our ecology started to punish the people in one form or the other. Depletion of ozone layer, melting of glaciers and vast sheets of ice in the Antarctic, sudden change of climate, the effect of El Nino across the world, dwindling agricultural production, rising temperature beyond normal levels and the perishing flora and fauna in their traditional habitats indicate the dangers we are facing now due to environmental degradation.

Several issues involving environment have direct bearing on human rights. Protection of environment and sustainable development issues had a stake on the life of millions of people. Unless these issues are addressed urgently by all stakeholders, one cannot imagine the threat we are facing now. Already some scientists argue that it is too late to balance the losses on ecology and environment by corrective measures.

It is estimated by a number of scientists who forecast a temperature increase of 6 degrees Fahrenheit at the end of 21st century.

They speculated that its effects could be catastrophic. The globe may experience widespread droughts and desertification, frequent devastating storms and a rise in ocean levels as much as 3 feet. Such a development naturally submerges heavily populated areas and cultivated lands.

From the collective wisdom gained over the knowledge of past happenings, scientists point out that nature will adjust itself shortly to manage the man-made chaos on earth. It means through natural calamities like earthquake, pestilence, sudden climatic change and unknown development millions of human beings and other life forms may wipe out from the face of earth. Once again the remaining humanity starts its onward march of civilization from scratch like the primitive man. He may not be a threat to environment till he scientifically advances to a level of today's man. It is believed that such occurrence is not a far away possibility but a hypothetical reality within this century. We are sitting on a ticking time bomb that may explode at any time. Unlike the dooms day prediction that recur frequently over a period of time, this warning on environmental threat is scientifically calibrated one.

There is a close relationship between men and nature. As long as this relationship is maintained without harming one another everything goes well. The environmental issue emerges due to variety of factors such as overindustrialization, deforestation, reckless mining for minerals, and unplanned urbanization at the cost of agriculture and overexploitation of fossil fuel. In all these issues violation of human rights exist that affect the life of millions of people. The third generation of human rights is particularly focusing its attention on issues like environment and sustainable development. In the long run, development that is not sustainable cannot help the community for which the development plan is initiated.

Several issues of human survival are linked with environment. Earlier, the Vedic Indians had a great love for nature and animal life. They showed great care in the preservation of what nature has bestowed on humanity. In this context Gautama Buddha said, "the forest is a peculiar organism of unlimited kindness and benevolence that makes no demands for its sustenance and extends generously the products of its life's activity. It affords protection to all beings, offering shade even to the axe man who destroys it."[127] Consequently, men developed intimate relationship with nature and benefited from such contact. The industrial revolution propelled humanity in a fast plane that brought unmanageable issues later. It provided employment and fuelled the growth of urban centres and transport facilities. When man earned more than what he needs for his sustenance, he started spending on several things that ruins his surroundings. Trees were cut to facilitate construction activities. It has its negative impact on raining, release of oxygen and number of other natural benefits we derive from lush forest cover.

Right to life is natural right but living the life happily involves several things. But what we are doing sometimes is contrary to the goal of achieving happiness. In his address to UN climate summit, the former Maldives President, Mohamed Nasheed pointed out that his country's greatest threat is due to climate change and raising sea level.[128] The Maldives faces an existential threat and its people are living on borrowed time. The President is making serious efforts to settle his country's population in other countries before sea swallow the group of islands. It is not a case in isolation and low lying areas in many parts of the world like Bangladesh, India and US faces the threat. However, contrary to this type of prevailing scientific opinion, a climate change conference organised by the University of Mumbai claimed that the sea levels were not rising and carbon dioxide did not pose a special threat to the climate. According to its report sea levels in the Indian Ocean were not rising. Prof. Nils-Axel Morner, Retired Professor from Stockholm University, said that the Maldives President's claim that his island nation was drowning was totally unfounded in observational reality.[129] He observed that the tide gauges of Mumbai and Visakhapatnam recorded a significant sea level drop during 1955-1962 followed by stable sea levels in the past five decades. To him, the locals in Lakshadweep were aware of the fact that the sea level was not at all in a rising mode today. But rather, new land had been added. Prof. Morner said that ignorance was terrible but exaggeration was dangerous. He stressed the importance of visiting the sites instead of creating computer modelling. He argued that there was clear evidence of strong coastal erosion but no rise in sea level. Nils Finn Munch-Perterson of the Nordic Institute of Asian Studies pointed out that Maldives was marketing its sea level rise that led to a significant income for the island nation in the form of foreign aid.

In Sikkim plant diseases, warm winters, glacial floods and dry streams indicate the impact of global warming. Sikkim which was the world's biggest producer of large cardamom produces 75 per cent of world's cardamom a decade ago. But its production fell to the level of 30-40 per cent. A blight epidemic reduced self-sufficient farmers to the level of daily wage worker. The summer temperature is increasing year after year. The farmers say that earlier they used to get at least one foot of snow. Now there has been no snow that normally acts as manure for the soil.

The people of Sikkim is experiencing change of seasons and glacial floods. Though the government is forming a commission to look into the issue, it is planning to construct 26 dams. People are afraid that these dams will destroy the fragile ecology of Sikkim. Indian forests represent one of the important 12 centres of biodiversity in the world. Any men made intervention in the name of development will destroy the life form preserved in the forest for millions of years. Every passing year witnessed the extinction of some species and plants due to human intervention. It must be halted to preserve the world for the present and future generations. The environmental degradation and challenges to ecology affect forest wealth.

Of late, the flowering season of certain wild varieties indicates change in the forest area. In Sikkim, the people also experienced unusually prolonged monsoon in 2007 that caused extensive damage. The Chief Minister Pawan Kumar Chamling added that "Sikkim is a mini theatre, which in a way displays how climate change triggered by non-natural forces at the global level could bring disastrous natural calamities."[130] The people of this area are worried a lot due to the developments in their environment that threatens their normal life. In course of time, if the trend continues it could be a matter of survival for millions of people whose life is invariably linked with environment. For the worrisome developments in Sikkim, we cannot blame a single incident or a wrong step taken in one place. Environmental degradation which is mounting up every-year due to hundreds of factors that are mostly man-made affects even far flung areas on earth. It affects the right to life and to live happily.

The depletion of ozone layer causes considerable concern among nations. Its short term and long term effects including global warming are felt everywhere. The green gas emission and the release of carbon monoxide that is termed as carbon footprint affects global environment. Countries which are developed or developing at a fast pace contribute for carbon emission. It led to global warming that affects nature very much. In countries like India people are consuming more than what they can actually produce. In other words, the development we are experiencing in different sectors is not sustainable in the long run. Hence, urgent steps are necessary to halt this regression.

Tourism Industry is the second biggest industry after oil industry in terms of generating revenue. Everywhere, the government and private agencies are interested in promoting tourism potential. This approach aiming only at revenue and employment creates several problems to the local environment where tourism is promoted. The tourist arrival also brings several problems to environment and livelihood issues of the local people. Throwing away of plastic bottles, carry bags and other waste pollutes the environment and blocks the free passage of waterways.

Due to commercialization of tourism industry thickly wooded forests are destroyed to construct infrastructure and buildings. The creation of concrete jungles amidst greenery and real jungle affects the ecosystem. It also led to the drawl of large quantities of groundwater by sinking several bore wells. The quantum of water consumed was more than the water generated in the natural process. Deforestation also contributes to less rainfall and climatic change that affects the livelihood of millions of people. Another important problem in this regard is the availability of potable water for human consumption. At the global level, the availability of safe drinking water is less than one per cent. Estimations suggest that 21st century may witness a situation in which the nations fight with each other not for oil, but for water resources. Industrial pollution coupled with the sewage discharged from towns and cities into the river system pollutes water and environment. We are ruining our own sources of drinking water and endangering the survival possibility of present and future generation.

Globalization brought both development and misery to millions of people. The development is also not sustainable and its reward is not shared among the communities rationally. It pushed economic activities in several countries that unleashed several complications. The name of commercialization of agriculture and several occupations, globalization created a vast environmental challenge. The introduction of mineral water, 'packaged drinking water' in pet bottles and large scale selling of beverages and bottled drinks adversely affects the water table across the country. It is estimated that worldwide water privatization is a multi-trillion-dollar industry in near future. It has produced huge misery for the poor. Shortage of water has led to the emergence of 'water Lords' who makes fortune at the cost of poor.[131] "Water is the stuff of life and a basic human right."[132] But despite several judgments passed to protect this right to life, the status of water as a fundamental right has not been recognized by the authorities in India.[133]

In Plachimada in Palghat district of Kerala, the Coco cola production unit ruined the livelihood of hundreds of farmers and public. By sucking millions of litre groundwater through giant bore wells the water table in that area went down at alarming level. The chemical wastage sludge from this bottled unit was sold to the local farmers as manure that caused soil degradation, water contamination and consequential loss to agriculture in the soil. The local people have successfully fought for the closure of the unit and sued the company for compensation. The Coco Cola Company was forced to supply drinking water in tanker lorries to the affected villages and take measures to contain pollution.[134] The story of this environmental hazard reached outside world thanks to the vigilant media. Following long drawn agitation by the local people, the media and environmental activists, the Kerala cabinet has decided to set-up a tribunal to adjudicate on compensation claims from the people affected by the plant.[135] There is increasing resistance to destructive development thanks to the awareness created by such incidents. The monks in Sikkim and the Arunachalese youth groups are fighting against mega-dams, farmers refusing to surrender their lands for Special Economic Zones (SEZs) and the Adivasis in Orissa keeping at bay powerful industrial groups such as Vedanta and POSCO. Such struggle and awareness on environment give some hope on human rights protection in this regard.

Because of the development of infrastructure, communication network and construction of several buildings and highways, the environment is affected. In addition to felling thousands of trees, the building activities damage the river and other water systems due to large scale removal of sand. The sand mafia is thriving on political patronage and corrupt system. The Tamil Nadu Government bans sand mining operations in the state by private parties but further action in this issue is delayed by court cases that have been initiated on the issue. The Madras High Court directed the State Government in 2002 to take steps to halt to illegal sand mining on river beds. In Tamil Nadu, the government is directly involved in the sand trade but several loopholes leads to the depletion of an important mineral, the sand.

Even the government officials trying to prevent the smuggling of sand were attacked by the mafia controlling sand trade. When sand is removed in large quantities it destroys the water body and ecosystem surrounding it. The water-table would be reduced to unmanageable level. Collection of sand takes hundreds and thousands of years through a slow natural process. When men disturbs it, the lifeline of water resources dries up since sand retains large quantities of water and purifies it.

When states like Kerala ban the quarrying of sand, its construction requirement is fulfilled by the interested groups operating from Tamil Nadu. One regular feature is that hundreds and thousands of lorries are shifting the precious sand from Tamil Nadu border to Kerala and Karnataka. Imagine the cumulative effect of this destruction on water sources in the near future. Tamil Nadu is already threatened by depleting water-table and most of its land is semi-arid in nature. The Israeli scientists who are known for their world class water management techniques warned that the state is moving towards desertification. Communist leaders like Nallakannu are fighting lone battle against the 'sand mafia' in Tirunelveli region in the courts.

The case of Palar River is an example in this regard. Originating from Karnataka, it touches Andhra Pradesh and passes through Vellore, Kanchipuram and parts of Chennai in Tamil Nadu. It was a perennial river providing water for agriculture and domestic purpose. Due to politics and man-made damage to this important river system, no water passes through its streams in the recent decades, except briefly during floods. The life of millions of people and their drinking water requirement depends upon the revival of this river. Agriculturalists are slowly selling their lands and migrated to other places for survival. It is the case in several parts of India where the ecology is badly affected due to man-made destruction. Drinking water, a basic necessity of humanity is denied to considerable section of the population. It is a gross human rights violation as it involves the right to life. Due to the unavailability of potable water the people are forced to consume the available polluted water with consequent health problems.

In cities and towns managing the garbage is a major problem affecting the rights of the people. The mounting garbage disposal is really a challenging task for the metropolitan administration. The heaps of garbage dumped at the city outskirts create a foul smell and damage the quality of groundwater. Clearing the garbage by fire also leads to air pollution. In addition to the existing wastes, a new trend is noticeable. Exporting waste illegally to poor countries has become a vast and growing international business.

When the Western countries imposed new environmental laws for recycling and disposal of waste, they simply export it to other countries. The law also stipulates that the waste should be recycled or disposed of in a responsible way. Otherwise the authorities imposed tax on waste generated. The waste includes electronic items, old wires, electricity meters, circuit boards and plastics in addition to household trash that contains toxic components. It is estimated that every year 20 million containers of waste is shipped to countries like China, Indonesia and India either legally or illegally.[136] Due to the need for raw material, the fast growing economies like China and India uses the waste imported from other countries. Electronic waste tends to go to African countries especially to Ghana, Egypt and Nigeria. But the recycling capacity of these countries highly varies. Despite ban on the export of waste in some European countries, the illegal shipment continues. This irresponsible greed affects the health of people as well as the environment in several developing countries.

Deforestation and mining have made several hilly towns bare. Cherrapunjee, the place known for the highest rainfall in the world is facing a peculiar problem due to the environmental degradation. In the adjacent town named Sohra acute water shortage haunts the people. Deforestation and mining made the town bare. The strong flow of water has eroded soil fertility making it difficult to revive agriculture. The peasants lament that the crops don't grow well and they are getting half the quantity they get around a decade ago. Harvests are destroyed by unseasoned rains. It also damages the flowers, fruits and nuts that fall-off from the tree. They are experiencing warmer winters and unpredictable climate that made the life more insecure. The pattern of rainfall is changing since the thick forest is cleared for mining purpose. The cooling effect of trees is missing. The people's income is steadily decreasing due to this drastic change in climate and production. Though the average rainfall remains the same the yearly fluctuations are greater. The people don't know whether the rains let them down or it arrives at the right time. The places like the slopes of Khasi hills have been stripped bare by logging and mining that compounded the misery of the local people.[137]

Biodiversity is the source of all ecological goods and services that form the source of living for all. India is enormously endowed with biological diversity. It is among the 12 mega gene centres of the world and two of the 31 global hot spots of biodiversity that includes the North-eastern Himalayas and the Western Ghats.[138] An estimated 8 per cent of all species on earth exist in India. Over the years, increasing global trade, tourism and travel have helped the movement of some species which have become invasive.

The swine flu outbreak in April 2009 caught the attention of people all-over the world. It reminded us about our vulnerability to invasive aliens which do not respect geographical boundaries. Globalization and expansion of human population besides other factors have facilitated the movement of species beyond natural bio-geographical barriers. When they become invasive they are considered as mainly responsible for biodiversity loss at the global level. Such species cause considerable environmental and economic damage that affects the people. It can directly affect human health. Infectious diseases are often traced to invasive alien species. When we use pesticides and herbicides to control them it pollutes water and earth. It is observed that these species cause flu, respiratory disorders, allergies and infertility among human and animal population. For example, parthenium was believed to have entered the country during the 1950s along with the supply of wheat given as aid by the US. It occupies 50 lakh hectares in India and has become a major health hazard.

During Second World War milkania was introduced in India to help soldiers to camouflage themselves. It grows around 9 cm per day and destroys small plants and affects larger trees. Likewise, the introduction of eupatorium as an ornamental plant in the middle of 19th century at the Calcutta Botanical Garden creates problem to entire South East Asian countries. It grows into a dense bush and depresses the growth and yield of crops such as rubber, mango, cardamom, tea and coffee. For the purpose of afforestation of dry and degraded lands, prosopis juliflora (kattu karuvelan) was introduced in India in the 20th century. Its capacity to grow in diverse ecosystem from coastal areas to desert region enables it to wipe out other plant species nearby.

The water hyacinth is threatening our fresh and marine water resources including the corals. Ponds, lakes and lagoons and other water sources are affected by this invasive plant. A fresh water fish, tilapia was introduced in 1950s and it is declared as invasive species in 90 countries. Its survival ability and rapid multiplication as well as its aggressive eating capabilities led to the starvation and death of native fishes. These invasive species creates lot of ecological damage and danger to the biodiversity of India. Needless to say, it also affects the people of this region in so many ways. With international cooperation, serious efforts have to be taken to deal with invasive alien species. Preventing the entry of these species is a service to mankind and to the protection of their right to survival.

India and Environmental Protection

From the arguments placed above, on the issues concerning environment and human rights, we may be tempted to ask a question whether India has been able to balance human welfare and prosperity with safeguarding its natural environment. In the 1970s and 1980s, a number of people's movement focuses attention on the concern over raising pollution level and the decimation of wildlife and forests. Especially, the Chipko Movement under Sundarlal Bahaguna is struggling to save the Himalayan forests by preventing the cutting of trees. Medha Patkar fought a valiant battle against the Narmada dam project that displaces Adivasis and tribal communities from the forest region which is a lifeline for their survival. In South India also strong protest against the construction of dams in places like silent valley saved the ecology. The Bhopal gas leak tragedy in 1984, and the delay in settlements for their rehabilitation created widespread condemnation in the aftermath of trial court's judgment after a delay of 25 years.[139] Following media and public pressure, the Government of India is making fresh efforts for the extradition of former Union Carbide Chairmen, Warren Anderson.[140] The Group of Ministers (GoM) on Bhopal recommends Rs. 1500 crores package for the victims to the Prime Minister. They suggested enhancement of compensation to the victims and prepared a road map to address the legal, medical, humanitarian and environmental aspects of the disaster.[141]

The government also responded positively and created the Ministry of Environment and Forests and passed several path breaking laws on wildlife forests and pollution. In the process of environmental decision-making considerable space was opened up for citizens and the civil society is included to advice the Environment Ministry. The judiciary also plays a very active role through progressive judgments on the issues concerning environment, pollution, mining and forests.

But these environmental gains are temporary as the process of globalization sets in during Narashima Rao's tenure as Prime Minister. When Indian economy was opened up to globalization, the liberalized regulatory environment helped the industry and commerce to push further. The outcome was that India should slowly move away from sustainable development because the production and export of minerals and fisheries jumped many fold. Recent studies suggested that an estimated 1.64 lakh hectares of forest land has been diverted for mining in India. Water is also used in large scale in certain mining process. In 2005-06 alone, around 77 million gallons of water was used in India for iron-ore mining which is enough to meet the daily needs of three million people.[142]

The estimate of Indian Institute of Metals in 2009 points out that around $300 billion is to be invested in the metals and mining sector in eastern India over the next few years. This amount is six times the investment made since 1947.[143] While it generates employment and economic opportunities for a section of people it has serious consequence on environment and on the livelihood options of millions of people. Illegal mining in India is another issue. For major and minor minerals, studies estimated that around 30,500 illegal mines are plundering the natural wealth in various parts of India.[144] It has a serious consequence for forests, land, water and coastal environment. When the Environment Ministry is attempting to impose stringent checks on mining, it provokes strong reactions. The corporate lobbies strongly oppose the Mines and Minerals Bill, 2010.[145]

In order to satisfy the demands of industry 1,00,000 hectares of forest land was given to mining since 1980. Undoubtedly, these areas were also home to several traditional native communities. The methods used by the government and the corporations include cajoling and bribing the community leaders to accept relocation. In certain places like Orissa force was applied to evict them. Other wildlife species also affected badly. Reports suggest that India's recorded diversity of 1,30,000 wild plant and animal species may be heading towards extinction.[146]

Unfortunately, the National Environment Policy announced in 2006 provides only justifications for placing economic considerations above environmental concerns. Ashish Kothari argues that according to the Global Footprint Network, India has the world's third largest ecological footprint after US and China and Indians are using almost twice what the natural resources within the country can sustain. In the recent decades the capacity of nature to sustain Indian population has declined sharply. But hardly any sign of basic changes visible in environment and development governance that affect millions of people. However, thanks to continued efforts by civil society programmes and the media, several positive laws such as the Right to Information Act, National Rural Employment Guarantee Act and the Forest Rights Act were passed. Despite limitations, a radical ecological democracy is entirely possible where all citizens have opportunity to participate in decision-making process that affects their livelihood issues. The Supreme Court has also embarked on environmental activism in recent years. It expanded the right to life and personal liberty to include environmental protection.[147]

The threat to environment is mostly man-made. Variety of factors contributed for the erosion of environment and ecological balance.[148] Nature has time and again warned us on crossing the limit to play with it. Protection of environment is directly related with the survival of mankind. Protection of human right cannot be dissociated from the issues concerning environment. One of the major challenges faced by 21st century is related to global warming and its ill effects on wide variety of human population settled across the globe. There is a clash of interest between the developing and developed countries over sharing the cost of environmental protection.[149] The global summits on this important issue failed to reach agreements that can at least halt the degeneration of environment to a point of no return. Any collective efforts to protect environment will naturally protect the human rights of millions of people.

HIV/AIDS and Human Rights

During the 1980s the knowledge on the existence of HIV/AIDS, a disease caused by a virus called Human Immunodeficiency Virus or HIV created apprehension. This virus destroys the immune system thereby minimizing the capacity of the body to fight diseases. AIDS is the last stage of infection by the virus and it is estimated that around eight to ten years period a person infected with HIV becomes a full blown case of AIDS. No vaccine has been invented even after a quarter century though advance research work is going on in this field. Once infected by this disease, there is no medicine available to cure it. However, significant advances made in the understanding of HIV infection and its end stage of AIDS helped the scientists to develop potent drugs to control HIV infection. The fatal course of HIV infection is now altered to a manageable condition that allows an infected person to lead a relatively normal life. These anti-retroviral drugs have radically changed the position of HIV infected person and the treatment regimen. In developed countries Highly Active Anti-Retroviral Therapy (HAART) provides solace to the patients. In US alone, the popular use of HAART since 1996 led to a 50 per cent decline in AIDS incidence, hospital admissions and death toll.

The spread of HIV/AIDS creates a situation in which the affected persons and their family experience variety of human rights violations. Lack of knowledge and awareness on the incidence of AIDS creates a near panic situation in the 1990s that stigmatized the disease. The HIV/AIDS affected persons and their spouses are treated with contempt. At times they are ostracized by the society and even by their family members. In several cases family rejection, public contempt, lack of awareness on the disease led to suicides. They experience ill-treatment at the place of work and in several cases dismissal from service followed suit. It complicated the living options of the patients. Since it spread mostly through sexual contact and by drug addiction a lot of stigma and taboo is attached to this infection that questions the morality of the patient.

The international documents widely accepted that human right is central to any nation's effective response to HIV/AIDS. In this context, it is important to access the role and importance of a human rights framework in responding to this disease. Human Rights are inherent and inalienable to every individual. This right makes the government and the larger society accountable to the citizen. Every individual has the right to live with freedom and dignity. The fellow citizens are duty bound to respect, protect and address this fundamental need. We must remember that human rights are not given by a society or by individual governments but are earned by virtue of being born human. Needless to say that dignity is the entitlement of all as long as life exists. Since the affliction of HIV/AIDS involves questions related to honour and dignity of individual, the protection of human rights is essential to safeguard human dignity at all level. The society must ensure an effective, rights based response to this dreaded disease. Addressing the epidemic with in a human rights framework involves the acceptance and non-discrimination of populations perceived to be more vulnerable to HIV/AIDS.

Reports suggest the increasing concentration of this epidemic in the developing countries. Developed countries like US took lot of steps to curb its further spread. Increased awareness, collective social response as well as the affordability of people for costly treatment in developed countries including HAART significantly reduced the spread of HIV. In developing countries the response to HIV is not only in protecting the rights and privacy of individuals but also involves other issues like poverty, gender and inequality. Such response will reflect the spirit of the Universal Declaration of Human Rights which regards poverty as the greatest denial of human rights.

A community response recognizing the vulnerability to the epidemic not just in terms of individual behaviour but also other conditions that led to this vulnerability. Such approach recognizes that the vulnerability of migrant workers, women, children, injecting drug users, sex workers and homosexuals, can be reduced through the protection of their human rights. When the stigma and discrimination faced by the affected person is eliminated they can be empowered to control their lives properly. Protection of human rights undoubtedly creates a supportive environment to encourage the vulnerable group to access health and HIV related social services. Such support mechanism would stimulate behavioural change.

The international response at first represents two diametrically opposed public health approaches. One is isolationist approach and the other is integrationist approach. In the isolationist approach compulsory HIV screening for all, disclosure of HIV status of those testing positive, and isolating the affected person through discriminatory practices were followed. The integrationist approach proposes voluntary testing and non-disclosure of patients' HIV positive status and equitable treatment for them through community health care. It also includes the protection of their employment and other important factors affecting the life. The basic idea behind this approach is that it would encourage people to come out and access health services that would increase the chances of behavioural change that reduce the chances of spread of HIV.

The counselling of HIV positive persons in a non-discriminatory, humane setting encourages their personal responsibility in preventing the spread of HIV further. In most countries of South Asia, at the earlier stage, the approach of disclosing the positive status of persons in order to protect the rest of the society was favoured. However, it was given up when such approach only fuelled stigmatization and violation of human rights of affected persons. In course of time, experience shows that help, support and protection extended for the infected persons is an important step in the battle against AIDS.

It is observed that the cost of treatment is beyond the reach of the vulnerable groups in South Asia. Especially sex workers, injecting drug users, women, children and migrant workers are socially disempowered groups that already experience the denial of basic rights. Enforcing positive rights in the socio-economic front and the law reforms sympathetic to them can help the group in controlling the spread of HIV.

In India HIV/AIDS related litigation is increasing day by day. When a worker was terminated from service on the ground of being HIV positive, even though he is functionally healthy, the Lawyers' Collective challenged it in the court of law. The Mumbai High Court in a landmark judgment in 1997 reinstated the worker in the service with back wages. The Lawyers' Collective also obtained a special order to suppress the identity of person involved since it affects his privacy. It facilitated the HIV positive litigant to sue his employer under pseudonym.[150]

In India, the most court cases involving HIV are related to employment. Regarding women the problem involves their maintenance, custody of children and property rights. The HIV also led to a number of divorce cases. It is felt that free legal service should be given to the HIV positive persons. Their individual complaints should be handled by a network of lawyers. Step must be taken to remove discrimination against people with HIV. The access to treatment is another important area which needs attention. We come across reports of denial of admission in hospitals for HIV/AIDS patients even when they are in the dire need of urgent treatment. Lack of awareness and fear of contracting HIV made even the health workers to deny the patients their basic human rights. The hospital authorities are concerned about the attitude of the other patients coming for treatment, who feared that going to such hospitals increase the risk of contracting HIV.

Denial or lack of proper health care to HIV positive group amounts to a violation of the basic human rights to life. Fortunately, the experience related to HIV/AIDS in the past quarter of century significantly reduced the stigma attached to it. The understanding on the HIV infection and its spread creates awareness against stigmatization. The scientific advancement in finding new drugs to control the dreaded epidemic raised the hope of HIV positive and their family members. The efforts of government and NGOs in spreading awareness on protective measures as well as the need for humane treatment of HIV positive persons slowly percolated to the social system. In countries like Brazil free and subsidized HAART treatment is given. It provides opportunities to counselling on proper treatment and prevention of its spread to other family members and society. But some developed countries are pressing the developing countries against the manufacture of generic alternative to these patented drugs. It will hamper the fight against HIV and increase the cost of treatment.[151]

By accepting the HIV positive persons as partners with health care providers in mitigating the impact of HIV creates a positive environment. Such approach is also gaining momentum in countries like India where large number of HIV/AIDS affected persons are suffering in silence. The medical needs of sex workers who are badly affected by this dreaded epidemic can be met in a non-discriminatory manner. It would facilitate them to share their intimate concerns about unsafe sexual practices and HIV in an environment of trust.

The free availability of condoms and the understanding of why and how they needed to be used prevent the spread of HIV further. In India several positive steps were taken to prevent the spread of HIV/AIDS that needs community understanding and participation. Providing free treatment for the economically marginalized group and making drugs available at affordable cost are other important steps to be taken to mitigate the sufferings of HIV positive persons. Even in science subjects at the high school level, lessons on HIV/AIDS can be incorporated to increase the awareness from the early stage of adulthood.

Questions

1. Write a note on the Rights of Children.
2. Give some suggestions for the eradication of Child Labour.
3. Evaluate the problems faced by the child soldiers.
4. Examine the concept equal pay for equal work.
5. Classify different types of crimes against women and punishment for such crime.
6. Write a note on female infanticide.
7. Briefly describe the issues related to 'Gender Bias'.

8. Explain Indian women's Right to divorce and remarriage.
9. Examine the condition of Dalits in India after independence.
10. Write a note on the Constitutional protections available to Dalits.
11. Who is transgender and narrate their human rights violations in contemporary society.
12. Write a note on the steps taken to help the transgender population.
13. Briefly analyse the causes of bonded labour.
14. Do you feel that the efforts of the government in the eradication of bonded labour are adequate?
15. Write a note on the problems faced by refugees.
16. Trace the International efforts for the protection of the rights of the refugees.
17. Bring out the attitude of India towards Refugees.
18. How terrorism violates human rights?
19. How political rights are violated in the name of national security?
20. Give your reasons for the abolition of Capital punishment.
21. How the protection of environmental issues involves the livelihood option of millions of people?
22. Write a note on the choice between market economy and sustainable development.
23. Examine the human rights violations faced by the HIV/AIDS affected persons in India.
24. Briefly explain the role of press in the protection of Human Rights in India.
25. Give an account of the functioning of Human Rights Commission in India.
26. Discuss the constitutional remedies available to protect fundamental rights in India.
27. Examine the proactive role played by judiciary in several landmark cases.
28. Give an account of custodial deaths and its impact on the victim's family.

Objective Type Questions

1. The Child Labour (Abolition) Act was passed in India in ....

(a) 1975 (b) 1979
(c) 1981 (d) 1991

2. .... is the surest means to eradicate child labour.
(a) public health (b) free education
(c) punishment (d) none of the above
3. The transit school for 'working children' project was funded by
(a) Amnesty International (b) ILO
(c) Asia Watch (d) PUCL
4. The Devadasi system was abolished due to the efforts of ....
(a) Raja Ram Mohan Rai (b) Jyotiba Phule
(c) Dr. Muthulakshmi Reddy (d) E.V.R. Periyar.
5. Articles 15 and 29 of Indian Constitution stressed equal educational opportunities to ....
(a) children (b) women
(c) refugees (d) transgender.
6. The 'Dowry Prohibition Act' was amended in ....
(a) 1961 (b) 1974
(c) 1980 (d) 1984
7. The Cradle Baby Scheme was introduced to raise female babies in ....
(a) Kerala (b) Karnataka
(c) West Bengal (d) Tamil Nadu
8. Vikam Satyagraha in Kerala was led by .... for the temple of untouchables.
(a) Ayodhya Dasa (b) E.V.R. Periyar
(c) Mahatma Phule (d) Narayana Guru
9. The Article .... of Indian Constitution abolishes the practice of Untouchability.
(a) 7 (b) 9
(c) 15 (d) 17
10. According to the Criminal Tribes Act ...., the Aravanis were regarded as criminal by birth by the British Government.
(a) 1847 (b) 1857
(c) 1858 (d) 1871
11. Among the various state governments of India .... provides lot of welfare schemes and support mechanism to the third gender.

(a) Maharashtra (b) West Bengal
(c) Tamil Nadu (d) Andhra Pradesh

12. The Bonded Labour System (Abolition) Act, ... was passed in...... to liberate all bonded labourers.
(a) 1956 (b) 1976
(c) 1979 (d) 1984

13. Dr. Nansen, known for Nansen passport was ....
(a) a passport officer
(b) High Commissioner for Refugees
(c) an Italian Prime Minister
(d) UN Secretary General

14. The Right to asylum is stressed in the Article .... of the Universal Declaration of Human Rights.
(a) 10 (2) (b) 12(1)
(c) 14(1) (d) 15 (3)

15. For its resettlement work and humane approach ....is awarded with Nobel Peace Prize twice.
(a) UNHCR (b) ECOSOC
(c) IRO (d) UNRRA

16. The terrorist attack on .... was an important turning point in the issues concerning global terrorism.
(a) Mumbai Taj Hotel (b) Beslan school
(c) New York World Trade Centre
(d) Indian Parliament.

17. The terrorist group which invented suicide bombing as a means to eliminate key opponents was ....
(a) PLO (b) LTTE
(c) Al Qaeda (d) HUJI

18. Nearly .... countries have either abolished or stopped the practice of awarding capital punishment.
(a) 76 (b) 84
(c) 112 (d) 138

19. Today .... executes more than 90 per cent of death penalties carried out worldwide.
(a) India (b) Pakistan
(c) China (d) USA

20. The country which is fighting for survival due to raising sea level is ....

(a) Sri Lanka (b) Maldives
(c) Russia (d) Nigeria.

21. The Sterlite plant which was ordered to be closed by the High Court is located at ....
(a) Plachimada (b) Tuticorin
(c) Kodaikanal (d) Niyamgiri.

22. The wheat which was supplied to India by .... led to the spread of parthenium.
(a) England (b) France
(c) USA (d) Russia.

23. The Chipko Movement to protect the Himalayan Forest was led by ....
(a) Medha Patkar (b) Sundarlal Bahuguna
(c) Arundhati Roy (d) None of the above.

24. The prevalence of HIV/AIDS came to the knowledge in the ....
(a) 1970s (b) 1980s
(c) 1990s (d) none of the above

25. The HAART treatment gives solace to the patients of ....
(a) heart disease (b) arthritis
(c) cancer (d) HIV/AIDS

Key to Objective Type Questions

1.	c	2.	b	3.	b	4.	c	5.	b	6.	d
7.	d	8.	b	9.	d	10.	d.	11.	c	12.	b
13.	b	14.	c	15.	a	16.	c	17.	b	18.	d
19.	c	20.	b	21.	b	22.	c	23.	b	24.	b
25.	d.										

POINTS TO REMEMBER

Child Labour

Being a vulnerable group, children are exploited all-over the world—UN convention on the rights of the child adopted in 20th November,

1989—it focuses attention on civil, political, social, economic and cultural rights of every child—The child has the right to survival, protection, education and participation—Child Labour is prevalent in almost all the countries especially in developing countries like India and China—a working child in the age group of 5 to 14 years either for payment or without payment is child labourer—It affects the physical and mental health of children—Lack of education prevents their escape from this trap—Causes includes poverty, preferences of children by employer, desire to continue the traditional occupation through the child and irresponsible parents—Types of child labour including bonded child labourer and child soldiers. Why the efforts of government are not successful?—Poor implementation of preventive Acts—Apathy of officials and the society—Different schemes of UNICEF, ILO and NGOs for the children.

Women's Rights

Secondary position of women through the ages—Devadasi system—efforts of social reformers like Raja Ram Mohan Rai, Jyotika Phule, E.V.R. Periyar and Dr. Muthulakshmi Reddy—efforts of UN and International Women's Conferences in Mexico, Denmark, Nairobi and Beijing. Several International instruments to protect variety of rights involving women—Indian Constitution gives equality of status, rights to education, social, political and economic rights—Social laws governing women covers marriage, dowry, adoption, guardianship, maintenance and the custody of child—Muslim women's right covered under Muslim personal law—rights given to women differ from religion to religion—Importance of Hindu Marriage Act, 1954 and the Special Marriage Act, 1955—Enhancement of Women's Rights since independence.

Crimes and violence against women, a major rights violation—types of violence—rape, cruelty, sexual harassment and domestic violence—different laws covering these violations and how it is implemented—inheritance and succession rights and the importance of Hindu Succession Act, 2004 in protecting women's property right—Its poor implementation—Female foeticide and infanticide issues—considerable progress in upholding the rights of women due to their education, vigilant media and the proactive judiciary—remarks of justice Markandey Katju on what is to be done to improve the position of women.

Dalit Rights

Manusmriti and four-fold division of the society—evolution of untouchability—role of great leaders like Mahatma Phule, Ambedkar, Gandhiji and EVR Periyar—condition of Dalits and the emergence of Dalit literature—problems of Dalits includes untouchability and discrimination in the allocation of jobs, land, basic resources and other amenities—rape of Dalit women and atrocities against Dalit including temple entry are some of the serious issues in independent India—Through Constitution Ambedkar attempted their protection—role of reservation and Constitution in their protection—Dalits position varies from state to state—role of Compulsory Education Act, 2009 as a positive step for Dalit children—gradual improvement of Dalits' position due to education, awareness and governments' positive discriminatory steps. Further efforts needed for their protection.

Rights of Transgender

Transgender's existence recorded from 9th century B.C.—Who is transgender?—mostly men and sometimes women carving for the body of other sex—physical and psychological problems—lack of family and social support led to complications—process involving the entry into the transgender group as member—Transgender's problem includes ill-treatment, lack of social support, opportunities for education and proper career and income etc.—problems of social prejudices and draconian laws that criminalize alternative sexuality—difficulties in getting civil and political rights—till recently they cannot get regular jobs, vote, marry, inherit property—forced by circumstances to live through begging, dancing and sex trade—discrimination in public place—states like Tamil Nadu is taking several measures for their support—creation of helpline and NGOs for their support—issue of ration card, housing schemes and support through Self Help Group Schemes—need for training and employment opportunities and other supports like old age pension etc.—need for awareness and sympathy from the public.

Bonded Labour

Bonded labour refers to the exploitation of labour by paying very poor wages for hard work using threat, and written bonds to make the labour submissive—It exists in almost all parts of India and in other developing countries—Using the illiteracy of the labour loan or advance amount given is used as a pretext to get the thumb impression in plain papers. Sometimes, they were given even below ¼ of actual wage—Unable to repay the debt they bring their children into the trap—It involves indebtedness and forced labour—Bonded labour is illegal but the workers are unaware of it—One can find bonded labourers in agriculture, brick kilns, stone crushing units, bangle making units, match factories, cracker units, construction and hosieries units, in *beedi* factories, lock making industries and in number of unskilled and semi-skilled works. Human history reveals its existence from early time—Pyramids as well as the Great Wall of China were constructed mostly with forced labourers or slaves—Under sections 21, 23, 39 and 49 of the Indian Constitution bonded labour is prohibited—Due to social system, caste hierarchy, illiteracy and poverty this system prevails—The government took several measures including the passage of Bonded Labour System (Abolition) Act 1976—The law includes rehabilitation measures to the victims and punishment to the guilty—District level vigilant committees were created—But they are ineffective, corrupt and non-functioning—Apathy of the officials and lack of interest hamper any progress in this issue—Sincere officials to be protected from the ruthless owners—Lack of accountability is another issue—Several state governments failed to treat it as a serious issue—The bonded child labour is another pathetic issue which needs attention—Several case studies suggest the cruel nature of the system.

Refugees and Human Rights

Mostly due to war, ethnic issue and for religious problems people migrated to unknown place as refugees—When there is no protection from their government people have no choice but to flee—In the 20th century millions of people were forced by circumstances to move out of their country—Work of Dr. Nansen as the High Commissioner for Refugees—Nansen Refugee Passport helped millions—Variety of refugees and their problem—Article 14(1) of UDHR stressed the need to give asylum for people suffering from persecution—Refugees have the right to international protection—the role of UNRRA in their support—The ECOSOC's special committees on refugees—Several convention, UN conferences and protocols to help the refugees—South Asian countries, African countries and even the European continent faced the problem—India's partisan, Afghan crisis and Sri Lankan ethnic issue created millions of refugees—The International efforts and the role of NGOs is not sufficient to solve this mounting crisis.

Terrorism and Human Rights

Terrorism involves the use of terror and unpredictable violence against governments, public or individuals to attain political objective—It erodes mutual trust and faith among communities—It is a very complex problem that eludes solution—The terrorist outfits justify the use of violence and try to integrate with the general public who experience violation of their rights—No country is insulated against terrorism—The terrorist act as well as the counter-terrorist measures of the state inevitably leads to human rights violation—Large scale terrorist acts are crime against humanity—Violence is a powerful instrument of control and the terrorists effectively use this—Terrorist Act disturbs the balance of entire society—Suicide bombing is new technique used by terrorist organisations—Sometimes, the special legislative measures to cure terrorism like TADA and POTA complicated the matters further—Israel usually gives disproportionate response to terror strike through large scale destruction—The US war on terror also creates concern since it affected large number of civilian population—When mighty nations overact and subject other nations to inhuman attack and subjugation it fuels further violence—Terrorism should be combated within the legal framework—Winning the hearts and minds of the affected community is most important—The counter-terrorism method should not involve fake encounters like Sorabuddin's case—The state must protect women, minorities and vulnerable groups from human rights violation.

Capital Punishment

Death penalty was given for even ordinary crimes earlier—Advancement of civilization added its impact on the approach towards capital punishment—Variety of methods were used for execution including hanging—less painful or humane method of capital punishment emerged later—The UN plays a key role on the changing perception of capital punishment—138 countries abolished death penalty—30 countries have not used this punishment for the past one decade—In countries like India death penalty is awarded on rarest of rare cases—In China even corruption is sufficient cause for death penalty—In Islamic countries stoning to death or beheading at a public places practiced—In India a mercy petition is delayed for a long time by the Presidents from 1997—The death penalty involving terrorist always creates public and media pressure—At the international level a strong debate exists on the desirability of capital punishment—One group argues the necessity of retaining capital punishment while the other group argues against it—But racial bias, political influence public pressure should not influence the decision on death sentence—in history death penalty was used as a tool of oppression—It can be used only in most series crimes—of late the judiciary is awarding capital punishment on very rare cases—we must give importance to the right to life and its value.

Environment and Human Rights

Today environment degradation not only affects the human rights of millions of people but also the future of humanity—The abuse of natural resources beyond sustainable level creates a dangerous situation—Market economy unleashed a force that devour forest and other mineral wealth including water—Deterioration of ecology led to melting glaciers and Antarctic ice in addition to sudden climatic change that includes El Nino effect—rising sea level may submerge vast areas in near future—unless series effects were taken the entire humanity is at risk—human survival is linked with the protection of environment—the wisdom of our forefathers in protecting environment is not respected in the greedy rush towards wealth—in Maldives and Sikkim people are fighting against sudden change in climate and in rising sea level—commercialization of tourism also affects environment—the water lords are making profit through mineral water at the cost of the poor—despite several judgments the right to water was not recognized as a fundamental right by the authorities in India—in Plachimada in Kerala the people successfully fought against the Coco Cola production unit—the media and the local people forced the company to close the factory and to give them compensation—Adivasis of Orissa have halted the plan of Vedanta to mine their hills—In Tamil Nadu the sand mafia is destroying the precious mineral through commercialization—it is affecting the water table and threatens the agriculture—judiciary is playing a proactive role in protecting environment and people's right—the Sterlite plant closure is an example—Western countries export its wastes to other developing countries—it is a major threat to Asian and African countries—several plants introduced from the Western countries are threatening environment in India—From 1970s due to increased awareness people's movement forced the government for suitable action—several important laws were passed to protect the wildlife, forests and to contain pollution—civil society is able to open up a space for active role but economic compulsions made the government to yield to the pressure of multinational companies—Bhopal gas tragedy warned us on the toxic industrial climate that prevails in India—The government allocates 1,00,000 hectares of forest land for mining since 1980. It affects the tribals, flora and fauna—The environmental activism of the Supreme Court is encouraging sign—men must understand that he should not play with nature—what is necessary is the sustainable development which needs collective effects and wisdom.

HIV/AIDS and Human Rights

HIV/AIDS is a major threat to the existence of humanity—no preventive medicine or total cure is possible for this health condition—it destroys the immunity of the affected individual that led to death after some time—due to fear and lack of awareness the HIV/AIDS affected peoples were ill-treated and denied support from the society—Even the medical fraternity denied treatment to these needy people—Ill-treatment at the place of work and dismissal from service complicated their living option—A lot of stigma and taboo attached to it—at the early years several affected persons committed suicide due to this attitude—need for human rights framework in responding this disease—every individual has the right to live with freedom and dignity—the society must respect and protect this fundamental need—a non-discriminatory approach towards the population vulnerable to HIV/AIDS is necessary—developed countries halted the further spread of this disease—the HAART treatment and collective social response played a significant role—in developing countries other issues like poverty, gender and equality should be addressed—who will bear the cost of medicine is a major challenge—need for non-discriminatory, humane approach to prevent the spread of HIV further—In countries like India HIV related litigation is increasing—Lawyers' Collective is helping them—denial or lack of proper health care to HIV positive group is a violation of human rights. Slowly the increased awareness on the treatment and the prevention is helping the fight against this dreaded condition—need for the free availability of condoms to limit the spread of HIV—Free treatment and creating awareness at the High School level on the disease is a necessity.

NOTES

1. B. Gopalakrishnan, *Rights of Childran* (Jaipur: Aavishkar Publishers, 2004), 78.
2. For details see. Rachna Suchinmaya, *Gender, Human Rights and Environment* (New Delhi: Atlantic Publishers, 2008), 103; and Ruma Ghosh Singh, Nikhil Raj and Helen R. Sekar, *Hard Labour at a Tender Age* (Noida: V.V. Giri National Labour Institute, 2002), 1.
3. Personal interviews with parents employing their children in their traditional occupation in Vellore district in Tamil Nadu, India.
4. For details see Kalpana Sharma, "Invisible Environmentalists", *The Hindu*, 13th June, 2010, Magazine section.
5. Ruma Ghosh Singh, 1-8.
6. U.N. Department of Public Information, *Human Rights: Children's Rights* (New York: U.N. Department of Public Information, 1996), 3.
7. Dharmalingam, "Female Beedi Workers in South Indian Village", *Economic and Political Weekly*, XXVIII: 27 and 28 (July 3-10, 1993.)
8. Kailash Satyarthi, "Child Labour: A major cause for poverty", *Health for the Millions* (November-December, 1998): 29.
9. UNICEF, *Focus on Child Labour: The State of the World's Children 1997* (New York: Oxford University Press, 1977), 20.
10. Human Rights Watch, *The Small Hands of Slavery: Bonded Child Labour in India* (New York: Human Rights Watch, 1997), 130.
11. *Ibid.*, 132.
12. "Interview of President Chandrika Kumaratunga", *Frontline*, January 1, 1999, 10.
13. *The Hindu*, 26th November,1999.
14. K. Mohanasundaram, "Human Rights and the Child Labour", *Third Concept*, 14: 157 (March 2000): 24.
15. Rekha Roy, *Women's Rights in India* (New Delhi: Akansha Publishing House, 2006), 8.
16. The girls also wore the sacred thread and performed Vedic rites and rituals. They also handled careers in medicine, business, defense and

administration. For details see, B.S. Upadhyaya, *Women in Rigveda* (New Delhi: S. Chand and Co., 1974), 44-46; and J.E. Llewellyn, *The Legacy of Women's Uplift in India* (New Delhi: Sage Publications, 1998), 27.

17. A. Devanesan, *History of Tamil Nadu* (Tamil) (Marthandam: Renu Publications, 1998), 93.
18. Dr. Usha Padhy, "Role of Women in Indian Politics", in *Women Empowerment*, ed. Rajib Lochan Panigrahy and Dasarathy Bhuyan (New Delhi: Discovery Publishing House, 2006), 48.
19. See, http://www.un.org/Women Watch/daw/sitemap/index. html.
20. Human Rights Advocacy and Research Foundation, *Basic Course on Human Rights Education for Teachers of Post Graduate Departments* (Chennai: Human Rights Advocacy and Research Foundation, 2003), 111-18.
21. Bipan Chandra, *India since Independence*, 642.
22. Shilpi Gupta, "*Legal Rights of Woman in Independent India*" in B. Goswami, 170.
23. *Ibid.*, 170-71.
24. Padma Iyer, *Human Rights of Women* (Jaipur: Pointer Publishers, 2006), 88.
25. *The Hindu*, 11th June, 2010.
26. Abdur Rahman Asshaha, *Islamic Concepts of Human Rights* (Delhi: Sipra Publications, 2004), 9.
27. S.A.H. Moinuddin, *Divorce and Muslim Women* (Jaipur: Rawat Publications, 2000), 40.
28. Kirti Singh, "Left in the Lurch", *Frontline*, April 9, 2010, 19.
29. B. Goswami, 168.
30. Ram Ahuja, 245.
31. Annie George, U. Vindhya, Swamy Ray, "Sex Trafficking and Sex Work: Definitions, Debates and Dynamics—A Review of literature," *Economic and Politically Weekly,* XLV: 17 (April 24, 2010), 65.
32. *Ibid.*
33. Markandey Katju, "The Ideal of Women's Emancipation", *The Hindu*, February 18, 2009, 13.
34. Lina Gonsalves, *Women and Human Rights* (New Delhi: A.P.H. Publishing Corporation, 2001), 121-23.
35. S.K. Pachawri, *Women and Human Rights* (New Delhi: A.P.H. Publishing Corporation, 1999), 165.
36. Kalpana Sharma, "Defining Sexual Assault", *The Hindu*, May 30, 2010, Magazine section, 3.

37. C.S. Anuradha, "Women Political Leadership and Perception: A Case Study of South Asia," *International Journal of South Asian Studies*, 1:1, (January-June 2008): 189.
38. S. Viswanathan, "A Silent Revolution", *Frontline*, June 6, 2008, 21.
39. B. Krishnakumar, "Feminisation of Panchayats," *Frontline*, June 6, 2008, 18.
40. Samiyendra Nath Dhar and Soumitra Sarkar, *Self-Help Groups: A Micro Financial approach to poverty reduction and establishment of Human Rights for Rural Women in Globalization and Human Rights*, ed. Anil Bhuimali (New Delhi: Serials Publication, 2006), 39-41.
41. Sharda Srinivasan, Arjuna Bedi, "Daughter Elimination: Cradle Baby Scheme in Tamil Nadu", *Economic and Political Weekly*, XLV: 23 (June 5-11, 2010): 17.
42. S. Mehartaj Begum, *Human Rights in India: Issues and Perspectives* (New Delhi: A.P.H. Publishing Corporation, 2000), 236.
43. T.K. Rajalakshmi, "Woman as Victim", *Frontline*, January 4, 2008, 4.
44. Indu Agnihotri, "Towards Equality", *Frontline*, April 9, 2010, 4.
45. *The Hindu*, 27th June, 2010.
46. K. Kartikeya, *Women Movements and Human Rights* (New Delhi: Navyug Publishers, 2008), 6.
47. Markandey Katju, 13.
48. Indira Parthasarathy, "Existential Dilemmas", review of Venomous Touch: Notes on Caste, Culture and Politics, by Ravikumar, *The Hindu* Book Review, June 6, 2010, 6.
49. Gyanendra Singh Rawat, *The Status of Dalit and Human Rights in India* (New Delhi: Sumit Enterprises, 2005), 261.
50. Gail Omvedt, *Dalits and the Democratic Revolution: Dr. Ambedkar and the Dalit Movement in Colonial India* (New Delhi: Sage Publications, 1994), 9-10.
51. S.N. Busi, *Mahatma Gandhi and Baba Sahib Ambedkar: Crusades Against Caste and Untouchability* (Hyderabad: Saroja Publications, 1997), 62-74.
52. Ram Ahuja, *Social Problems in India*, (Jaipur: Rawat Publications, 1999), 170.
53. A. Viswanathan, "Temple car and caste tension", *Frontline*, August 15, 2003, 37-39.
54. S. Viswanathan, "The fall of a wall", *Frontline*, June 6, 2008, 123-25.
55. S. Viswanathan, "Untouchability Unlimited", *Frontline*, March 28, 2008, 39.
56. T.K. Rajalakshmi, "Fire of Aggression", *Frontline*, September 23, 2005, 124-28.

57. For details see, Shireen Moosvi, "Domestic Service in Pre-colonial India: Bondage, Caste and Market", *Proceedings of the Indian History Congress*, 64th session, 2003 (Patna: Indian History Congress, 2004): 560.
58. Quoted from Gyanendra Singh Rawat, 89.
59. M.M. Adhikary, S.K. Acharya, S.K. Musiar Ali, *Empowerment and Entitlement of Rural Women in the Panchayat System* (Udaipur: Agrotech Publishing Company, 2009), 21.
60. Gyanendra Singh Rawat, 267.
61. Meera Velayudhan, "Cut off by Caste", *Frontline*, April 9, 2010, 30.
62. Surinder S. Jodha, "Dalits in Business: Self-Employed Scheduled Castes in North-West India," *Economic and Political Weekly*, XLV:11 (March 13, 2010): 48; and Kumar Anshuman, "D Companies", *The week*, January 22, 2012, 16-20.
63. For the evaluation of Dalit emergence in India see. Christophe Jaffrelot, *India's Silent Revolution: The Rise of the Low Castes in North Indian Politics* (Delhi: Permanent Black, 2003), 493-96.
64. Mandira Moddie, "Development: Dreams within Reach", *The Hindu*, June 13, 2010, Magazine section, 4.
65. Vidya Venkat, "From the Shadows", *Frontline*, February 29, 2008, 104.
66. Ibid., 103.
67. A. Mangai, *Ethiroliekum karavaoligal; Aravanigalum Manithargale*, (Echoed hand claps; the Aravanis are also human beings) (Chennai: Bharadhi Puthakalayam, 2009), 13.
68. Dorairaj, "Seeking Identity", Interview with Priya Babu, Transgender activist, *Frontline*, January 1, 2010, 101.
69. Vidya Venkat, "Sex-reassignment surgery", *Frontline*, February 29, 2008, 102.
70. For details see, *Hijra* (South Asia) Wikipedia, the free Encyclopaedia.
71. Vidya Venkat, "From the Shadows", 101.
72. *Ibid.*, 103.
73. *The Hindu*, 14th March, 2009.
74. S. Dorairaj, 101.
75. The following associations are notable for their services:
    Asha Bharathi is the President of Tamil Nadu Aravanigal Association in Chennai and the South India Positive Network is looked after by Noori. In Kanchipuram, the Sudar organisation is doing a good work. Tamil Nadu Aravani Rehabilitation Centre, Trichy and Aravani Welfare Society, Thiruvnnamalai are some other Aravani organisations working for their welfare. Besides, several such organisations are working in other districts also.

76. Some of the popular documentaries in this regard are: Bombay Eunuch; Between the Lines: India's Third Gender; India's Ladyboys;, Jareena, Portrait of a Hijda; Middle sexes HBO documentary includes segment on modern Hijda; The Hijras of India, BBC radio documentary; and The Hijras: India's Third Gender.
77. Ram Ahuja, 481.
78. For conditions of slaves and labourers, see, A.K. Kalimuthu, *Colonial Economy and the Lower Peasantry—Tamil Nadu Since 1801-1947* (Trichy: Archana Publications, 2004), 60–73.
79. Human Rights Watch, *The Small hands of Slavery*, 135.
80. *Ibid.*
81. India: Debt Bondage—A Concept Paper, 1.
82. For details see, S. Dorai Raj, "Kilns of Bondage", *Frontline*, July 17, 2009, 85-87.
83. Purnima S. Tripathi, "Child Rights: Audit Shock," *Frontline*, June 4, 2010, 104-05.
84. Ishtiyaq Ahmed, "Refugee Problems in India", *Third Concept*, 10: 110-11, (April-May 1996): 27.
85. Arjun Dev, 31.
86. Amnesty International (Australia) *www.amnesty.org.au*.
87. For details related to the issues involving the refugees see, Ramachandra Guha, Indhiya Varalaaru: Gandhikku Piragu (Part 1) (India after Gandhiji) (Chennai: Kizhakku Pathippagam, 2009), 147-164; and Kuldip Nayar, "They left behind their Homes ... and Hopes," (India: Special issue) *The Hindu,* August 15, 1997, 30-31.
88. For details see, G. Palanithurai and K. Mohanasundaram, *Dynamics of Tamil Nadu Politics in Sri Lankan Ethnicity* (New Delhi: Northern Book Centre, 1993), 57.
89. Sumita Das, "The Role of UNHCR in Sri Lankan Tamil Refugees Repatriation during 1992-1995", Proceedings of *South Indian History Congress*, 22nd Annual Session, 2002, 76-79.
90. Simon Tisdall, "A 'new deal' is needed for refugees", *The Hindu*, October 16, 2010, 9.
91. S.D. Muni, ed. *Responding to Terrorism in South Asia* (New Delhi: Manohar Publishers, 2006), 16.
92. Ted Robert Gurr, *Why Men Rebel* (New Jersey: Princeton University Press, 1970), 36.
93. David Kennedy, "Terrorism and Human Rights", *Harvard Human Rights Journal* (Spring, 2002): 1.
94. Walter Laqueur, "The Terrorism to Come", *Public Review* (August and September 2004): 51.

95. Hasan Suroor, "Striking at London," *Frontline*, July 29, 2005, 15; and Praveen Swamy, "Maximum Terror and its Mechanics," *Frontline*, July 28, 2006, 6-7.
96. Noam Chomsky, "Dominance and its Dilemmas," *Frontline*, November 21, 2003, 11.
97. Hans Van Ginkel and Ramesh Thakur, "International Perspective on Global Terrorism," U.N. Chronicle (Online Edition) xxxviii: 3 (2001): 11.
98. Praveen Swami, "Catch them Young," *Frontline*, December 7, 2001, 68-69; and Nirupama Subramanian, "The LTTE's 'baby brigade'", *Frontline*, December 7, 2001,70-71.
99. The White House Office of the Press Secretary. *Bush outlines U.S. Strategy against Terrorism.* (Washington: The White House Office of the Press Secretary, October 28, 2005), 4.
100. United Nations General Assembly (Forty-ninth Session), Agenda item 100(b). Resolution adopted on the report of the Third Committee (A/49/610/Add. 2), 49/185 on Human Rights and Terrorism, (6th March, 1995), 2.
101. David Kennedy, 1.
102. Sukumar Muralidharan, "POTA: Untold Stories", *Frontline*, April 9, 2004, 44-45; T.S. Subramanian, "POTA: Bail in Tamil Nadu", *Frontline*, January 16, 2004, 24-25; and T.S. Subramanian, "Bail for Nedumaran", *Frontline*, January 30, 2004, 32.
103. Sukumar Muralidharan, 44.
104. *The Hindu*, 26th July, 2006.
105. V. Venkatesan, "In the Normal Course," *Frontline*, December 2, 2005, 22-23.
106. Gabor Rona, "Legal Frameworks to Combat Terrorism: An Abundant Inventory of Existing Tools", *Chicago Journal of International Law*, 5:2 (Winter 2005):499.
107. *The Hindu*, 28th July, 2006.
108. Anjali Kamat, "Turning the Clock Back on Lebanon", *The Hindu*, July 20, 2006, 8.
109. Siddharth Varadarajan, "Beware the 'new order' Israel is Imposing", *The Hindu*, July 29, 2006, 10.
110. Gilles Kepel, *Jihad: The Trial of Political Isalm* (London: I.B. TAURIS, 2003), 376.
111. Jason Burke, *London Sunday Observer*, May 18, 2003, quoted in Noam Chomsky, 10.
112. United Nations General Assembly, (Fifty-seventh Session) Agenda item 109(b) Resolution adopted on the report of the Third Committee (A/57/556/Add.2 and Corr.1-3), 57/219, on the Protection of Human

rights and fundamental freedoms while countering terrorism, (27th February 2003), 2.

113. The International Covenant on Civil and Political Rights, the European Convention on Human Rights, and the Council of Europe Guidelines on Human Rights and the Fight against Terrorism, 2002, were some existing International legal guidelines available in this regard. For details see, Japp de Hopp Scheffer, "Human Rights and Terrorism", (Statement at the Seminar on Human Rights and Terrorism, The Hague, September 18, 2003), 2.
114. Julio Ribeiro, "Local realities of Terrorist Threats", in *Science and Technology to Counter Terrorism*, ed. Roddam Narasimha and Arvind Kumar (Washington, DC.: The National Academies Press, 2007), 88.
115. For details see, "Anupama Katakam", In Cold Blood, *Frontline*, October 9, 2009, 10-13.
116. Ramesh Thakur, "The growing threats to Human Rights", *The Hindu*, 5th December, 2009, 8.
117. New World Encyclopaedia, 3.
118. "The case against Death Sentence" (Editorial), *Economic and Political Weekly*, XLV: 20 (May 15-21, 2010):8.
119. R.K. Raghavan, "A Judicial Murder", *Frontline*, October 21, 2011, 131.
120. *The New Indian Express*, 28th June, 2010; and Syed Nazakat and Vijaya Pushkarna, "Pardoning President". *The Week*, June 17, 2012, 48-49.
121. Bikramjeet Batra, "Justice or revenge?", *Frontline*, June 4, 2010, 21.
122. T.S. Subramanian, "Reprieve from Death", *Frontline*, September 23, 2011, 127.
123. Vijaya Pushkarna, "Dead men waiting", *The Week*, September 25, 2011, 40.
124. T.S. Subramanian, "Reprieve from Death", 128.
125. T.R. Ardhyarujina, "Mercy petitions: inhumane procrastination", *The Hindu*, 30th June, 2010,12.
126. Gurucharan Singh, *Pollution to Purity of Environment* (New Delhi: Deep & Deep Publications, 2005), 20; and Wayne C.Mc Williams and Harry Piotrowski, *The World Since 1945: A History of International Ralations* (New Delhi: Viva Books, 2012, 450.
127. Quoted in Dr. M.R. Biju, "Eco Tourism in Kerala", *South Asian Journal of Socio-Political Studies*, 5:(December 1, 2004):102.
128. For the original text see, Muralidhar Reddy, "A Sinking feeling", *Frontline*, October 23, 2009, 65.
129. *The Hindu*, October 15, 2011, 24.
130. Dionne Bunsha, "Withering Heights", *Frontline*, July 18, 2008, 45.

131. Sainath, "Thirst for Profit", *Frontline*, April 21, 2006, 5; and Lyla Mehta, *Politics and Poetics of Water* (New Delhi: Orient Longman, 2005), 17.
132. United Nations Development Programme: Human Development Report 2006—Beyond Security: Power, Poverty and the Global Water Crisis (New York: UNDP, 2006), 1.
133. Jayanta Bandyopadhyay, R. Rajesh Babu, "Regulating the stuff of Life", review of *Water and the Laws in India*, by ed., Ramasamy R. Iyer, *Economic and Political Weekly*, XLV:17th April, 24-30, 2010, 30.
134. R. Krishnakumar, "The Village and the behemoth", *Frontline*, January 15, 2010, 114.
135. *The Hindu*, 1st July, 2010.
136. Elisabeth Rosenthal, "Gateway for trash", *Frontline*, October 23, 2009, 112.
137. Dionne Bunsha, "Clouds of misery", *Frontline*, August 1, 2008, 49-53.
138. K. Venkataraman, "Alien invasion", *Frontline*, July 3, 2009, 65.
139. R. Ramachandran, "Lethal Aftermath", *Frontline*, July 2, 2010, 20.
140. J. Venkatesan, "Gas Leak: Centre to file curative petition", *The Hindu*, 27th June, 2010, 11.
141. *The Hindu*, 22th June 2010.
142. Venkitesh Ramakrishnan, "Plunder and Profit", *Frontline,* July 16, 2010, 4.
143. C.P. Chandrasekhar, "Liberalising loot", *Ibid.*, 9.
144. R. Sreedhar,"The way ahead", *Ibid.*, 13.
145. Ajoy Ashirwad Mahaprashasta, "Mining tussle", *Frontline,* July 16, 2010. 29; and V. Venkatesan, "For a New Law", *Ibid.,* 25.
146. Ashish Kothari, "Sustainable Future?", *Frontline*, January 15, 2010, 107.
147. In Vrendra Gaur vs. State of Haryana 1995 (2) SCC577, the Supreme Court of India observed the need for the protection of environment. See, Bhavani Prasad Panda, *Human Rights, Development and Environmental Law* (Delhi: Academic Excellence, 2007), 281.
148. L.K. Singh, *Ecology, Environment and Tourism* (Delhi: Isha Books, 2008), 54.
149. Neil Pudukone, "Climate Change in India: Forgotten Threats, Forgotten Opportunities," *Economic and Political Weekly*, XLV:22 (May 29-July 4, 2010): 47-49.
150. Jyotsna Tiwari, ed. *Scope and Categories of Human Rights* (Delhi: Isha Books, 2006), 248.
151. Gopal Bhargava, *Human Rights: Conflict Build Peace* (Delhi: Kalpaz Publications, 2003), 105.

CASE STUDIES

Child Labour

Dada Peer is 12 years old boy who was working in the puffed rice making unit (Mandakki bhattis) in Bhatti Layout in Davangera town in Karnataka. Paddy is socked in water and de-husked before dried in the sun. The rice is then salted and poured into a cauldron containing heated sand. It is heated to 800 degree centigrade by an underground oven using husk and tyres. Dada used the rough salt to rice and also looked after the fire in the oven. The work near the cauldron left scares on his body. In December 7, 2004 Tahir Ali, a 13 years old boy working in such a Bhatti fell into a cauldron and died. The UNICEF estimated that more than 36 per cent of the children working in such units have respiratory problems also. Thanks to the child labour elimination project of UNICEF, 900 children were rescued from child labour and put in schools in the last five years. Now Dada is undergoing a bridge course for 8 months after which he will be put in a class appropriated to his learning level. But he is aloof and he is longing to return to his family. Though he was happy to be in the boarding school he misses his family and any enquiry about his home emotionally upset the boy. He is fortunate that he can dream about his future, thanks to the schooling. The work handled by him was even not suitable for an adult and if anyone is working for 4-5 hours a day for 15 years he is as good as condemned. The UNICEF is trying to create child labour free Gram Panchayat in this region. It has a child tracking system till X standard and conducts periodic rights to rescue child labourers. (Refer N. Bhanutej, "No Childs Play", *The Week*, August 17, 2008, pp. 22-24.)

Violence Against Women

Gita Naik from Banavasi in Karnataka is one among the several victims of acid attack. Due to this attack Gita is deaf in one ear and left part of her body is burnt. She narrates how she forced to make a number of trips to the district surgeon to get a medical certificate and several trips to Bangalore to get the initial compensation of Rs. 10,000 from the government. Though she has a diploma in education no one is willing to give her a job. Another woman, Haseena Hussein from Bangalore has to undergo more than 15 surgeries to correct her face to some extent. Her boss poured sulphuric acid on her. Even though she is completely blind she is determined to work. Women like them are fighting a valiant battle to get justice. Due to more than 65 cases of acid attacks reported in Karnataka, an organisation named Campaign and Struggle against Acid Attacks on Women was created to support them. The acid attack survivors narrated details of their struggle in hospitals, in court rooms and to the society. In Tamil Nadu also we come across the frustrated roadside Romeos attacking college going innocent girls with acid, who refused their romantic overtures. (Refer M.R. Maithreyi, "Burnt, Not Defeated", *The Week*, August 17, 2008, pp. 32).

Child Marriage

Shakunthala Verma, an anganwadi supervisor in Dhar district of Madhya Predesh was attacked by a group of persons with a sword and nearly one of her hand got severed. What was her crime? As per the direction of the government she tried to stop the possible 15 child marriages in her area.

Female Infanticide

A recent study titled 'Planning Families, Planning Gender', with the support of Action Aid India and International Development Research Centre, Canada describes how even the wealthy and literate parents are eliminating their infant daughters in some of the most prosperous states with high literary rate like Punjab, Haryana, Gujarat, and Maharashtra. The researchers staying in each village for more than six months in north India where there is a lowest sex ratio, they have come across the cruel method through which an infant girl is eliminated. They either use any of the following methods—filling the infant's mouth with tobacco or throw the infant into a drain. In Dholpur, poisonous seeds were fed on infant girls or they are dropped from a height. In Morena, a midwife named Motti Bhua was usually asked to kill infant girls soon after their birth. She used to keep one leg of the stool on the neck of the infant and sit on it. She used to say 'go bitto (baby) you go and send your brother'. Unfortunately, the agents for eliminating daughters are mostly women—either midwives, mother-in-law or sometimes their mothers. It is partly because the women are rarely empowered to make independent choices. (Refer:

Harsh Mander, "Unwanted Daughters", *The Hindu*, 29th August, 2010, (Magazine, 3).

Female Foeticide

Despite the efforts of Government and civil society groups, female foeticide continue among various communities all-over India. In Parli, Maharashtra's Beed district, one Munde hospital thrives on sex determination of foetuses and female foeticide. The local people call it as the 'slaughter house'. The hospital was run by Dr. Sudam Munde and his wife Dr. Saraswati Munde. It was reported after a sting operation by social activist Varsha Deshpande, who runs the NGO Lek Laadki Abhiyan, that female foeticide was a common feature of the hospital. The hospital allegedly maintains several dogs which are feeding on foetuses. Only under pressure, FIR was registered seven months after the complaint. The local authorities are reluctant to take action against the doctor couple due to political pressure. They got bail and upon their release hiked their rates for female foeticide due to the risk quotient. People also observed that in the nearby Sangam Nullah, a drain, some women found female foetuses. Possibly after the sting operation, they are throwing away the foetuses in the drain as well as in two wells. Even 24 weeks old weak babies were aborted and thrown away. It was discovered that Dr. Sudam was among the biggest purchasers of abortion drugs in Maharashtra. Hospitals like these are thriving in the Beed region. The Census 2011 indicates that only 801 girls exist for every 1,000 boys under the age of six in Beed district. It was 894 in the 2001 Census and possibly through the foeticide 93 girls are missing for every 1,000 boys in the district. Unfortunately the Medial Termination of Pregnancy Act, created for the benefit of women is misused and has been working against the women and their health. Civil society activist are demanding the creation of special, fast track court to deal with these types of cases effectively. (Refer: Swagata Yadanar, "Lethal Prescription", *The Week*, June 10, 2012, 39-43).

WOMEN'S RIGHT

Gudia's Choice

In 2004, a soldier married a girl named Gudia during a short vacation, and returned to duty 10 days after the marriage. He never returned home and there was no news about his whereabouts. His case was regarded as 'missed in action' and the bereaved family's search ended in vain. Gudia waited for 3 years with the hope of a happy reunion. When the hope turned into despair her family arranged for her remarriage with another person. When she was pregnant and happily leading a married life, her first husband returned from Pakistan prison and reclaimed his wife. The tormented Gudia, preferred to stay with her second husband. But the local Panchayat consists of elders favoured the claim of the soldier and asked her to go with him. Since it was a sensational case, the media followed it with lot of focus and sided with the soldier. As desired by the soldier husband, it was decided that she has to hand over the baby after its delivery to the second husband. The heartbroken Gudia was forced by the circumstances to go with her first husband. She died during the child birth with the infant. No doubt, the case of the soldier is painful from the beginning, but who cared about the feelings of the girl—Moongi Gudia? (Refer: *The Hindu*, 3rd October, 2004.)

In Manipur, the Armed Forces are given special powers to curb militancy. Unfortunately, there were violations in which the innocent persons of this region suffer. Armed with this special power, the armed force allegedly violates the dignity of individuals. Following the rape and murder of a woman allegedly by the security forces, a group of women agitated in front of the security forces camp by removing their own dresses and shouted slogan to rape them too like the innocent victims. There was a widespread condemnation against the misuse of Armed Forces (Special Powers) Act which gives sweeping powers to the armed forces. There is a demand for its repeal since there are stories of fake encounters, missing children and illegal arrests and rape. Irom Chanu Sharmila an ordinary girl who was shocked to see the picture of 10 peoples shot dead by the armed forces allegedly in retaliation to a bomb attack decided to use the only weapon she had—a hunger strike from November 4, 2000 demanding the repeal of the Armed Forces Act. She argued that "there was no other means to stop further violations by the armed forces against innocent people." With grit and determination she is continuing her fast for the past twelve years. When her condition deteriorates she was arrested on the charges of attempting to commit suicide and force feed through her nose. For the past ten years she was under medical observation and is kept alive by force feeding vitamins and laxatives through a nose tube. She refused even to swallow water and brushes her teeth with wet cotton. Despite her pathetic bedridden condition she continued her struggle and is facing the court trials in Delhi and other places. She became a symbol of human rights and has become the icon of peace and non-violence across the globe. But she has the best years of the youth in forced captivity in the security ward of Jawaharlal Nehru Hospital, Imphal. Sharmila was given several awards all-over the world including the Rabindranath Tagore Award 2010 which carries 51 lakh in cash, a gold medal, a citation and a shawl. She was also the recipient of South Korea's Gwangju Human Rights Award. She donated the money to organisations fighting human rights violations and terrorism. She was a model fighter through the Gandhian method of fasting. "I will eat rice from my mother's hand once the Act is repealed" was the hope of Irom Sharmila. She is still waiting. When the fasting of Anna Hazare attracted popular media attention and pressurised the centre to act on the Lok Pal issue, she appealed to this Gandhian leader to lend support to her agitation against the Armed Forces Special Powers Act. The social activists Medha Patkar launched 'Save Sharmila Solidarity Campaign' in Sri Nagar to support her cause. (Refer: Mandira Nayar, "Irom Sharmila—Living Martyr, *The Week*, August 23, 2009, 26-27. *The Hindu*, May 12, 2007, 12; *The Hindu*, September 13, 2010, 11; Kalpana Sharma, "Manipur, Once more", *The Hindu*, (Magazine) August 23, 2009, 3; and Sanjoy Hazarika, "Mainland Discourse: The media ignores basic facts about the Northeast, J & K in its insurgency chatter", *Outlook*, November 1, 2010, 96-100 and *The Hindu*, October 17, 2011.)

Despite India's Independence and development, the tribal women are still facing the worst type of humiliation. A Maha Panchayat of the tribal community was conducted to look after the tribal issues within the community. It was inaugurated by the Fisheries Minister from Madhya Pradesh. While the tribal leaders are addressing the vast gathering of tribals, Basanta, a young woman was standing on a heap of sharp edged blue metal carrying a grinding stone on her head. Like her several other young women like Devaki are also punished to stand with heavy load on their head for more than a day. The punishment is meted out to these hapless women due to their choice of marriage. Basanta married a man from another tribal community and had children. Her marriage was not accepted by her community elders. In the Maha Panchayat the tribal elders forcibly annulled her marriage and auctioned her along with other defaulters. An old man from the community took her for a sum of eight thousand rupees ignoring her protest. The money thus collected from 'such auction' was used for community feasting and liquor in the Maha Panchayat. Following media attention on this shocking incident, human rights activists are pursuing the matter through a legal battle. Due to media focus, these women now live with their husbands.

Six decades after independence, the tribal woman has no choice and is auctioned like cattle. (Refer: Deepak Tiwari, "Women for sale, "*The Week,* January 26, 2003; and "The auction", "*The Week,* March 18, 2012, 18.)

Widows of Maharashtra Farmers who commit Suicide

In the recent decades a large chunk of rural India is facing the jaws of the agrarian crisis that tearing its veins apart. We have reports of suicide by farmers of Maharashtra that left their widowed wife and children in search for survival options. Kavita Devi Das of Kharakdo in Maharashtra was forced to handle the financial situation after her husband committed suicide by swallowing pesticide. It was a nightmare for her and her two daughters. Rs. 30,000 compensation package of the government was took away by two of her brother-in-laws who also usurped her six acres of land. Adding insult to injury, she was raped in the fields by one of them. When she refused to be their mistress they then threw her out of her house. She now leads a pathetic life in her village Pandharkawada in Vidarbha region. Though she is earning some money as daily wage labourer and gets some support from her brother she is sexually exploited by other villagers. There are number of cases like that of these poor widow who has to fight for survival. (Bidisha Ghosal, "Silent Sufferers", *The Week*, September 14, 2008, 22-26.)

Environment

Lingaraj, instead of pursuing an ambitious career like most of his classmates from Jawaharlal Nehru University took the road less travelled. He spearheaded a movement to save Gandharmardan hills from becoming a bauxite mine. Due to his untiring efforts and the protest of the Adivasis, the Bharat Aluminium Company (BALCO) was unable to push the project into operation. The hills spread over to Bargarh and Bolangir districts are home to a number of endemic species of fauna and flora. Nearly 200 streams originate from these hills. The place is linked with Ramayana and two ancient temples are also located there. Hence, it was a holy place to the Hindus. Despite several attempts by BALCO and later in 2007 by National Aluminium Company, Lingaraj with the support of people whose livelihood is threatened thwarted their attempts to mine the area. He is also protesting the proposed bauxite mines in Niyamgiri hills. He lives with his school teacher wife and son and is dedicated for the cause of the poorest of the poor in western Orissa. However, the recent decision by the Union Minister of State for Environment and Forests, Jairam Ramesh banning the mining of Bauxite in Niyamgiri hills by Vedanta Resources is a matter of immense relief to the people of the region. (Refer: Deepak Tiwary, "Lingaraj: Anti-mine force", *The Week*, August 23, 2009, 27; and *The Hindu*, 6th September, 2010.)

In 2005, people from 150 villages including its tribal residents protested outside the Orissa Assembly against the authorization given to Vedanta Alumina for bauxite mining by the government. Following such protest the Norwegian Government, citing environmental reason withdraws investments in Vedanta Alumina's parent company in the United Kingdom. Norway was worried about the serious damage to people and the environment in India by its projects. The fund was estimated to be more than nine million euros. (Refer: Prafulla Das, "Mines of Trouble", *Frontline*, December 7, 2007, 41-42.)

Mercury Poisoning

R. Vijayalakshmi who is 38 years old is visiting a dentist and hospitals treating on other illness. She was strong and healthy at the age of 21 before entering into the service of Hindustan Unilever thermometer factory in Kodaikanal as a temporary worker. She said that after working for three months she felt the stomach pain, giddiness and blood in her urine. Despite the advice of the doctor known to the family, she goes back to work in the factory since the family needed the Rs. 135 given as daily wages. She is one among the 550 men and women who claimed that their work in the factory caused irreparable damage to their health. The affected employee's welfare association members say that 23 of their colleagues died young and the cause of death is related to mercury exposure. It led to lung problems, heart problems and kidney failure that resulted in their death. The remaining workers of this factory still report various health problems that include head-ache, skin, eye problems, chest pain, bleeding of the nose, vomiting, blooded urine, breathing problems, impotency, irregular menstruation, miscarriage, giddiness and other problems. Dr. Linda Jones of Massey University commented that these symptoms are classic symptoms of occupational mercury poisoning. Mercury is the third most toxic element in the world after arsenic and lead. Even though the Kodaikanal Thermo meter factory was closed following the discovery of mercury contaminated scrap, the workers are unable to meet their health bills and are fighting through PIL in the Madras High Court for economic rehabilitation and health care treatment. They also wanted to see the Hindustan Unilever prosecuted. Unfortunately the 360 kilos of mercury remain spread over the site despite the removal of mercury bearing waste by decontamination experts. It was send to US for special disposal in 2003. It will affect the forest soil and reduces the microbial activity. The environmentalists and the local people have feared the consequence when mercury will convert into an even more dangerous form, methyl mercury and moves into the food chain. The workers have reported that they were not informed of the dangers in working the factory and were not provided with proper personal equipment. Even though the Hindustan Unilever claimed that it had incurred Rs. 22 crores for the clean up process, it had the profits of Rs. 2,202 crores at the end of 2010 financial year. It appears that the company took advantage of the insensitivity of the law and the lack of critical examination by the regulators. In its article the *Frontline* reveals how a global corporation using the lax laws of a developing country like India to run a second hand plant with aging equipment that compromised on safety. Scientists from DAE and JNTU, Hyderabad found detectable levels of methyl mercury in the Kodaikanal Lake. Unfortunately, these companies failed to forget their social responsibilities and are insensitive to the protection of environment.

(Refer: Sarah Hiddleston, "Poisoned Ground", *Frontline*, September 24, 2010, 4-21.)

Rights of the Children

No one would believe until recently that Payal Bag, a five year old girl was an enemy of the state. At the age of three during the Singur agitation in 2007 against the Nano Car Factory she was arrested with her mother Krishna, and spent a month in Chinsurah District Jail.

Later the court asked the police to remove Payal's name from the list of suspects. Payal Bag's family had sacrificed two acre land for the Nano Car Factory. When her mother agitated in the BDO office, Payal picked up a pebble and through it on the BDO. The enraged officer informed the police and around 50 women protesters were arrested. Payal Bag and her mother were arrested from their home at night. Payal's mother Krishna observed that she did not say anything when they arrested her but when they recorded the arrest of the child she wept. She wonders how the authorities could believe that the three year old little girl had schemed to bomb offices. Though the case against Payal was dropped following the direction of the court her mother visits the court every month to fight her own case. To her classmate Payal is a symbol of courage. (Refer: Rabi Banerjee, "Baby Bomber", *The Week*, October 11, 2009, 20-21.)

Child Labour

V. Manikandan, a thirteen year old boy wondered that he cannot believe that he is free and can see day light. He was free from a mastra weaver in Kanchipuram, a major silk weaving centre in Tamil Nadu. More than 150 children between the age of 6 and 15 were released from the bondage. In Kanchipuram and Thiruvannamalai districts they are thrilled to know that they are out of the loom pits in which they had been to working from dawn to dusk without proper rest for several years. The Kanchipuram district administration as well as a non-profit voluntary organisation Social Action Movement helped them to come out of child labour. For loans ranging from Rs. 1,000 to 10,000 received by their parents from the master weaver they were kept in bondage. In the case of Manikandan he was working as a bonded labour for five years since his father could not repay Rs. 5000 borrowed. The district administration started two special schools after they were released under the Bonded Labour System (Abolition) Act, 1976 to integrate them into regular schools later. A sum of Rs. 20,000 was deposited in the name of each child. Several schemes are launched to help the released child labourers from the funds received from the National Child Labour Project. The US Government and the ILO contributed for this fund. In order to increase the income of the parents the administration is making efforts to establish more than 500 Self Help Groups to train women in different occasions. For every child taken away from work and send to the regular school, Rs. 100 is deposited every month in a Nationalized Bank. In order to ensure the continuous attendance of the child in school, the deposited amount will be given to the family only if the child remains in school. Providing supplementary income to the families may ensure the children's education. Regarding the implementation of the Bonded Labour Abolition Act, the fear of parents to give the details of the persons employing their children is a major hurdle. (Refer: Asha Krishnakumar, "Child Labour: Out of Bondage", *Frontline*, July 4, 2003, 97-98).

Domestic Child Slaves

Bubli a 10 year old girl child labour rescued from domestic work has learnt to laugh when she talks about her former employer Chandini and her impossible demands. Since Chandini is working at the air port she will go to work at 3 a.m. or 4 a.m. and she would not allow the child servant to sleep until she goes out for work. Again from 5 a.m. the domestic help has look after the day to day work. She has to stand near the dressing table holding the make-up set and lipsticks. She expected Bubli to know which shade of lipstick she was going to wear each day. If she made a mistake she will be beaten with anything which comes to her hand—broom or missiles—from kitchen. She kicks and slaps the girl even for small errors. Since Bubli's mother paid a visit when she was bleeding after severe beating in one such a day she was able to escape from the clutches of Chandini. Of course, a team of activist and the police had to intervene to rescue her. Otherwise, Bubli could have ended up like 10 year old Sonukumar who was tortured before she was killed. Her fault was that she was trying a lipstick belonging to the mistress. This senseless brutality on innocent domestic help would shock anyone. If anyone pays a visit to the Mukti Ashram, a transit hostel-cum school for rescued children, every child has a horror story to tell. Most of the domestic child workers are female and faces sexual, emotional or physical abuse. Even educated persons, enjoying a sophisticated life are employing child labourers as domestic help and treat them miserably. One little girl who worked in the home of a nurse was made to stand in a plate full of diluted acid whenever she commited even small mistakes.

An IAS officer severely beaten up a seven year old boy Ashraf, who drank some left over milk and the matter was brought to the notice of National Human Rights Commission. It promptly wrote to the government, suggesting that all government servants should be prohibited from employing child workers as domestic help. The Central Government and at least 18 State Governments have ruled against employing minors by the government servants. Unfortunately, despite the order children are ill-treated, raped and even murdered by their employers. Reports suggest that the underage girls who migrate to cities in search of work are first raped by the placement agent before they face the ordeal of domestic help. At least 2 lakh girls in Delhi either have been trafficked or have migrated from other neighbouring states. Living workers are often treated as 24 hour slaves by their masters. The ILO describes domestic works as a new form of slavery. Domestic workers are unfortunately disadvantaged in comparison to other type of workers. It is because they are not covered by laws such as Industrial Disputes Act, the Equal Remuneration Act and the Minimum Wages Act. (Refer: Annie Zaidi, "Domestic Slaves", *Frontline*, August 11, 2006, 107-108.) The Government of India is finally making necessary preparations for a Comprehensive Sexual Offences Bill, 2011 to protect children from sexual abuse. But the Bill, from the viewpoint of activists has a major flaw regarding sexual consent that needs to be immediately addressed after consulting the stakeholders. [R. Krithika, "Defining 'Consent'," *The Hindu*, October 9, 2011, (*Magazine*) 4.]

Terror Strike and Corporate Responsibility

In the Mumbai slum Govandi, Momima Khatoon lived with her husband Md. Umar and three children. When terror struck the Taj Mahal Palace on 26th November, 2008 it also struck a blow to her peaceful life. Her husband died inside the taxi he drove on that day due to the bomb blast. The family without the sole breadwinner suffered beyond description. Momima struggled to meet the expenses on monthly rent as well as for other expenses including food. The Rs. 5 lakh compensation given by the government is slowly evaporating. In this dire situation the Taj Public Service Welfare Trust set up days after the terror attack came to her rescue. For every month Rs. 10,000 is given to her for the last seven months. Momima thankfully narrated her condition that she has "no idea of what the future has in store for her. Without this support from the trust she could have killed herself". Besides, her children's education is funded by the trust. Even though the trust offered her a job she is unable to accept it due to her responsibility to look after her young children. Like her, the trust is helping 138 victims and their families. The Taj Public Service Welfare Trust was the brain child of Ratan Tata. The trust identified the victims from the police records and surveyors from the Tata Institute of Social Sciences went to the victim's houses to access their requirement. They also evaluated their emotional and psychological condition. Later properly trained Councillors were sent to the victims, houses to give them hope for the future. The trust also wants to see that the families stood on their own leg. It provides support in the form of monthly sustenance, hospitalization and medical needs, education of the children and assistance to set-up micro enterprise so that they can live with hope. From the Tata's point of view these steps are a tribute to those who lost their lives in the attacks. Taj, a victim is sharing its emotions. Money came from different quarters including from the Tata Company, HDFC as well as from individuals and trusts. It also offers employment to the family members affected by the terrorist attack. In India such a noble gesture from a corporate house rarely happens. This type of humanitarian approach to man-made calamities created goodwill and profound impact on those who are behind such benevolent steps.

(Refer: Nandini Oza, "Wah Taj!", *The Week*, October 3, 2010, 32-34.)

6

Development of Human Rights Concept in India

Introduction

The people of Indus Valley Civilization naturally enjoyed freedom. The Society was not stratified as in the later period of Indian history. Women enjoyed all the rights like men and were respected. But in the succeeding centuries the society underwent several changes. The concept of right also changed. If we analyse the history of India, from the earliest time till date, we can understand how the political and economic changes had its impact on the human rights concept. Great souls like Buddha, Mahavira and Asoka deeply influenced the early Indian thought on human rights and just society.

During and after the foreign invasions, the people of India experienced the deterioration of their rights. The entry of Mughals and their way of approach in granting rights to their subjects was another phase in the history of rights in India. Emperor Akbar's benevolence and grace fortified human rights during the medieval phase of Indian History. The compassion and grace of Sufi saints, the thought process of Kabir, Ramanujar and Thirumullar blended with the society. They preached the oneness of God and mankind and stressed the need for compassion towards fellow beings. The entry of British and the influence of western education led to the awakening of Indian leaders. The exploitation of the British and the denial of basic human rights increased the tempo for independent struggle. Mahatma Gandhi introduced Satyagraha as a means to achieve his goal. He demanded rights and self-respect for the people of India from the British. Gandhiji also wish to liberate the untouchables from the clutches of caste discrimination. They toiled under oppressive social practices which treats them with contempt.[1]

The Indian National Congress passed several resolutions demanding fundamental rights. It demanded the inclusion of certain basic rights in the Constitution of India. The Motilal Nehru Report was an important milestone in this direction. When India attained freedom, all these basic rights were incorporated in the new Constitution of India. It contains an elaborate list of rights. Democracy and the observance of human rights are two inseparable elements. It was experienced in India. People can enjoy the fruits of freedom and human rights only under a sovereign republic.

India and Human Rights

In India, we have references to the practice of human rights from the Vedic Age. During this period women enjoyed equal status with men and there was no practice existed on untouchablity.[2] The *Atharva Veda* highlights the existence of certain inalienable rights and stressed the duty of men to respect them. It stresses that "Man is not an individual. He is a social organism. God loves him only who serves the other being: men, cattle and other creatures… he is linked with every individual of society whether near or far… man thus lives, works and dies for society possessed of certain inalienable rights."[3] But the post-Vedic Age experienced variety of human rights violation in the name of *varna* and caste.[4] The entry of Aryans into Indian social system brought many changes and the stratification of society became the order of the day. The entry of caste led to serious violation of human rights. Untouchability became a major scourge of Indian social system. Gautama Buddha preached universal peace and brotherhood and helped the removal of several practices against human rights norms. As early as 4th century B.C., *Arthasastra* described the need for maintaining the poor, widows and orphans.

Emperor Asoka introduced the seven principles that contain the essence of human rights. His order that non-slaughter of animals, non-injury to the existing creatures were highlights on human rights. Asoka tried to abolish war as an instrument of state policy. His message was peace, goodwill and harmony. Asoka concentrated on the material and moral welfare of his subjects. The Asoka Dharma stressed the need for giving respect to elders, truthfulness and kindness towards animals. He emphasized non-violence as a basic principle and there was no place for caste differences. Asoka's primary aim was human happiness everywhere and he spread this message to the entire South and South East Asian region. Following the decline of Mauryan Empire, the Human Rights Jurisprudence also witnessed a downfall. The frequent foreign invasions created disturbance. Emperor Harsha Vardhana also promoted the welfare of his people. Like Asoka he was also deeply influenced by the high moral principles of Buddha. In South India the celebrated Tamil book on philosophy, *Tirukkural* which was wrote around two thousand years ago, touches upon almost all the civil, political, social, economic and cultural rights.

The medieval period witnessed a setback to the concept of human rights in India. The Muslim rulers distinguished between the Muslims and Hindus and tax them accordingly. But, Emperor Akbar represented benevolent despotism. His period witnessed a new era in the history of human rights. He introduced a policy of universal reconciliation and tolerance, concerned with the welfare of his people. Akbar respected all faiths and allowed his Rajput princess, the freedom of worship. He never forced others to follow his Din Ilahi. People from various communities were given their due share in the decision-making process of his administration. His reign period witnessed the glorification of universal toleration. But this trend was reversed during the period of Emperor Aurangzeb.

The indifference to human rights and values under the succeeding rulers led to the rise of Bhakti Movement in India. It revived the Indian value of truth, righteousness, justice and morality. Saints like Tulsidas, Kabir, and Guru Nanak re-established the supremacy of Vedic values. They reiterated Natural Law with religious fervour. But strangely it also led to persecution of the believers belongs to non-Hindu faith like Jainism and Buddhism. In Tamil Nadu, there are several references available on this sordid happening which targeted other religious beliefs. These are aberrations and there are references avilable on such occurrences in other parts of India as well.

When the people of India resisted the British rule they demanded civil and political rights as well as fundamental freedom. The British violated the human rights in all possible ways. They humiliated and discriminated the native population. The British exploited the wealth of the nation and never bothered about the welfare of their subjects.[5] They allowed millions of people to die during famine and pestilences.

It was not a welfare government but aimed only on collecting taxes and maintaining law and order. Leaders like Gandhiji termed the British rule as unjust and violent. He propounded the theory of Satyagraha to achieve independence.

The Indian people launched non-violence struggle to achieve self-government and fundamental rights for everyone. In 1895 itself the Constitution of India Bill prepared by the Indian National Congress demanded fundamental rights. It also demanded equality before law, respect for liberty, life and property. In 1918, it demanded the principle of self-determination as a basic right. The Madras session of the Indian National Congress demanded a declaration of fundamental rights in any future constitutional framework. The Motilal Nehru Committee Report in 1928, demanded fundamental rights. When India got independence, its constitution incorporated ten rights enumerated in the Motilal Nehru Committee Report. The Simon Commission rejected the demands of this report. Due to its historic significance, the Motilal Nehru Report is briefly analyzed below.

In the succeeding years the Indian National Congress proposed the necessity to incorporate fundamental rights in the Constitution. Later, the Government of India Act of 1935 disappoint the Indian leaders. The Sapru Committee in 1948 insisted on the need for fundamental rights. The demand of Indian leaders for the grant of these rights was not honoured during British rule. The Indians had to wait till the liberation of their nation. The new Constitution of Independent India incorporated the natural law rights in the Preamble. It also incorporated fundamental rights.

Motilal Committee Report (1928)

The Indian National Congress played a crucial role in demanding fundamental freedoms from the British rulers. It also demanded civil and political rights for the people of India. In 1895, it prepared a document known as the Constitution of India Bill. It stressed the need for a Constitution that guarantees basic human rights to the people of India. In 1918 and 1925, the Indian National Congress in its sessions demanded equality before law, protection of life and property, respect for liberty, freedom of speech and press and the right of association. It also demanded the right to self-determination. In any future Constitutional arrangement, the Congress demanded the inclusion of fundamental rights.

The Indians boycotted the Simon Commission when it visited India. In response to a challenge by the Commission to draft a Constitution acceptable to all parties, the Congress organized an all party's conference. It appointed a sub-committee under the Presidentship of Motilal Nehru to draft a Constitution. Subhash Bose, Sir Sapru, Sahib Qureshi, Sardar Mangal Singh and M.S. Pradhan were the other members of the Committee. The Nehru Report favours Dominion status and full responsible Government. It rejected the communal electorate. The report argued that sovereignty belonged to the people. It should be exercised through their representatives in accordance with the Constitution. To ensure freedom to the individual, the report highlights 19 fundamental rights to be included in the Constitution. Among these rights the notable rights were the equality of men and women and the freedom of faith of every individual. Some of the rights highlighted in the Nehru Report were as follows:

1. Personal Liberty, inviolability of dwelling place and property;
2. Freedom of conscience and profession and practice of religion subject to public order and morality.
3. Right of free expression of opinion and to assemble peaceably and without arms to form association and union's subject to public order and morality.
4. Right to free elementary education and in the matter of admission into any educational institution maintained and aided by the State without distinction of caste or creed.
5. Equality for all citizens to the law and civil rights.
6. Right to every citizen to the writ of *Habeas Corpus*.
7. Protection of respect of punishment under *ex-post facto* law.
8. Non-discrimination against any person on grounds of religion, caste or creed in the matter of public employment, office or power of honour and in the exercise of any trade or callings.
9. Equality of Right to all citizens.
10. In the matter of access to and use of public roads, well and other places of public resort.
11. Freedom of combination and association for the maintenance and implementation of labour and economic conditions.
12. Right to keep and bear arms in accordance with Regulations, and
13. Equality of Rights to men and women as citizens.

According to Zachariah, the Nehru Report was a masterly report. For the "first time in the India's History all the parties laid their heads together to discuss Constitutional problems and their mutually agreeable solutions. No greater tribute can be paid to it than that it supplied the blueprint of the present Indian Constitution". The report was accepted by the all parties' conference at Lucknow.

Indian Constitution and Human Rights

Several historic documents that uphold human rights values had its influence on the making of Indian Constitution. The framers of Indian Constitution were influenced by the Bill of Rights of the American Constitution, the Declaration of the Rights of Man and Citizen in France and the Declaration of Human Rights by the United Nations. They also wanted to remove Untouchability because of the crusade launched by Mahatma Gandhi[6] and other leaders. The Constitution of India contains an elaborate list of fundamental rights. When the Constitution guarantees such elementary rights to every individual it gives a moral character to the state. It also puts a check on its absolute power. Naturally, it could prevent the government from becoming despotic. The fundamental rights are above all other laws of the land. Their observance by the state was ensured by the Supreme Court, which is the custodian and watchdog of the Indian Constitution. One positive feature of the role played by courts in India is that while interpreting the meaning and scope of the Constitutional provisions, they normally referred to international instruments on Human Rights including UDHR.[7] Especially, the apex court is protecting the human rights of the marginalized, deprived and weaker sections of the society.[8] It has revolutionalised the criminal justice system to protect the interest of the bonded, underpaid and exploited labourers. Judicial activism is felt in the protection of human rights.

The sovereignty of the people of India is emphasized in the Preamble of the Constitution. It also secures all its citizens, social economic and political justice. It ensures freedom of thought, expression, belief, faith and worship, equality of status and of opportunity to everyone of its people. It ensures the dignity of the individual. The use of the words, "We, the people of India" in the preamble indicates that the actual authority of the Government of India is derived from its people. In the Preamble, the concept of secularism, socialism and integrity are also found mention.

The Constitution ensures the availability of a long list of fundamental rights to its citizens. The concept of economic freedom stresses the avoidance of concentration of wealth. For both men and women equal pay for equal work should be given.[9] Children and young men and workers are to be protected against exploitation. The workers must be given reasonable wages and provided with just and humane condition of work. Everyone has the right to work, right to education and public assistance in case of unemployment, old age, sickness etc. The children can be provided with free and compulsory education. The Constitution guarantees all its citizens freedom, equality and right to religion. It assures the right to property, culture and Constitutional remedies. The Directive Principles stressed that the State shall strive to promote the welfare of the people.

Nature of Fundamental Rights

The makers of Indian Constitution keep the fundamental rights in a high pedestal. The Constitution provides for machinery which guarantees those fundamental rights in actual practice. By Article 32, the Supreme Court is appointed as the guardian of fundamental rights. Whenever a fundamental right is infringed by any authority, the Supreme Court shall ensure that the individual is allowed to enjoy it.

The fundamental rights guaranteed by the Constitution are not absolute rights. Many reasonable restrictions have been placed on its enjoyment. Article 19 guarantees the right to freedom of speech and expression, and peaceful assembly of people. They can form association and practice any profession and trade or business. In the interest of the integrity of India, security of the state, certain restrictions can be imposed on this right. For the protection of any Scheduled Tribes and in the interest of general public the state can put reasonable restrictions on the fundamental rights. Even though personal liberty is guaranteed in Article 21, the state can keep a person under preventive detention in some cases. Right against exploitation is guaranteed but compulsory service for public purposes is accepted. Depending upon the circumstances these rights can be suspended or restricted by the state.

The fundamental rights are restrictions on the powers of the three organs of the government. Whenever the legislature is making any law it should not in any way infringe on any fundamental rights. The court must safeguard the fundamental rights from any encroachment by executive action. The fundamental rights were placed in part III of the Constitution and could be enforced by a court of law. The non-enforceable rights were placed in part IV of the Constitution and were termed as Directive Principles of State policy.

The Constitution under various headings covers the fundamental rights. Some of the important rights are given below:

Right to Equality

The Right to equality is covered in the Articles 14-18. This right gives equal protection of laws and prohibits the discrimination against any citizen on grounds of religion, race, caste and sex etc. It also ensures the removal of disability or condition with regard to access to shops, public places like wells and bathing ghats, etc. It provides equality of opportunity for all citizens in public appointments. The Right to Equality abolishes untouchability and makes it as an offence punishable under law.

Right to Freedom

The Articles 19-22 of the Constitution guarantees Right to freedom of speech and expression, right to peaceful assembly, the right to free movement in any part of India and the right to protection against conviction except for the violation of the law. It also guarantees the right against arbitrary arrest and indefinite detention.

Right Against Exploitation

The Constitution prohibits traffic in human beings and forced labour. It also prohibits the employment of children in factories. These rights were guaranteed in the Articles 23 and 24.

Right to Freedom of Religion

Article 25 deals with the freedom of conscience, practice and propagation of religion. Article 26 guarantees freedom to manage religious affairs.

Cultural and Educational Rights

The protection of interests of minorities in the field of language and culture is covered in the Articles 29 and 30. It also provides for the right of minorities to establish and administer educational institutions.

Right to Constitutional Remedies

The Constitution makers made necessary arrangements for the realisation of Fundamental rights. For the enforcement of these rights, a citizen has the right to approach the Supreme Court. The High Courts and the Supreme Court are empowered to issue writs in the nature of *Habeas Corpus*, Mandamus, prohibition, *Quo Waranto* and Certiorari. The President of India has the power to restrict these rights during the times of emergency.

There are some other rights which are not included in the list. It includes right to citizenship and right to Franchise. The Constitution also protects the interest of minorities. The right to education and right to work were also covered in this section.

Directive Principles of State Policy

One important difference of this section is that the provisions contained in this Part shall not be enforceable by any court. But the principles are fundamental in nature and the state must apply these principles while making laws. It stressed the state to secure a social order for the promotion of people's welfare. It directs the state to follow certain principles of policy like gender equality, adequate means of livelihood, distribution of material resources of the community to serve the common good, prevention of concentration of wealth, equal pay for equal work for both men and women and the protection of children and the youth from exploitation.

This part of the Constitution also stressed the need for equal justice and free legal aid to the citizens. It suggests the necessity of Village Panchayats and a uniform civil code for the citizens. Free and compulsory education for children and the promotion of educational and economic interests of SC, ST and other weaker sections are some of the guidelines given in this section. Finally, it stressed the need for protection of environment[10] to safeguard the forest and wildlife in India. Protection of monuments, separation of judiciary from executive and the promotion of International peace and security were other areas covered in the guidelines. The state should try to incorporate these key issues while framing the policies.

Human Rights Commission in India

Under the protection of Human Rights Act, 1993, the National Human Right Commission was constituted in October 1993. It is a fully autonomous body. The method of appointment of the members, the fixing of tenure, the status accorded to this Commission and its financial powers indicate its full autonomy status.

Composition

The Commission consists of a Chairperson, who has been a chief justice of the Supreme Court, one member who is or has been, a judge of a Supreme Court, one member who is or has been, the Chief Justice of a High Court, two members to be appointed with knowledge and practical experience in matters relating to Human Rights.

The chairperson of the National Commission for Minorities, the National Commission for SC and ST and the National Commission for Women shall deem to be members of the Commission. There shall be a Secretary General who shall function as the Chief Executive Officer of the Commission. The Headquarters of the Commission shall be at Delhi. The members were appointed by the President of India on the recommendations of a committee headed by the Prime Minister. The other members of the committee are the Speaker of the Lok Sabha, Minister of Home Affairs, Leader of Opposition in the Lok Sabha and that of Rajya Sabha and the Deputy Chairman of the Rajya Sabha.

By an order of the President of India, the Chairperson or the members of the Commission can be removed from the office. Such a step should be recommended by the Supreme Court on the basis of proved misbehaviour or incapacity. The term of office of the Chairperson and members will be five years from the date of assumption of office or until the age of 70 years, whichever is earlier.

Functions

The following functions devolve on the Commission under the Act:[11]

(a) Inquire, on its own initiative or on a petition presented to it by a victim or any persons on his behalf, into complaints of—
   (i) Violation of human rights or abetment thereof; or
   (ii) Negligence in the prevention of such violation, by a public servant.

(b) Intervene in any proceeding involving any allegation of violation of human rights pending before a court with the approval of such court;

(c) Visit, under intimation to the State Government, any jail or any other institution under the control of the State Government, where persons are detained or lodged for purposes of treatment, reformation or protection to study the living conditions of the inmates and make recommendations thereon;

(d) Review the safeguards provided by or under the Constitution or any law for the time being in force for the protection of human rights and recommend measures for their effective implementation;

(e) Review the factors, including acts of terrorism that inhibit the enjoyment of human rights and recommend appropriate remedial measures;

(f) Study treaties and other international instruments on human rights and make recommendations for their effective implementation;

(g) Undertake and promote research in the field of human rights;

(h) Spread human rights literacy among various sections of society and promote awareness of the safeguards available for the protection of these rights through publications, the media, seminars and other available means;

(i) Encourage the efforts of non-governmental organisations and institutions working in the field of human rights; and

(j) Such other functions as it may consider necessary for the promotion for human rights.

How Complaints are handled

The Commission expects that the complaints are self-contained. They may be in Hindi, English or in any language included in the Eighth Schedule of the Constitution. No fee is charged on complaints.

Depending upon the necessity, the Commission may ask for further information and affidavits to be filed in support of allegations. The Commission may, in its discretion, accept telegraphic complaints and complaints conveyed through FAX.

Ordinarily, complaints of the following nature are not entertained by the Commission:

(a) in regard to events which happened more than one year before the making of the complaints;
(b) with regard to matters which are sub-judice;
(c) which are vague, anonymous or pseudonymous;
(d) which are of frivolous in nature;
(e) those which are outside the purview of the Commission; and
(f) which pertain to service matters.

Inquiry Powers

The Commission vested with wide ranging powers relating to inquiries and investigation under the Act. While inquiring, the Commission could exercise all the powers of a civil court. It has the following powers:

1. summoning and enforcing the attendance of witnesses and examining them on oath;
2. discovery and production of any document;
3. receiving evidence on affidavits;
4. requisitioning any public record or copy thereof from any court or office;
5. issuing commissions for the examination of witnesses or documents; and
6. any other matter which may be prescribed.

Investigation Staff

The Commission has its own investigating staff for investigation into complaints of human rights violations. Under the Act, it is also open to the Commission to utilize the services of any officer or investigation agency of the Central Government or any State Government. In addition, the Commission envisages the association in appropriate cases of outsiders as investigators or Observers.

Inquiry into Complaints

The Commission may call for information from the government or other organisation within such time as may be specified by it while enquiring into complaints of human rights violations. If the required information is not received within the stipulated time it may proceed with the inquiry. If the Commission is satisfied that no further inquiries required or suitable action was taken already by the authorities concerned, it may not proceed with the complaint further.

Steps After Inquiry

After the completion of inquiry, the Commission may take any of the following steps:

1. In the inquiry the negligence of the public servant to prevent the violation of human rights is found, the Commission will recommend the government for suitable prosecution or action;
2. Approach the Supreme Court or the High Court concerned for such directions, orders or writs as the court may deem necessary;
3. Recommend to the government for the grant of immediate interim relief to the victim or the members of his family;
4. The Commission shall provide a copy of the inquiry report to the Petitioner;
5. The Commission may send a copy of its inquiry report to the concerned Government for its comments on the report with the action taken in the case; and
6. The Commission shall publish its inquiry report together with the comments and action taken by the concerned government or authority.

The Commission also follows some procedure with respect to armed forces when they violate human rights of individuals or groups. After receiving the complaint it may make its recommendation to the government. Within three months, the Central Government shall inform the Commission of the action taken in this regard. The Commission may publish its report together with its recommendations and the action taken by the government. The Commission is required to submit an annual report to the Central and State Governments concerned. Whenever necessary it may submit special reports on any matters. The Central and State Governments should place the annual and special reports in the Parliament or the State Legislature along with the details of action taken in the concerned cases.

However, the future of National Human Rights Commission, which has done commendable work in the recent years, appears uncertain. It is because the vacancies in the Commission remain unfilled. In comparison to similar institutions in other countries it has a relatively heavy case load since it handles a large number of complaints of human rights violation. It received 3,06,975 complaints for a period of nine years from 1993 to 2002 and 2,95,072 complaints were taken up for consideration. But dealing with a complaint was only one of the 10 major functions assigned to the Commission. Despite its heavy workload it did a commendable work in protecting economic and social rights. When cyclone devastated Orissa in October 1999, the NHRC intervened to ensure the rights, the affected people were protected. It monitored the relief and rehabilitation work following a devastating earthquake in Gujrat in January 2001. It also worked for the most vulnerable section of the people affected. Following the Godhra Train Tragedy and the widely reported Anti Minority Pogrom carried out by the Hindu Right Wing organisations, the NHRC pointed out the failure of the state government in protecting the rights of the people, their dignity and liberty.[12] It worried about the lack of credibility in the charge sheets filed by the police in which the victims were defected as the provocaters. It also intervened later in attempts by right wing groups to sensationalize the Godhra tragedy.

In India, the National Human Rights Commission stressed the importance of linking the issue of providing adequate food, health and education to that of human rights. It also pursued its recommendations with the Government of India at the highest level in other important matters such as tobacco control, nutrition and HIV/AIDS. The Commission also stressed the necessity to remove the gender and caste based discrimination. On individual complaints, the Commission directed the institution to pay interim relief to the victims of human rights violation. If any public servants are responsible for such violation, it recommends the departmental proceedings and prosecution against them. Generally speaking, the guidelines and recommendations of the NHRC is by and large been observed by the agencies concerned. Naturally, it strengthened the Commission, institutional legitimacy. It also plays a constructive role in educating the public on the issues related to the enactment of Prevention of Terrorism Act (POTA). Since the commission came into conflict with the Union Government on several occasions, the government was less enthusiastic in filling the vacancies in the NHRC in time.

State Human Rights Commissions

There is an enabling provision in the Act for State Human Rights Commission to be constituted by the respective State Governments. The State Commission shall consist of:[13]

1. Chairperson who has been a Chief Justice of a High Court;
2. One Member who is, or has been, a Judge of a High Court;
3. One Member who is, or has been, a District Judge in that State;
4. Two Members to be appointed from amongst persons having knowledge of, practical experience in, matters relating to human rights.

There shall be a Secretary who shall be the Chief Executive Officer of the State Commission and shall exercise such powers and discharge such functions of the State Commission as it may delegate to him. The headquarters of the State Commission shall be at such place as the State Government may, by notification, specify.

Constitution of the Commission

The Chairperson; and other Members of the Commission shall be appointed by the Government after obtaining the recommendations of a Committee consisting of—

(i) The Chief Minister—Chairperson
(ii) Speaker of the Legislative Assembly—Member
(iii) Minister-in-charge of the department of Home in that State—Member
(iv) Leader of the Opposition in the Legislative Assembly—Member

Where there is a Legislative Council in a State, the Chairman of that Council and the Leader of the opposition in that Council shall also be members of the Committee. No sitting Judge of a High Court or a sitting District Judge shall be appointed except after consultation with the Chief Justice of the High Court of the concerned State.

The Chairperson or any other Member of a State Commission can only be removed from his office by an order of the President in accordance with the procedure envisaged for the National Commission.

The term of office of the Chairperson or Member will be five years from the date of assumption of office or at the age of 70 years, whichever is earlier. A Member is however eligible for reappointment for another term of five years subject to the age limit of 70 years. On ceasing to hold office, the Chairperson or a Member is ineligible for appointment under the Government of the State or under the Government of India.

Officers and Staff of the State Commission

The concerned State Government shall make available to the State Commission an officer not below the rank of a Secretary to the State Government who shall be the Secretary of the State Commission and such police and investigative staff under an officer not below the rank of an Inspector General of Police and such other officers and staff as may be necessary for the efficient performance of the functions of the State Commission. The State Commission may appoint such other administrative, technical and scientific staff as it may consider necessary.

Functions

A State Commission may inquire into violations of human rights only in respect of matters relating to any of the entries enumerated in List II (State List) and List III (Concurrent List) in the Seventh Schedule of the Constitution. However, if any such matter is already being inquired into by the National Commission or any other Statutory Commission, the State Commission shall not inquire into the said matter. Subject to this, the powers, the procedure of investigation, inquiry and steps to be taken thereafter are comparable to those of the National Commission.

Reports of the Commission

The State Commission shall submit Annual Report to the respective State Governments and may, at any time, submit Special Reports on any matter which in their opinion is of urgency or importance. It is enjoined on the State Governments to cause to lay on the Table of the respective State Legislature the Annual and Special Reports of the State Human Rights Commission.

Human Rights Courts

The Act envisages that for the purpose of providing speedy trial of offences arising out of violations of human rights, State Governments may with the concurrence of the Chief Justice of the concerned High Court specify for each District Court of Sessions to be a Human Rights Court to try such offences. For every Human Rights Court, the State Government shall specify a public prosecutor or appoint an advocate of at least seven years standing as a Special Public Prosecutor for the purpose of conducting cases in that Court.

Miscellaneous

The National Commission as well as the State Commission shall not inquire into any matter which is pending before a State Commission or National Commission as the case may be or any other statutory Commission.

If the Government considers it necessary, it may, notwithstanding anything contained in any other Law, constitute one or more special investigation teams consisting of the requisite police officers for purpose of investigation and prosecution of offences arising out of violations of human rights.

The Central Government as well as the State Government concerned may make rules to carry out the provisions of the Act. The Rules so made are required to be laid before each House of Parliament for a total period of 30 days as regards the National Human Rights Commission and appropriate State Legislature in respect of the State Commissions.

The development of Human Rights concept in India shows various phases of development. Great souls like Buddha and Emperor Asoka contributed for the spread of human right ideas through their preaching and practice. The foreign invasions and the entry of new races had its impact on the society and on the observation of human rights. Among the Mughal rulers Emperor Akbar demonstrated compassion and respect for other religious beliefs. The exploitation under the British and their gross human rights violation intensified the struggle for independence. The Indian National Congress starting from its inception demanded the inclusion of basic human rights in the Constitution. Motilal Nehru Report highlighted the necessity of having a set of fundamental rights for the people of India.

When India attained freedom, all these thought process find expression in the pages of Indian Constitution. It also enshrined the essence of Universal Declaration of Human Rights. Only under a democratic republic, people can enjoy the real benefits of human rights. The evolution of human rights in India indicated various stages. India enacted legislations to create a mechanism to supervise the implementation of suggestions on the protection of human rights. The National Commission on Human Rights and the State Human Rights Commission were created for this specific purpose. Despite heavy workload the Human Rights Commissions in India are doing a commendable job in protecting the rights of the individual. Whether it is communal riot, failure of the government machinery or the individual officials responsible for human rights violation, the NHRC took note of the situation and recommended suitable action against the erring official. By and large the directions of the NHRC are adhered and it strengthened its institutional legitimacy. Such institutions should be strengthened to uphold the dignity and rights of the individual. Filling up the vacancies in the Commission and respecting the direction of the Commission by the Government are other important requirements.

Questions

1. Briefly analyse India's practice of human rights from early times.
2. Bring out the rights highlighted in the Nehru Report.
3. Write a note on fundamental rights and its importance.
4. Examine the importance given to human rights in Indian Constitution.
5. Analyse the composition and functioning of Human Rights Commission in India.

6. Bring out the Constitutional remedies available for human rights violation.

Objective Type Questions

1. In India human rights was practiced from ....
   (a) Vedic age (b) Sangam age
   (c) Medieval period (d) Modern period.
2. .... session of the Indian National Congress demanded fundamental rights at first.
   (a) Bombay (b) Surat
   (c) Delhi (d) Madras
3. The .... guarantees freedom, equality and right to religion to the citizens of India.
   (a) Parliament (b) Constitution
   (c) Supreme Court (d) State Assemblies.
4. The Nehru Report highlighted .... fundamental rights to be included in the Constitution.
   (a) 19 (b) 20
   (c) 22 (d) 23
5. According to Article 32 .... is appointed as the guardian of fundamental rights.
   (a) Lok Sabha (b) Rajya Sabha
   (c) Supreme Court (d) Election Commission.
6. The Chairperson of the Human Rights Commission in India can be a person who has been a ....
   (a) Judge of the Supreme Court
   (b) Chief Justice of the Supreme Court
   (c) Judge of a High Court
   (d) Chief Justice of a High Court.

Key to Objective Type Questions

1. a 2. d 3. b 4. a 5. c 6. b

NOTES

1. Ramachandra Guha, *India After Gandhi*, 569.

2. R. Sathianathaier, *History of India* vol. 1 (Madras: S. Viswanathan, Printers and Publishers, 1985), 42-43.
3. Quoted in Asish Kumar Das, *Human Rights in India*, 4.
4. Sukhadeo Thorat, *Ambedkar's Role in Economic Planning, Water and Power Policy* (Delhi: Shipra Publications, 2006), 30-36.
5. Bipan Chandra *et al.*, *India's Struggle for Independence* (New Delhi: Penguin Books, 1989), 93-97.
6. Shweta Mehra, *Human Rights: A Gandhian Perspective* (New Delhi: Sarup & Sons, 2006), 37-44.
7. Umesh Bhatt, *Human Rights: Achievements and Challenges* (Delhi: Vista International Publishing House, 2005), 200.
8. Bhanwar Lal Harsh, *Human Rights Law in India* (New Delhi: Regal Publications, 2008), 147.
9. Anu Saksena, *Gender and Human Rights: Status of Women Workers in India* (Delhi: Shipra Publications, 2004), 162-163.
10. For details on the importance on the right to a healthy environment see, Antonio Augusto Cancado Trindade, "Human Rights and the Environment" in *New Dimensions and Challenges for Human Rights*, ed. Janusz Symonides (Jaipur: Rawat Publications, 2003), 117-145.
11. For details see, Arjun Dev, 173-182.
12. V. Venkatesan, "Human Rights: A Commission in Limbo", *Frontline*, February 14, 2003, 121-22.
13. *Ibid.*, 182-186.

7

Law Enforcing Agencies and Human Rights

The role of law enforcing agencies in the protection of human rights is an important aspect of any civilized society. The Constitution stresses the need to protect the rights of people irrespective of their caste, creed, language, religion or sex. In developing countries like India one can notice the increasing nexus between the criminals, politicians and the police. Needless to say that such a grouping of vested interest would hamper the rights of the common man. While a considerable number of personnel in the law enforcing agencies are doing their duties in accordance with the guidelines of the service, they face all sorts of pressure from their superiors and from their political bosses. Inevitably such a trend would demoralize the law enforcing agencies.

In the past two decades the market economy and its forces led to the pumping of money in a scale one cannot imagine earlier. The multi-national companies and the neo-riches in the country employ all the techniques to exploit the wealth of the nation, whether mineral or human resources. The market force disturbs the balance and equilibrium of the society for its own selfish reasons. The law enforcing agencies are lured to serve the interest of these new dominant forces. Another trend is the increasing communalization process sets in the Indian polity that victimizes religious minorities and other marginalized groups. The Right to Information Act is a notable positive development to check some of these violations. But here again the whistle blowers are either killed, maimed or silenced by the criminal elements with the active connivance of the police.

In recent years the terrorist threat is looming large over every nation's horizon. Especially after the twin tower attack in USA the focus on terrorism and counter-terrorism measures increased many fold. Inevitably in several countries it brought misery and destruction to millions of people. In the name of protecting the security of the nation, large scale human rights violations are reported. The problem is finding a balance between containing terrorism and preventing the rights abuse. Sometimes, the security laws like POTA, TADA and the Armed Forces (Special Powers) Act (AFSPA) empowering the law enforcing agencies with lot of special powers were misused to target political opponents and innocent victims. The AFSPA has come in for widespread criticism in Jammu and Kashmir, Manipur and other parts of North East due to its association with human rights abuse.[1] Of course, every terrorist act would have its impact on the police and they have to answer the government as well as the powerful media and public. When a quick solution is not available it led to encounter killings and false cover-up arrest of innocent people. In addition, mafia groups and powerful business groups also uses the encounter killings as a means to settle personnel scores.

The fake encounter of Sorabuddin by the Gujarat police on the request of marble traders of Rajasthan and the alleged involvement of Amit Shah, a Minister in the Narendra Modi's Government and higher police officials highlights this trend.[2] Due to his criminal activities, Sorabuddin earned the wrath of the marble traders of Rajasthan. When they wanted to eliminate him, they got the assistance of the top Gujarat police officers who killed him and claimed that they have killed a dreaded terrorist on a mission to assassinate the Chief Minister, Narender Modi. It appears that these encounter killings for personal reasons were used to get rewards from the government for their bravery in eliminating 'hardcore' terrorists with plan to assassinate top leaders. The police can also get the handsome payment from those who wanted to end his life. Mukul Sinha, lawyer and founder of a Civil Rights organisation says that crores of rupees was paid for the elimination.[3] Sorabuddin's wife Kausar Bi was allegedly raped and killed in a farmhouse before her body was disposed of by the police. An associate of Sorabuddin, Tulsi Prajapati who was an eye-witness to this killing of police was also killed later. The shocking incident exposes the highhandedness of the senior I.P.S officers and the cool manner in which they acted as henchmen for private traders and political leaders. The case is still at the investigative stage but exposes a murky story of extortion, contract killing, rape, bribery and corruption involving the political bosses, businessmen and the police. Amit Shah was arrested following evidence gathered by the CBI on his attempt for derailing the investigation of the killings by the CID, as the Minister of State for Home.[4]

In this context many lawyers and activists argue that unless the Union and State Governments commit themselves to zero tolerance on encounter killings the Sorabuddin investigation may turn into one-off event. In the name of immunity, police officials and their political bosses cannot be granted free hand to do whatever they like. The CBI investigation has exposed the operation of small group of officers, which allegedly planned, executed and benefited from several illegal activities. It also underlines how sincere officers who refuse to carry out illegal orders are punished. It resulted in a polarized administration.

Ishrat Jahan along with three others was killed near Naroda in Ahmedabad on June 15, 2004. The police claimed they were operatives of Lashkar-e-Taiba, planning to kill the Gujarat Chief Minister. But the human rights activists claim that she was innocent. The Pakistan-American terrorist David Headley has reportedly told his interrogators that Ishrat was a Lashkar operative. However, the Ahmedabad Metropolitan Magistrate, S.P. Tamang said the encounter was *prima facie* a false one and there was no evidence to link Ishrat and others with the Lashkar. The crime branch police kidnapped them from Mumbai on June 12, 2004 and brought them to Ahmedabad to eliminate them. The motive of the officers, according to the Magistrate was career promotion and appreciation from the Chief Minister, Modi. Some of the officers involved in the encounter were already arrested in the Sorabuddin encounter case.[5] In Gujarat, several officials 'loyal' to the administration were rewarded through appointments to positions of power. Likewise, those who sincerely did their work despite pressure from their higher ups met with punishment postings.[6] But there are officers who refuse to budge to the pressures and are fighting the rot from within.

The Court of Law is also playing a positive role in punishing the police officers guilty of fake encounters. In October 2010, a CBI Special Court in Kerala sentenced a former Inspector General of Police, K. Lakshmana, to life imprisonment for ordering the killing of Varghese, in the Thirunelli forest in Wayanad district 40 years ago. According to the prosecution, Varghese was a common man who was branded as naxalite and shot dead in cold blood with his hands tied behind in a fake encounter.[7] The matter surfaced only when a former police constable, P. Ramachandran Nair made a statement 28 years after the incident in 1998, that he shot dead Varghese on the orders of then SP Vijayan and DSP Lakshmana.

There are human right activists, like the proactive courts, are fighting against the corrupt system that has eaten into the vitals of the society. Teesta Setalvad, a lawyer activist is waging a battle on those who play a major role in killing innocent minorities and others in communal violence as well as in encounter killings. On the progress of some of the cases she has observed that "What we are witnessing for the first time is the transparency and accountability process for mass crimes within a democracy."[8]

On the 62nd year of Independence Day, Rabina Devi, a pregnant woman going to the market was shot dead as the police chased a young man. The police at the same time pushed a "suspected militant" into a pharmacy and shot him. When the police denied their hand in it, a photographer leaked the killings to the magazine *Tehelka*.[9] This incident happened in a crowded market area in broad day light. It led to the agitation of public, demanding justice and an end to the impunity granted to security forces under the AFSPA. One notable feature of this agitation is the mobilization of women and their fearlessness. The women are calling this as another 'Nupila' (woman's war). Chaoba Devi, a women leading the agitation said that the situation reached a point beyond tolerable limit. That is why "we have come out unitedly to get ourselves killed or get arrested by the police."[10] They are worried about the effect of curfew on education and the livelihood of thousands of poor people who depend on daily wages.

Torture of Adivasis

Today, India is facing the Maoist threat which was more serious and widespread than the Naxal movement. Several states including Chhattisgarh and Andhra Pradesh face the worst threat from Maoists. In several districts of these states virtually their writ runs large and they are running their own parallel government. Through Kangaroo courts they punish those who act against Maoist group that includes execution. The law-enforcing agencies created a network with local village support against the Maoist group. They were given weapon and support that led to lot of bloodletting. The Maoist targeted these groups that led to further violence. There were allegations that the Border Security Force (BSF) personnel have tortured Adivasis in Kanker, Chhattisgarh, into confessing that they were Maoist cadres.[11] Following complaint, the Chhattisgarh Commission for Scheduled Tribes has initiated an enquiry into the incident. The Adivasis accused that the BSF assaulted forty men and molested two women in which one of whom is a minor during search operation.[12] Some of the Adivasis in the hospital have hairline fracture on their feet that indicates the possibility of torture. The BSF is conducting a parallel inquiry and its Director informed that anyone found guilty would not be spared. But despite such assurance, rights violations on the tribal people continued. In October 2010, a young tribal woman alleged that she was sexually assaulted by the Koya Commando unit of the Chhattisgarh Police in the Bade Bidme Panchayat of Dandewada district. The woman carry her torn blouse and inner cloth and a lock of her hair that was cut off by the police.[13] A raid was conducted by the police on that night that began with eight hour blackout. The Adivasis accused that their valuables were stolen by the search party.

While the Maoist threat is very serious to the integrity of the nation, the law enforcing agencies must handle the issue with caution that any major human right violation would only strengthen the Maoist cause. The tribal communities should not be pushed to the Maoist side. There is no denying the fact that some tribals are helping the Maoist cadre either due to their frustration with the government or due to threat perception from the Maoists.

In Tamil Nadu, during June 21-23, 1992 the forest department officials, with the help of revenue and police personnel searched the forest area for sandalwood smugglers. They have brutally attacked the tribals in Vachathy village near Harur in Dharmapuri district. Women were raped, men assaulted, houses were looted and destroyed and cattle were killed in the name of upholding law and preventing the smuggling of sandalwood. In total, 18 women including a 13 year old girl student were raped and beaten. All the men escaped to the nearby forest and stayed there for a month due to the fear of police action. During the search operation that tribal population was beaten and ill-treated. The raped women were taken into the forest office and were ill-treated. The CPI(M) took a proactive legal step to procure justice for the tribal victims.[14] Strangely, the police department never filed an FIR in this case. Due to public pressure, a CBI enquiry was ordered. The CBI brought to book all the 269 accused and after a prolonged battle of 19 years the Dharmapuri district court declared that all the accused were involved in the crime that includes violence and rape. All the 215 persons excluding the 54 accused, who died naturally in the course of enquiry, were found guilty of the crime and punishment was given in accordance with the level of their involvement.[15] The court appreciated the tenacity of CBI in solving the case and awarded it with 1 lakh special reward. However, the tribals felt that the compensation of Rs. 15,000 for each of the 18 rape victims was inadequate due to the trauma of the incident. They have planned to fight for enhanced compensation as prescribed in the various sections of the Scheduled Castes and Scheduled Tribes (Prevention of Atrocities) Act, 1989. *The Hindu* in its editorial dated October 1, 2011 observed that *"while men in the lower ranks indulged in violence, senior officers watched from a distance. The subsequent attempts at denial and cover-up were indicative of sanction for the attack from elements at the higher levels of the government... The wait for justice might have been long and tiresome, but was finally rewarding. The peoples struggle have a decisive impact on the course of justice was clearly demonstrated in the Vachathi case. The verdict ... shoud serve as a reminder that the rule of law will have to be upheld everywhere, including in the remotest of villages. Civilised India cannot afford a repeat of Vachathi."*

Over the years, during which Armed Forces Special Powers Act has been in operation, the army opened fire on countless times and killed hundreds of people. When the killed people were terrorists or insurgents there have been no major public outburst of emotions. But when the army killed unarmed civilians the voices get raised against AFSPA. When fake-encounter incidents like Pathribal and Macchhil is reported in Kashmir the public strongly reacted against the misuse of the Act. In the Pathribal case, the CBI observed that "abducting and killing unarmed civilians in cold blood could not be considered part of official duty."[16] The officials concerned prevented the prosecution of the case on the ground that they have not granted sanction to prosecute according to Section 6 of the Act. It is argued that the law enforcing agencies has every right to use the deadly force against the enemies of the state. But they should not shy away from allowing the courts to step in when doubts arise.

In several cases the legal proceedings got blocked due to the denial of official sanction. The officers can be protected from criminal proceedings to protect the work environment. But it should not be used as a pretext to the killing of innocent unarmed civilians. In 2004, following the death in custody of Thangjam Manorama and scores of others like her by the paramilitary forces, Manipur raised in a major protest against the Armed Forces Act and the way in which it was misused. Scores of women stood in front of the army camp in Imphal without any dress carrying banners that cry 'Indian Army Rape us'.[17] It shows the intensity of the feeling against the Armed Forces that ravages their life. The Armed Forces Special Powers Act empowers soldiers to kill on suspicion and still they can escape prosecution for murder.

In Kashmir too, the public rose in revolt against the army when two young Kashmiri women were allegedly raped and killed before dumped in a stream by the law enforcing agencies. It intensified the struggle against AFSPA as well as on the security agencies. The public, including women and children started pelting stones and the government found it very difficult to assuage the feelings of the public. Concerned over the violent protest, Prime Minister, Manmohan Singh observed the need for non-lethal crowd control measures since nearly 60 civilians have died in police action while controlling the stone pelting crowd.[18] The Prime Minister favoured re-calibration of the promotion system in the police force to reward those who perform better, especially in troubled areas. Likewise, commenting on the need to regulate the behaviour of police and the protection of human rights, the former NHRC Chairperson, Justice K.G. Balakrishnan observed that "policemen do not directly or indirectly, become violators of human rights. Only then they can act as protectors of human rights. They should be sensitive and sympathetic to the plight of victims of crime".[19] He pointed out that the image of police got a dent in issues involving police encounters and custodial violence. He asked the police chiefs to give leadership to the force for zero tolerance to custodial violence. He suggested that guaranteeing the basic human rights of the police and basic amenities of the service were the best way to motivate the police force for proper discharge of their duties. In addition, transparency, impartiality and accountability create strength to the police force. To him, democratic policing based on the idea of the police as protectors of the rights of citizen ensures the safety of everyone. Justice Balakrishnan was interacting with senior police officers for the first time, in an annual conference organised by the Intelligence Bureau, for sensitizing the police officers about creating a security environment that promotes good governance and upholds human rights value.

Due to number of grievances including the threat to their livelihood options by the MNCs, that destroy their traditional habitat for commercial exploitation, the tribals are fighting for their right. In Orissa and in number of hilly regions the mining operations threatened the survival of this marginal group. The MNCs with the support of local police either cajole or force these communities to evict the forest land after accepting monetary compensation. One Khond tribal women lamented that "what is the use of money? We don't need it and what is sufficient is our life depending on the forest resources." What they need for their simple sustenance is allowing them to utilize the forest resources that helped them to survive for thousands of years. In Kerala, activists like Janu are fighting for the traditional rights of Tribals to live and use the forest resources for their survival. The law enforcing agencies are disturbing the survival possibility of these tribal groups.

Communal Violence and Law Enforcing Agencies

The way in which the law enforcing agencies are handling communal violence in certain states needs scrutiny. Especially, the secular democratic India has witnessed three pogrommes against all three significant minorities—Sikhs, Muslims and Christians. In 1984 when Indira Gandhi was assassinated by her Sikh bodyguards, the entire Sikh community in Delhi bears the brunt of violence which was organised in nature. The role of the political leaders in the violence is well documented. The police either took no action against those who killed, raped and looted the property of the Sikhs or they played a supportive role in the mob violence.[20] Likewise, the Gujarat pogrom also targeted another important minority community, the Muslims. In the name of revenge for Godhra incident, large numbers of innocent Muslims were tortured. V.R. Krishna Iyer Tribunal brought out the sadistic, inhuman nature of the Gujarat killings. He observed that "the widespread violence that targeted Muslims in urban and rural Gujarat was marked by utter bestiality and brutality." He added further "that the administration reversed its Constitutional role, and by omission and commission, engineered the loot, ravishment and murder which were methodically perpetrated through planned process."[21] In most cases, the police were mute spectators or connived with those who targeted the Muslims.

Justice was denied to most of the innocent victims, partly due to police harassment and partly due to their fear over the politician and administration that prevented them from seeking justice. But there are some notable exceptions like Bilkis Yahoob Patel who was raped along with her pregnant sister Shamim who delivered a baby on the way to escape. The Hindu neighbours caught them and killed the group that includes her two year old daughter Saleha. The unconscious Bilkis was the lone survivor surrounded by 14 dead bodies. She decided to fight the case despite the attempt of Gujarat police to hush up it. They closed her case with the note that "the case was true but undetected due to lack of sufficient evidence".[22] A CBI team found that the local police officials had hidden the bodies of Bilkis family. As Bilkis has no faith in getting a fair trial in Gujarat, the National Human Rights Commission intervened and the Supreme Court transferred the case to Mumbai on her request. After a painful trial, the court finally convicted 11 of the 20 accused. They were held guilty of rape and murder and sentenced to life imprisonment. One police constable was held guilty of destroying evidence in the case while five other police personnel who played a role in hiding the bodies are acquitted. Bilkis wanted to fight till all the policemen involved got punished.

R.K. Raghavan, former CBI Director, commenting on this judgment pointed out that "it is significant in many ways and deserves to be studied in detail by policemen, lawyers, prosecutors, human rights activists and trial court judges all-over the country".[23] He further argues that when a police force is under the thumb of the State Government, one cannot expect professionalism from the police. In Gujarat one may ask the question that how many women victims have the tenacity and courage of Bilkis to get justice despite all sorts of threats and pressure. The CBI did a commendable job through scientific investigation with the help of Central Forensic Science Laboratory. Under trying circumstances the CBI made possible the examination of witnesses that led to conviction. One important provision in our criminal law that helps victims like Bilkis is the *in camera* deposition. It helped the victim to narrate the details of the attack on her in a cogent and uninhibited manner that convinced the Judge that she was speaking the truth. The 11 convictions in the Bilkis case was more or less on oral evidence and that indicate how Judge Dalvi was humane and pragmatic.[24]

The Best Bakery case was also tried outside Gujarat and the accused got punishment. Thanvir Jafri, who was the son of a Congress M.P. killed in the communal violence, pointed out that the verdict in Bilkis case is heartening, but "the policemen should also be punished since they consciously tried to derail the investigation". To him it will sent out a strong message to other police personel that they cannot defy the rule of law and get away with it. In several other cases related to the communal violence in Gujarat, the police have hidden evidence and failed to properly record the testimonials. More than half of the cases were closed as 'true but undetected'. But the Supreme Court ordered the Gujarat police to reinvestigate all the cases. The convicted persons in several cases harass the witnesses when they are back in the village on parole. There are also reports about the transfer of judges who convict the accused.[25] It tarnished the image of the state administration.

When 43 of the communal violence victims from Orissa, testified before the National People's Tribunal on Kandhamal, which is headed by former Chief Justice of the Delhi High Court, A.P. Shah, their narrative on the violence chilled the audience. One of the victims Priyatama Nayak said that her husband Abhimanyu was tied to a tree and burnt in her presence. The mob looted her house and destroyed it amid religious chants. Her young son went to the local police station and begged for their assistance. The police reached the village only after 10 days and the stray dogs preyed on the body of Abhimanyu. (FIR No. 90 u/s 147/148/436/506/302/149, dated August 31, 2008).[26] The police made no arrest despite Priyatama named her husband's killers. Following threat from the accused, she took the case to the Orissa Human Rights Commission which ordered enquiry and action against the errant policemen.

Another victim Narsingho Digal testified that how a 600 strong armed gang destroyed his house after looting it. His mother was gang raped and later killed with his father. Like many other Kandhamal Christians he also faces a social boycott. The rioters demanded that he must reconverted back to Hinduism to facilitate his return to native village. The local BJP MLA was spotted among the rioters and he was later sentenced to seven years rigorous imprisonment. The Orissa violence in Kandhamal targeted Dalit-tribal Christians in which 38 persons were killed and several people were injured. In addition to violence and killings in all the three pogroms involving the minorities, Vidya Subrahmaniam observed that abuse of women is rampant. In most cases, the women were gang raped in front of their family members not for lust but as a demonstration of power and to humiliate the male relatives of the victims. On September 30, 2008, a catholic nun was stripped naked and raped in front of a police post. 12 police men present at that place watched the whole tragic incident while a catholic priest with the victim was mercilessly beaten for refusing to join with the gang in dishonouring the nun.[27]

However, when this issue was taken to court of law the nun was reluctant to testify. After repeated summons she appeared for cross-examination. The defence counsel after cross-examination in the trial court said that she is giving incoherent statements. She is giving different versions of the incident at different stages of investigation. Truth will prevail only after the final verdict from the court.

Vrinda Grover, a member of the Jury of the Kandhamal tribunal remarked that the Orissa rioters had "used women's bodies as sites for punishment". The tribunal observed the "institutionalized bias of State agencies, their deliberate dereliction of constitutionally mandated duties, their connivance with communal forces, participation in and support to the violence, and a deliberate scuttling of the processes of justice ...." in the riots.[28]

In addition to the role of law enforcing agencies in communal violence and in fake encounters, we have reports of several human rights violations committed by them on individual civilians. There are number of cases involving custodial rape and death committed by the police in several states. There is a steady decline in the efficiency of the police in handling cases involving rights violations. Besides, sexual harassment of women subordinates by the police officers is also reported. When the police officials are hesitating to face enquiries on the ground that entertaining such allegations by women subordinates would destroy the morale of the entire police force, the Madras High Court bench observed that police officer should not hesitate to face sexual harassment probe.[29] In a case of sexual harassment lodged by a women Sub Inspector against fellow police officers, the learned Judges observed that the officers are certainly entitled to defend and come out of the allegations. But it would be inappropriate for them to expect that no enquiry should be held. The police officials should not escape for their crime related to women in the name of service protection or demoralization of the service.

R.K. Raghavan talked about the charges on police insensitivity to crimes against women. To him, training methods have very little impact and women police wing have brought in only marginal relief as they themselves are believed to indulge in unethical practices. He was worried about our movies that systematically promote harassment of women. Generally, eve teasing is presented as fun and frolic and such tendency is not good for the society at large. Those who are in the film industry must take note of this observation and should avoid such negative exposure of women.

In July 12, 2009 issue, *The Week* exclusively exposed India's secret torture chambers that are compared with the notorious US controlled Guantanamo Bay detention centre, where thousands of terror related suspects were tortured to get information.[30] According to this expose, these centres exist in Jammu, Kashmir, Gujarat, Kolkata, Mumbai and in different parts of Delhi where far away from the eyes of the law, the 'enemies of the state' are made to 'sing'. There is variety of torture techniques used to get the required information. The method of torture includes the roller, the aeroplane, electric shock, hot and cold treatment, water-boarding and administration of pethidine injection that makes a person crazy and deprives him of sleep. A Srinagar based photo journalist, Maqbool Sahil was interrogated for 15 days in such detention centre and after the cruel experience he wonder that it was a miracle that he is alive today. After their torture anyone will breakdown and confess to anything was his observation. The concerned human rights activists pointed out that there should be an open debate on illegal detention centres. Like the US, the Indian Government should also come forward for an open debate. The security of the nation and its people is important and terrorism should be crushed without affecting the innocent lives. But some of the retired officers in IB argue the necessity for such secret detention centres. It facilitates them to interrogate the suspected terrorists as long as necessary without any restriction imposed by the legal system.

In 2008, the NGO People's Watch brought out a report that indicates that around 1.8 million people are victims of police torture every year in India. So far, there was no official denial to this important report from the government side. A former DGP of police, Tripura, Dr. K.S. Subramanian who served in different capacities in IB and other related services, agreed that during 1980-85, a number of Naxalites were killed in police action. But on enquiry with the state chief secretary it turned that the 59 people killed in the incidents were not Naxalites. Most of those killed were members of a peasant organisation fighting for social justice.[31] While answering the difficulties of the police in dealing with terrorism and the compulsion to uphold the principles of human rights, Subramanian pointed out that there are set rules for the police to follow but some police officers believe that while dealing with suspected terrorists they are not obliged to follow Constitutional norms. He highlighted the need for attitudinal change among the police officers.

The people in the Maoist or Naxal affected areas feel that they are like a sheet of paper caught between the pair of blades of a scissor i.e., the police and the Maoists. There is a constant pressure on the tribals and the people living near the sensitive areas from the law enforcing agencies as well as the Maoists. There is a drive to recruit these local populations to the police force, to counter the menace of the Maoists. But the Maoists are threatening the new recruits of the local area. They are also pressuring the youth to join their movement. It creates a very difficult situation for the people as it threatens their survival options. In some families, the youth who joined the Naxal movement or the police force were killed in encounters. The people suffer if they take sides; they are hit if they don't. It is reported that in West Bengal, women are forced to attend Maoist meetings and they are beaten if they are not brisk enough at reaching the venue in time.[32] Those who stay at home are molested and robed by some jawans.[33] The children have no school to go since the school buildings are used by the Para-military forces as their hideouts. Hence, the Naxals destroy the pucca buildings with dynamite. Even if there is a building, no teacher dares to handle the classes. A Maoist squad dragged the Head Master of a village's only primary school out of the class and shot him dead in front of his terrified students.[34] Invariably, the people in the Maoist dominated area suffer human rights violations in the hands of law enforcing agencies and the Maoists.

In India, the law enforcing agencies are criticized for the violation of human rights. There are reports as discussed earlier on the fake encounters, custodial killings and rape by the members of law enforcing agencies. There is no doubt that the police is working under enormous pressure to perform against a variety of problems that cropped up in the recent decades. The multi-national companies are trying to exploit the mineral wealth in the hilly regions dislocating thousands of tribals and other marginalized communities. When they resist such move it led to attack on them. Maoism spreads in such areas where there are genuine grievances against the lack of plan, or failure to deliver schemes that support the people. There is urgent need to tackle the Maoist menace that is slowly spreading to other parts of India. The Prime Minister, Manmohan Singh himself agreed that the greatest challenge faced by the nation is the threat from Maoists. The failure of tackling number of basic issues related to the survival of tribals only aggravates their grievance against the ruling establishments. Unless these issues are handled properly, such areas become germinating ground for militancy that would threaten the integrity of the nation.

The communal violence directed against the minorities and the way in which the innocent people are made to suffer highlights the failure of the law enforcing agencies. Even though such violence involves political game plan, the police only served its masters without bothering much about their duties and the rights of the innocent victims. Politicians are using the power of transfer as well as other rewarding methods as an effective tool to manipulate the police force. Of late, the Right to Information Act is effectively used against corruption as well as on key postings that were made with ulterior motive. But the whistle-blowers are facing reprisal from vested interest.[35] There are number of activist victims like Amit Jethwa from Gujarat, Dattatraya Patil, Arun Sawant and Vitthal Gite from Maharashtra, Sola Ranga Rao from Andhra Pradesh and Shashidhar Mishra from Bihar. They were eliminated by those who were threatened by the RTI Act.[36] Arvind Kejriwal, who was an RTI activist and Magsaysay award winner, resigned his post to fight the system to bring just, transparent and accountable governance.[37] He is of the opinion that the government must set-up an independent commission to probe corruption cases exposed by this Act. Only through people's power we can force the government to change the situation.

While evaluating the performance of police force in other countries R.K. Raghavan took the case of UK police. He argued that the fundamentals of policing have remained the same in the past three decades. The police are now undeniably more transparent and accountable than before. The police officials in UK attribute this to the role of media, which have become an integral part of the monitoring mechanism available to the polity. In India, some newspapers play a consistent role in bringing informations that help the public to evaluate the performance of law enforcing agencies. But following the onset of market economy, most papers, from the viewpoint of journalist themselves, are interested only in making profit and are not interested in 'real events'.[38] Sumir Lal pointed out that "instead of looking at the many aspects of an unequal nation in transition, the media indulged in petty deceit. To Sanjoy Hazarika, the media ignores basic facts about the Northeast, Jammu and Kashmir in its insurgency coverage. He laments that India is deploying the army and paramilitary forces for over 50 years in the Northeast and for over two decades in Kashmir without much success. The growth of Maoist campaign is mostly due to the acute frustration at the lack of delivery on promises, from bad government and governance, from the system's failure to provide basic health, education and livelihood opportunities 65 years after independence."[39] The insurgency and bad governance are part of the same coin, the same story and at times the media misses this point. On the other hand, the men in uniform wonder why the media focuses on them and not the anti-national activities of those who oppose to the idea of India.[40] Regarding the media focus on issues such as the draconian Armed Forces Special Powers Act, the metro media has made the mistake of focusing primarily on AFSPA as in Kashmir, forgetting that the Act has been in place in the Northeast for over 50 years, where the people are suffering under it. Sanjoy Hazarika feels that the television is totally inconsistent and uncommitted in following up the matters pertaining to the changing nature of the conflicts in a sustained manner.

However, in the Northeast the journalist has been the target of arbitrary killing and intimidation by armed non-state actors for their courage in reporting the truth. They also expose the secret killings of relatives of ULFA members during the regime of Prafulla Mahanta.[41] Such reporting inevitably led to backlash. Due to the killing of reporters in India, Reporters Sans Frontieres ranks India in the scale of 105 out of 175 nations at the global level. The thrust of the argument is that the Indian media can play a very active role like their western counterparts in bringing the issues concerning the rights violations by the law enforcing agencies. When USA is confronted with the torture cells in the Guantanamo Bay detention centre and on Wikileake exposure on human rights violations by the US troops, the media forced the government to accept its error. It led to enquiry and the closure of the Guantanamo Bay detention centre that would punish the violators of human rights.

Commenting on the need for the change in the police behaviour, Shri Dharma Vira, Chairman of National Police Commission, observed that "We may modify our laws to safeguard human dignity or talk loudly about such dignity or rights but so long as the police behaviour in our country remains as it is today, all such provisions and declarations would prove to be only on paper and not in reality."[42] The general attitude prevailing among the civil police is a thinking that they are above law and the system will protect them. Modern scientific methods of interrogation are not available at the grass roots level in police that led to physical torture. Inadequate police training as well as supervision by the higher officials and corruption in the police are some factors leading to human rights violations. When police officers who violated human rights and indicted by court of law for their violation of rights are awarded with promotions and medals, what type of image it would create among other police personnel? It is generally believed that almost all cases of custodial deaths and police misbehaviour are quietly buried after the initial media frenzy. The cases on police officials are investigated and charges framed in such a manner that provides enough loopholes for the guilty to escape. The politicians manning the government are made to believe that if the police force is taken in to task through enquiry or punishment that would demoralize the force.

In independent India, a large number of commissions of enquiry were constituted to enquire the complaints of torture and death in police custody and human rights violations committed during police operations. In addition, the lack of effective criminal justice system also helped them to behave as they can do anything and escape the legal consequences. But the government is reluctant to implement the recommendations of these commissions. V.V. Chandra Chud, former Chief Justice of India observed that "Police officers alone, and none else, can give evidence regarding the circumstances in which a person in their custody comes to receive injuries. Bound by the ties of a kind of brotherhood, they often prefer to remain silent to such situations and when they choose to speak, they put their own gloss upon times and pervert the truth."[43] The society also generally has the opinion that the police can use violence on the suspect to get the truth which emboldens the police behaviour. There are several good police officers who use variety of factors other than third degree methods to obtain confessions from the accused. But such psychological handling needs time and the police are under pressure to complete the enquiry in a short time given for custody. When some of the dreaded criminals who are apprehended with much difficulty and risk, got bail in the court and jump it easily, a kind of frustration sets in. Ashish Kumar Das argues that the police brutality and violations of human rights are symptoms of a sick society. Despite punishment meted out to several army personnel for their human right excesses in Jammu and Kashmir the violation continues even today.

In India, human right as a subject is slowly integrated into the curriculum of higher education. The law enforcing agencies should incorporate this subject while giving training to the personnel during recruitment process. With periodic interval they must update their knowledge on the cases related to rights violation. The CBI Special Court verdict on the fake encounter of Varghese and the life imprisonment awarded to the then Inspector General of Police, K. Lakshmana for ordering the killing, can act as a deterrent in the behaviour of the police force. More than anything, the cases like the Bilkis Patel and the verdict of the learned judges should be taught, so that they cannot take the law into their own hands and the rights and honour of women as granted. As in UK and other Western countries, the awareness of the public on their rights and the vigilant media can help the public in shaping the outlook of the law enforcing agencies to some extent. The criminal, police and political nexus is a major threat to the rights of the individual. The court of law, as the guardian of the Constitution and the protector of rights of the people, is playing an active role that must continue. Creation of public awareness on their rights is another important task before the rights activists and NGOs dealing with Human Rights issue.

Rights Related to Arrest

When a person is arrested he/she must know that they are entitled for some basic rights to ensure their well-being in custody. In the *D.K. Basu* vs. *State of West Bengal* case, in 1987 the Supreme Court clearly laid down certain conditions to be followed by the police for arrest, detention and interrogation of any person.[44] This particular judgment strengthens Constitutional and statutory safeguards related to rights and dignity of the arrested person. The Indian Constitution (Article 21) lays down that no person can be deprived of his/her right to liberty, except in accordance with the due procedure established by law. The police in India do not have any power to detain a person for questioning unless he is arrested with or without warrant. Warrant is a document in writing, signed by the presiding officer of the court that must have the seal of the court. The warrant should contain the name of the person to be arrested, his address and points out the offence with which he is charged. If any of the above details are missing, the warrant is not in order and an arrest made on the basis of such warrant is illegal.[45] A police officer has the power to arrest a person even without warrant, if he is suspected of having committed a serious crime (cognizable offence) such as murder, rape, robbery, waging war against the state etc. In case of investigation by any police officer of any male below 15 years or any women can be made only at the place of residence (Sec. 160 Cr.P.C.).[46] When a person is arrested he has the following rights:

1. The arrested person has the right to know why he was arrested. (Fundamental Rights: Article 22 and Sec.50 Cr.P.C.)
2. When a person is arrested he has the right to see the warrant. (Sec.75 Cr.P.C.)
3. The arrested person has the right to consult a lawyer of his choice. (Fundamental Rights: Article 22)
4. He must be produced before the nearest Magistrate within 24 hours of arrest, excluding the time taken for travel.[47] (Fundamental Rights: Article 22)
5. The arrested person must be told that whether he/she is entitled to be released on bail. (Sec.50 Cr.P.C.)
6. He/She has the right to inform a relative, friend or well wisher who may take interest in his/her welfare, about the arrest and the place of detention.[48]
7. A woman accused cannot be arrested during the night time except with prior permission of a Magistrate.
8. As far as possible, a woman can only be arrested in the presence of a woman police officer and the arrest must be carried out with proper dignity.
9. While arresting a juvenile or a child no beatings or force can be administered.
10. Regarding handcuffing, according to the ruling of the Supreme Court, normally an arrested person should not be handcuffed unless there is sufficient reason. If the accused is violent or likely to escape or commit suicide the officer can handcuff him.
11. A poor person, when arrested can get free legal assistance from the Legal Services Authority. (Article 39 A, Constitution of India).

12. If a woman is arrested, the medical examination has to be made only by a female registered medical practitioner.
13. If a person is arrested on a groundless basis or kept in illegal detention he/she is entitled for compensation.
14. The police should not arrest a person on mere suspicion. (145 Cr.P.C.)

Rights Related to Bail

1. If a person is arrested on the charges of a bailable offence, the police officer should inform that he has the right to be released on bail.
2. An accused person has the right to bail or demand judicial custody when surrendering before the Magistrate.
3. Subject to the nature of the offence, the provision of bail to women, sick and old age persons should be given priority.
4. Once the accused is given bail by invoking Section 205 Cr.P.C., the person need not attend the court—unless it is a condition of bail—before charge sheet is filed and process issued.
5. If no charge sheet is filed before 60 days or 90 days, depending upon the case may be, the accused in custody has a right to be released on bail.
6. If the Magistrate remanded a person to judicial custody on Sunday or holiday his bail application should be considered on the holiday itself.
7. If charge sheet is not filed within a period of 60 days, in non-bailable offences, the Magistrate has the power to release a person on bail, without notice to the other side.[49]

NOTES

1. Siddarth Varadarajan, "A modest proposal on AFSPA", *The Hindu*, September 6, 2010, p. 8.
2. Anupama Katakam and Venkitesh Ramakrishnnan, "The Lid is Off", *Frontline*, August 27, 2010, p. 4.
3. Anupam Katakam, "Planned by the State", *Frontline*, August 27, 2010, p. 11.

4. Anupama Katakam and Venkitesh Ramakrishnnan, "The Lid is off", *Frontline*, August 27, 2010, p. 4.
5. Lyla Bavadam, "Dreaded group", *Frontline*, August 27, 2010, p. 14.
6. *Ibid.*, p. 16.
7. *The Hindu*, October 29, 2010, p. 15.
8. Anupama Katakam, "Indian system could deliver", *Frontline*, August 27, 2010, p. 19.
9. Kalpana Sharma, "Manipur, once more", *The Hindu*, (Magazine) August 23, 2009, p. 3.
10. *Ibid.*
11. *The Hindu*, September 14, 2010, p. 10.
12. *Ibid.*
13. Amen Sethi, "Fresh allegations of sexual assault by security forces in Chhattisgarh", *The Hindu*, October 26, 2010, p. 11.
14. Kavin Malar, "Vachathy Pain", (Vachathy vali—Tamil) *Ananda Vikadan*, October 12, 2011, pp. 76-78.
15. *The Hindu*, October 2, 2011, p. 4.
16. Siddharth Varadarajan, "A modest proposal on AFSPA", p. 8.
17. Sanjoy Hazarika, "Mainland Discourse", *Outlook*, November 1, 2010, p. 96.
18. *The Hindu*, August 27, 2010, p. 12.
19. *Ibid.*
20. Vidya Subrahmaniam, "Three pogroms held together by a common thread", *The Hindu*, September 4, 2010, p. 11.
21. *Ibid.*
22. Dionne Bunsha, "Fight goes on", *Frontline*, February 18, 2008, p. 32.
23. R.K. Raghavan, "Hope for the victim", *Frontline*, February 15, 2008, p. 128.
24. *Ibid.*, p. 129.
25. Dionne Bunsha, "Fight goes on", p. 32.
26. Vidya Subrahmaniam, "Three pogroms ..." *op. cit.*, p. 11.
27. *Ibid.*
28. *Ibid.*
29. *The Hindu*, September 4, 2010. p. 4.
30. Syed Nazakat, "India's Secret torture chambers", *The Week*, July 12, 2009, pp. 25-31.
31. *Ibid.* p., 27.
32. Rekha Dixit, "The cross-fire people", *The Week*, August 22, 2020, p. 23.
33. *Ibid.*
34. Rabi Banerjee, "Lalgarh: Nights of terror", *The Week*, August 22, 2006, p. 36.

35. Venkitesh Ramakrishnan, "Martyrs to transparency", *Frontline*, September 10, 2010, pp. 4-8.
36. *Ibid.*, pp. 5-12.
37. Purnima, S. Tripathi, "For an Independent probe agency", *Frontline*, September 10, 2010, p. 18.
38. Sumir Lal, "Why I Quit the Media", *Outlook*, November 1, 2010, p. 36.
39. Sanjoy Hazarika, "Mainland Discourse", *Outlook*, November 1, 2010, p. 98.
40. *Ibid.*
41. *Ibid.*, p. 100.
42. Asish Kumar Das, *Human Rights in India*, p. 15.
43. *Ibid.*, p. 16.
44. Syed Nazakat, "India's secret torture chambers", *The Week*, July 12, 2009, p. 29.
45. Rohan http://content.msn.co.in/MSN Contribute/Topic.aspx? Topic Id=2.
46. *Basic Course on Human Rights Education for Teachers*, p. 72.
47. Arjun Dev, *Human Rights*: A Source Book, pp. 156-157.
48. Nikita Anand, "Rights Relating to Arrest in India", http:www. mighty laws.in/wp- content/uploads/arrest.jpg.
49. *Basic Course on Human Rights Education for Teachers*, p. 74.

8

Conclusion

The Human Rights of what we are enjoying today is the fruits of struggle carried over millennia by humanity under very trying circumstances. The wandering men moved to civilized habitat and organised his life through regulated governance. When state emerged as a protector, the limitless freedom of individual was curtailed to benefit the society at large. A civilized code of conduct emerged through a process of learning that lasts over millenia. This process is not uniform in the entire horizon in which the nations and city states are dotted here and there. Despite the domineering forces like religion and absolute monarchy men fought for his rights and survival. The Magna Carta, the American Declaration of Independence and the triumph of ideals like liberty, equality and fraternity took humanity to new heights in realizing their long suppressed freedom. These revolutions and the assertion of rights had profound impact on the evolution of human rights.

The industrial revolution which created opportunities for millions of men and women in new cities also opened new ways of exploitation and injustice in a massive scale. The unbearable living conditions forced upon the masses led to their fight for justice and basic rights. The working class demanded their masters to give them at least a semblance of basic rights for survival. The period following industrial revolution experienced the violation of human rights in a massive scale. The 20th century which was regarded as the century of human rights actually witnessed the worst form of human right violations against millions of innocent people due to the outbreak of two World Wars. The League of Nations which was created after the First World

War failed in its primary goal of preventing the outbreak of another World War. But the International Labour Organisation under its wing did much in improving the working conditions of labourers. The vast data gathered by ILO on the workers helped the nations in several issues on labourers. The rehabilitation work as well as the exchange of prisoners of war and Nansen's passport issued to the refugees by the League needs special mention. It constituted a Permanent Slave (Eradication) Commission in 1923 and the League's constructive work in other areas of human rights protection needs appreciation. But before any further development in this respect, the outbreak of Second World War led to the collapse of the League of Nations.

The horrors of rights violation in extermination camps like Auswitz under the Nazi Germany and in camp 10 under Japan exposed the villainy of rulers in terminating the life of millions without any sense of guilt. The terrible cost of war in relation to the loss of men and material and its impact on innocent civilians forced the leaders to find mechanisms to prevent the outbreak of another major war. Inevitably, they are concerned about the protection of human rights for the future generations. The UNO was created with the avowed goal of eternal peace on humanity. The birth of UNO is great turning point in the evolution of human rights. A systematic work followed suit to uphold the values of human rights. The UNO carried the burden and started the onerous task of evolving universal norms to uphold human rights. The Universal Declaration of Human Rights was the first major document elaborating on the rights everyone can enjoy cutting across the artificial national boundaries that divide humanity. It was followed by a number of such documents that covers every aspect of human right in relation to men, women, children, refugees, prisoners and other groups including the sexual minorities.

In comparison to earlier experience, the period after the formation of UNO witnessed the efforts of collective will to implement at least the core of human right values across the globe. Though the cold war politics and the authoritarian regimes create conditions not conducive for the protection of human rights, considerable segment of populations started enjoying at least the basic rights. The UNO with its limitations on its dependency on the donor nations did a commendable job in alleviating the miseries of people especially in the Third World countries. The high cost of peace keeping had its effect on the finance of the UNO. Serious fund shortage and the pressure of countries like USA to control the activities and priorities of UNO, hamper its freedom. Despite these shortcomings, the UNO is playing a key role in lifting the human rights standard. The UN High Commission for Human Rights and number of other related organs are doing lot of works on the people's right to development and inclusive growth. The Vienna Declaration and Programme of Action led to the establishment of a High Commission on Human Rights. The UNHCHR is playing a constructive role in the matters related to human rights.

While leaders representing different nations created UNO for protecting peace and human rights some individuals and Non-Governmental Organisations entered the scene. Especially Peter Benson, a London Lawyer was instrumental in the creation of Amnesty International. It systematically oversees human rights violations all-over the world and exposes it. Amnesty International is particularly concerned about the rights of political prisoners or others who are in prison because of their faith in certain ideology. It projected the failures of the governments and other agencies on human rights front. Its annual reports contain informations on violations of rights in individual countries and are respected for its almost unbiased contents. It also assists the asylum seekers who are at risk at their own countries. More than anything it tries to ensure proper control of international military, security and other law enforcing agencies within the parameters of legal framework. It made several countries to bring legislation against torture and other human rights violations. Today, there are hundreds of NGOs working in almost all the countries for preserving the dignity and the rights of the individual.

In order to take the first step for the collective enforcement of several rights enshrined in the UDHR, the European Union took the first step. The European Convention on Human Rights gives legal content to human rights. It also made necessary arrangements to oversee the enforcement of the rights among the nations that signed the instrument. The European Commission of Human Rights and the European Court of Human Rights will oversee the enforcement of these rights. The Helsinki Charter led to the move for greater economic scientific, military and social cooperation between the east and west. It also covers cooperation in the field of humanitarian issues and protecting the environment. Likewise, the Vienna and Copenhagen Conferences evaluated the progress made in human rights since 1948 and examined the link between development and the enjoyment of economic, social, cultural, civil and political rights. Its significance lies in the recognition of the interdependence between democracy, development and human rights. The African Human Rights System specifically recognizes the importance of collective rights. The African Charter on Human and People's Rights provides for the creation on African Commission on Human Rights. It organizes seminars, conferences and creates awareness on human rights. These International Human Rights Conferences cover wide ranging issues that include child welfare, advancement of women, support to marginalized groups and the protection of environment and human rights. The individual and the development of the society take the centre stage. In addition to the above endeavour, the International Commission of Jurists also plays a crucial role in the implementation of international law that advances human rights. The ICJ is an impartial and authoritative legal body that protects human rights through the rule of law. It provides legal assistance at national and international level. The sixty eminent jurists who are selected from all-over the world as its members represent various legal systems. It works closely with governments and NGOs. It also encourages the creation of ICJ's national section in any country. It assists the defenders of human rights with specialized training.

In the contemporary society, we come across the problems faced by different sections of the populations that include children, women, refugees, transgender, Dalits and persons with HIV/AIDS. Today we face the problem of terrorism and the human rights issues involved in capital punishment as well as the viewpoints of human rights activists on this sensitive issue. The issues related to environment are another area that includes both the developmental concern as well as the rights of millions of people. In these important issues, we come across a variety of violations. Especially in the developing countries of Asia and Africa, poverty and lack of awareness led to large scale exploitation. In countries like India, the period after independence witnessed the growth of a legal system as well as awareness on issues related to human rights. But due to the vast population size and the existence of medieval thinking and practices, progress achieved in the maintenance of human rights is limited. The exposure to mass media and other communication facilities sometimes encourage the affected people to ventilate their grievances in public domain. But human rights violations occur everywhere that mostly affect the marginalized groups.

Since the children are helpless in most cases, the UNO is taking all possible steps to protect their rights. The UN Convention on the rights of the child was acceded by the Government of India. It gives particular attention to civil, political, social, economic and cultural rights of every child. The exploitation of the child is a very common occurrence in almost all parts of the world. Needless to say in the developing countries they suffer much. In South Asia alone more than 90 million children are working as child labourers that prevents their education and future development. The government is passing several laws to protect them. Apathy of the officials in implementing these laws and lack of awareness limited the chances of eradication of this important problem. Since it is linked with poverty and family problem, the public is mostly unconcerned about the seriousness of the issue. The problem of the street children and child soldier are very pathetic and there is no guarantee for their survival.

Education is the surest way to tackle child labour and other related problems. The availability of free, compulsory and quality education is a key factor in the fight against the child labour. The recent efforts of government in making education as a fundamental right and giving compulsory, free education is a positive step. But how it is going to be implemented is another issue. In the past six decades, India considerably moved forward in the economic field. But the system of distribution is not able to serve the poorest of the poor. From the Nehruvian era of borrowing foodgrains we have moved to the level of producing surplus food stock that is rotting in the FCI godowns. But millions of people in several parts of India are unable to have a square meal per day. The irony is that the rotten foodgrains are sold for a meagre sum to the distilleries for producing liquor. The Supreme Court of India expressed its displeasure in this issue and directed the government to distribute the foodgrains free of cost to the poor. The government expressed its unwillingness on legal terms. The gap between production and distribution is a major concern in countries like India.

Like the children the women also face many problems that invariably affects their rights. All-over the world they experience discrimination in the male dominated societies. Their status and position is not uniform over the periods of history. The women who enjoyed almost equal status with that of men in the Vedic period found their position degenerated in the succeeding centuries. Though women are praised as Shakti she is treated like a commodity. Due to the secondary position given to women, the birth of male child is preferred and celebrated even among the educated, wealthy families. Female infanticide and female foeticide is practiced in rural as well as urban areas of India despite the existence of specific laws against such practice.

In 19th and 20th century several social reformers fought for their emancipation. In Tamil Nadu E.V.R. Periyar insisted on the need to give education to women folk. Dr. Muthulakshmi Reddy was instrumental in the abolition of Devadasi system. Independent India witnessed remarkable changes in relation to the advancement of women. The Hindu Code Bill was passed despite strong opposition from conservative Hindu communal organisations. Over the years, several progressive legislations replaced the age old belief system and practice. Today according to the law, women are entitled for equal share in the family property. But in practice they are not demanding it due to customary practice and sentiments. The Domestic Violence (Prevention) Act, 2005 gives special protection to women. In India, women in all the states are not equally enjoying the rights even though it is guaranteed under the Constitution. Recent studies at the national level suggest that Tamil Nadu has emerged as one of the safe states in terms of female security. The state also scored high on the well-being index as well. Unfortunately, it was not in the case of several well off states like Punjab, Haryana, Delhi and U.P.

In progressive states women took up education and employment as a surest mean to elevate their position. But studies suggest that despite education and employment in several states women continued to experience rights violations. In states like Kerala which is a model state in several respect women continued to feel the burden of age old practices that discriminate them. But they are steadily overcoming the hurdles and working for a better tomorrow. In the name of caste a variety of atrocities are committed on women in different parts of India. However, the women's organisations as well as a proactive judiciary is working in tandem in bringing relief to the women folk. The political participation of women at the grass roots level is giving them enormous confidence in tackling the problems of the local area that hampers inclusive growth. The difficulties in getting reservation for women at the legislature shows the impact of the male dominated societies mindset. The impact of cinema and tele-serials in projecting women in bad light and as an object of fun and frolic only encourages crimes against women. The producers have a moral responsibility but bad taste and male dominated social thinking in their psyche promote such works. The mass media must exhibit seriousness in handling issues affecting the welfare of women. As Justice Markandey Katju rightly pointed out that being in a transitional age our society is still largely male dominated and the women do not have real freedom. Spread of scientific thinking on a massive scale and awareness against superstitions and backward thinking is the need of the hour. We don't know when our nation will have the strength and determination to sweep away all remnants of the disgusting feudal and medieval practices and mentality in respect of women. Both men and women must work together for this collective goal.

In comparison to other countries, India has the notorious distinction of maintaining caste prejudices. In other countries it was race or colour that subjects people under rights violations. In India, the stratification of society on the basis of Manu Smriti degraded the lowest segments of the population. Even though these marginalized and ill-treated communities are referred in different names from region to region, today they preferred the terminology Dalits. Several leaders like Mahatma Phule, Gandhiji, and E.V.R. Periyar fought for the liberation of the untouchables. Dr. B.R. Ambedkar made it as a life mission to emancipate the millions of untouchables toiling under the rigid caste oriented social system. His untiring efforts granted them reservation in education and in employment. Ambedkar safeguarded the rights of the Dalits through Constitutional means and urged them to capture the power of law-making. Today the Dalits are emerging as a formidable force. No political party worth the name can ignore their vote bank and their issues. Leaders like Mayawati are demonstrating their political acumen and shrewdness. Considerable sections of these marginalized groups are experiencing the new found freedom and are emerging as potent content in the social ladder.

Reservation in education and employment helped them to come up in life in several states of India. As Justice Mandal has rightly pointed out, the pioneering work of leaders and social movements in states like Tamil Nadu keeps the backward and oppressed communities in forefront. But this benefit is not enjoyed by all those belong to the oppressed communities. They are able to educate their children in places where the social rigidity permits to move forward. Millions of Dalits, especially Dalit women needed all the help and support in liberating from the shackles of feudal social norms and customs. The bonded labour system traditionally keeps these communities in a very pitiable state from which they cannot easily escape. Despite the relative freedom enjoyed by this marginalized section in towns and urban areas, they are forced to live under a variety of rights violations and caste prejudices including the 'double tumbler' system. Periyar waged the Vaikom Satyagraha for the temple entry of untouchables during the British period. Six decades after independence there are places in Tamil Nadu where the Dalits are fighting for their right to enter the temple as well as using the road to burial grounds. Manual scavenging is another problem faced by this community in several parts of India. Despite the law banning this practice and the directives of the Supreme Court, this inhuman work is forced upon the Dalits. Unless we come out of this dehumanizing practice, there is no meaning in boasting about the possibility of India emerging as a superpower in the near future.

The Union and State Governments are taking several positive steps to alleviate the problems of the Dalits. Due to education and employment opportunities Dalits are relatively coming up in life after independence. Through organised efforts by their caste associations and political outfits the Dalits are trying to protect their community's interest. But where educational opportunities are not accessible due to variety of factors they toil like their forefathers. Lack of awareness on the importance of education is one another issue. The existing social customs and abject poverty keeps a large number of Dalit children away from schools. They ended up their life in debt bondage and the vicious circle suck their off-springs as well.

Regarding the Dalits who entered into the mainstream through education and employment opportunities are the one who realized the benefits of reservation. These benefits must seep through the community to reach the poorest of the poor Dalits cut off from the mainstream social life. In order to escape from social prejudices sometimes they even renounce their identity. It is observed that in some cases, the upward social mobility in terms of affluence and status associated with education and employment makes them to carve for new identities. There are cases where when they marry from other caste Hindu groups they tend to maintain the caste Hindu identities. It is not possible in a village or in a small town but in cities one can create a new identity after marriage. Even though one can understand the logic and pain behind such decisions, it would not solve the problems encountered by the community. Dr. B.R. Ambedkar is a role model for every Dalit who aspired to lead his community. Despite

Ambedkar's achievements in the academic and political career which a Dalit cannot imagine during the first half of 20th century, he maintained his Dalit identity to win over solid concessions for the community he belongs. Further, a Dalit who is fortunate enough to get the concessions guaranteed under Constitution that elevate his/her position must strive for the emancipation of fellow beings. They must think about their brethren toiling under poverty and ignorance. They have a moral responsibility to uplift the voiceless millions cut off from the path of development. They must act like a catalyst in broadening the social justice dreamed by leaders like B.R. Ambedkar through a process of empowerment. It is a complex process that involves careful analysis and concerted community effort through social support. Otherwise, like the backward class, a creamy layer would form that alone have more chances to enjoy the fruits of emancipation from caste hierarchy.

Exploitation of people for economic gain is an age-old problem and we have references about slavery and other types of bondage existed in history. Slavery is abolished in the modern period but great leaders like Abraham Lincoln has to wage a war for its eradication. But slavery existed in other indirect forms that include bonded labour. In developing countries, especially in India this flagrant violation of human rights exists. It kept millions of people in abject poverty and the family may never come out of debt bondage unless a strong outside support is provided. It exists in almost all parts of India and using the bonded labour system is embedded in the Indian psyche. The system involves indebteness and forced labour in which the worker may get only a poor wage that trap other members including children in the family into this vicious circle. It is observed that a small percentage of bonded labour exists due to customary social obligations.

The Indian Constitution prohibited bonded labour and the Bonded Labour (Abolition) Act failed to solve the problem since prosecution and conviction are rare. It is possibly due to the acceptance about the inevitability of its practice and apathy of officials. Data on the steps taken to eradicate this evil practice through legal action indicate the unwillingness or lack of concerted action on the part of state governments and its officials. Proper protection of sincere official is necessary due to the risks involved from ruthless owners of bonded labour. Child bonded labour represent the decay and malice in the society. Eradication of bonded labour system involves a very complex process in which the economic vulnerability of the poorest section should be addressed in addition to the improvement of their awareness to come out of bondage. Of course, it is not an easy task and education is the surest means to eliminate this system in the long run. Even though media reports highlights their flight the freed bonded labours enter again into bondage due to the non-availability of genuine rehabilitation packages. When the country advances in other fields, equal attention should be paid to eradicate this social evil through the cooperation of all stakeholders. Proper prosecution and conviction of those who encourage this evil exploitation is the need of the hour.

The problems of transgender community are neglected for a long period and the society refused to accept them as a part of its own. The emergence of this sexual minority community is embedded in the historical past. They are denied many basic rights and there is no separate enumeration to count their actual size. Due to their vulnerable position and lack of proper identity they have to struggle to keep the spirit of body and mind. Till recently they were not entertained in public places due to the general image that they will create nuisance to the public. In parts of India, especially in places like Mumbai, their blessings is regarded as essential during the birth of children and some social ceremonies. But by and large they have depended on sex work for sustenance. It is heartening that in certain states like Tamil Nadu several welfare measures are taken in recent times to address their pressing problems. A separate welfare board is created and facilities are made for their regular education. They also have responsibility to utilize the support of the government to make their life respectable through normal work and earning. The society must look at them with concern and extend help if they genuinely wish to earn through hard work like others. Other state governments can also follow the welfare programmes initiated by government of Tamil Nadu in this regard. Through self-help groups they are organizing some economic activities that need encouragement. Such steps would create a positive image on the third gender population. Unfortunately, the third gender population is not taking education as a means to come out of its difficulties. They must ponder over the changing scenario and effectively utilize the opportunities open to them.

Another important area that involves human rights violations is the refugee issue. The problem of refugee is not new but references are available on this issue from early history. Ethnic and religious issues, war and other problems force millions of people to migrate to unknown places for survival. When their government is not interested in protecting them they have no other choice except flee their mother land. Under Nazi Germany, the Jewish people fled to other country to protect them from sure death. In India, partisan led to communal violence and large scale migration of refugee started. The Tibetan Lamas, people from Burma and Bangladesh besides the Tamil refugees from Sri Lanka seek asylum. In South Asia and in Africa the refugees are constantly searching for a safe place to survive. Their problem is particularly pathetic since in most cases they don't have any documentary proof of their citizenship due to the compelling circumstances under which they escape. All-over the world millions of refugees are suffering due to the lack of basic amenities including a square meal per day.

The League of Nations and the UNO did considerable rehabilitation work to ameliorate the problems of the refugees. The UDHR stresses the refugees' right to asylum and the refugees have right to international protection. It is roughly estimated that millions of people live outside the country of their birth as refugees. It shows the enormity of the refugee's problem. Even though the UN High Commission for Refugees is assisting the refugees in all possible way it is not sufficient to meet all their basic demands. Today due to civil wars between different militant groups and the governments large number of people are forced to flee. Lack of concern for fellow beings, greed for natural resources and hatred towards other religious ethnic groups aggravate refugee's issue. The UN which is doing a commendable job is facing financial constraint and the politics of big powers. Only compassion and kindness from fellow human beings can help them from the wretched life they are living. Unfortunately, in international politics aid and assistance are mostly linked with the politics of power. Sectarian violence brings hatred and put helpless people in a miserable condition. One can only pray that better sense will prevail over hatred and vengeance.

One of the most dangerous problems faced by humanity today is terrorism. It became a popular terminology in the 20th century. Terrorism is a very complex problem that eludes proper solution due to the availability of difficult choices. No civil society is insulated against its horrors and every act of terrorism is a violation of human rights. Whatever may be the justness of the cause espoused by the terrorist, there is no justification for the act of violence. While terrorism affects the rights of common man who was the victim of violence, the counter terrorism measures of the law enforcing agencies victimizes often the innocent people. Our question in this context is whether even government has the right to violate human rights flagrantly while taking punitive action for a terrorist attack. Is it possible to tackle terrorism within the existing national and international legal framework?

The past experience of bringing draconian anti-terrorism legislation has failed to contain terrorism. Rather its misuse by the law enforcing agencies and their political masters only aggravated the situation. From Manipur to Kashmir, a large number of cases involving the victimization of innocent people earned the wrath of the people. Women in Imphal went to the extent of barring their bodies in protest against the army for the misuse of the Act. Irom Sharmila, a young girl became a symbol of protest against the misuse of the Act. She is fasting for the past ten years and force fed through her nose and still she is determined to carry out the Satyagraha type protest against the counter-insurgency measures that affects innocent people. A large number of fake encounter cases and communal violence directed against the minorities will only add fuel to fire. As Julius Ribeiro rightly pointed out that unless the people themselves decided against terrorism it is very difficult to stop its occurrence. The counter-terrorism measures carried out in a shoddy manner discredits the state machinery and its credibility. Protection of minorities, vulnerable groups and women from this type of violence is a necessity in a composite culture like India.

The existing national and international legal framework is sufficient to handle the terrorist issues as demonstrated by the successful prosecution of several cases. There is no short cut to the overall happiness and peaceful atmosphere in a democracy. The law enforcing agencies which are working under a trying circumstance must understand the value of human rights while executing their duties. Media exposure and popular participation of civil right groups create an awareness that hampers knee jerk reaction from the police force. Experience from western countries indicates how such positive pressure works on the behaviour of police men in respecting the rights of others. Judiciary is playing a proactive role in protecting the rights of the individual affected in counter-insurgency measures as well as in terrorism related issues.

When mankind started an organised way of life, he has to regulate the behaviour of individual in relation to the society. Hence, punishment for crime emerged as a deterrent to control the society for its collective good. Capital punishment was given even for ordinary crimes during the early period. As civilization advanced, the attitude towards the quantum of punishment also changed. However, for major crimes the capital punishment is used as a norm to safeguard the society. In the 20th century, human rights activists insisted the need for more humane legal approach in this issue. Following the creation of UNO, the perception of capital punishment also underwent considerable change. Nearly 138 countries have either abolished or stopped the practice of awarding death penalty. In 30 countries this punishment is retained but has not been used at least for a decade. In 68 countries the death penalty is retained and used. In countries like China which carried out 90 per cent of executions happening at the global level, even cases of corruption led to death penalty. In USA and in Singapore capital punishment is executed regularly. In India, the past two decades marked the decline in the cases of execution. It is partly due to the delay in deciding the mercy petitions by the Presidents of India. In a Parliamentary democracy the power of President is limited on deciding the mercy petitions. However, they have played a significant role by delaying the decision for long time. Today, there is a strong debate going on the desirability to continue the capital punishment. Those who argue against it pointed out that mostly the poor who cannot defend themselves properly in the court get death sentence. Racial bias, political influence, public pressure and media attention at times may tinker with the decisions related to capital punishment. The history of capital punishment indicates how it was abused as a tool of oppression over the progress of humanity. Its abolition or usage for only most serious crime is definitely a progressive step in the onward march of civilization. The rarity with which the capital punishment is awarded indicates how the legal system gives importance to the right to life and its values. But there are situation that warrants this stringent punishment even though it is an unfortunate option to preserve justice and social order. When we create a social order and a system that nurtures compassion for fellow beings, the chances for capital crime may decline.

The problems related to environment are very serious as it threatens the very survival of humanity. The exploitation of natural resources beyond the sustainable level creates a very dangerous situation. The destruction of forest and other natural wealth due to growing population and greediness gradually impacted upon the environment. Unless a collective action is taken at the global level far-reaching consequences awaits humanity. Depletion of ozone layer, melting of glaciers and vast sheets of ice in the Antarctic, sudden change of climate, effect of El Nino, dwindling agricultural production, raising temperature levels and the perishing of flora and fauna in their traditional habitats are indicators of deteriorating environment. Protection of environment involves the future of humanity and it is an important human right related to the right to life. Especially, the third generation of human rights is focusing its attention on issues like environment and sustainable development.

All-over the world, there are serious warnings given by nature that mankind is destroying the environment. Unless it is halted, the near future is very bleak. Globalization and the resultant economic activities unleashed several complications that challenge the environment. Commercialization of drinking water is one of a major threat to the poor that may result in serious water shortage. Mining of minerals and sand in several states including Tamil Nadu reduced the water table to a critical level. Disposal of industrial waste by exporting them to other developing countries creates new complications. Despite a ban on the export of waste in some European countries the illegal shipment continues.

When globalization process sets in, the greed for natural resources increased manifold in India. Deforestation and mining have made several hilly towns bare. The Adivasis and the tribal communities living in the forest area are facing the existential threat. Construction of mega dams destroys their traditional habitat and the flora and fauna. The development plan which is not sustainable may not serve the purpose. While multinational companies are making quick money through the exploitation of natural resources beyond a sustainable level its effect is felt. But there are real leaders like Sundarlal Bahuguna and Medha Patkar who fight for the rights of the poorest of the poor.

The Indian Government is passing several path breaking laws on wildlife, forest and pollution. Especially, the Bhopal gas leak tragedy and its impact are felt in the corridors of power. The present Minister of Environment Jayaram Ramesh is very active in the issues related to environment. Despite pressure from MNCs like POSCO and Vedanta he denied permission to mining that threatens environment and the livelihood options of the marginalized sections of the society. But the national environment policy announced in 2006 justifies economic considerations rather than environmental concerns. However, due to continue efforts by civil society programmes and the media several positive laws were passed. Despite limitations a radical ecological democracy is entirely possible where all citizens having opportunity to participate in the decision-making process that affects their livelihood issues. The Supreme Court also embarks on environmental activism in recent years. It expanded the right to life and personal liberty to include environmental protection. There is a clash of interest between the developing and developed countries over sharing the cost of environmental protection. Any collective efforts to protect environment from further degradation will naturally protect the human rights of millions of people.

During the 1980s, the mankind came to know on the existence of HIV/AIDS. Since there is no medicine available to cure it, the infected persons are ill-treated with contempt. Since it spreads mostly through sexual contact stigma is attached to the infected person. The spread of HIV/AIDS creates an alarming situation in which the affected persons and their family experience variety of human right violations. Mostly they are ostracized by the society and even by their kith and kin. In several cases family rejection, public contempt, lack of awareness on the disease and guilt conscience led to suicides. The affected persons experience ill-treatment at the place of work and some of them were dismissed from service. While fighting an unknown disease, the above developments complicated the living option of the patients.

It is generally accepted that human rights is central to any nation's effective response to HIV/AIDS. Every individual has the right to live with freedom and dignity. The fellow citizens are duty bound to respect, protect and address this fundamental need. Human rights is not given by a society or government but are earned by the virtue of being born human. Needless to say, the dignity is the entitlement of all human beings as long as life exists. Since the HIV/AIDS involves questions related to honour and dignity of individuals, the protection of human rights is essential. The society must ensure an effective, rights based approach to this dreaded disease. Addressing the epidemic within a human rights framework involves the acceptance and non-discrimination of populations vulnerable to HIV/AIDS. In developed countries like USA, the incident of HIV/AIDS indicates that its spread is halted considerably. The HAART treatment significantly reduced the spread of HIV in addition to the awareness level in developed countries. In several developing countries such treatment is not given free of cost. In countries like India several NGOs and the government is taking some positive step to treat the affected persons. The children affected by this dreaded condition are given medicine and scholarship to continue their studies. In comparison to the 1980s, the awareness on HIV/AIDS is increasing. Hence, there is a change of attitude noticeable at the societal level. The awareness that the HIV/AIDS is not killing people in few years and there are medicines available to prolong the life for some more years increased the hope of affected persons.

In countries like Brazil free and subsidized HAART treatment is given. Besides, the patients are given opportunities to counselling on proper treatment and prevention of its spread further. Some developed countries are pressing the developing countries against any attempt to manufacture the cheap generic alternative to the patented drugs. It will increase the cost of treatment and hamper the fight against HIV/AIDS. The medical needs of sex workers who are badly affected by this dreaded epidemic can be met in a non-discriminatory manner. The free availability of condoms and awareness on its proper use to prevent the spread of HIV is a necessary step in developing countries like India. Providing free treatment for the marginalized groups and the availability of drugs at affordable cost are other important steps to mitigate the sufferings of HIV positive persons. At least from the High School level lessons on HIV/AIDS can be incorporated to increase awareness from the early stage of adulthood.

In India the development of human rights concept shows a varying trend in which the rights enjoyed by all sections of the people changes due to other factors. The people of Indus valley civilization naturally enjoyed freedom since the society was not stratified and the women enjoyed all the rights like men. Over the millennia the socio, political and economic changes had its impact on the human rights concept. Great souls like Buddha, Mahavira and Asoka deeply influenced the early Indian thought on human rights and just society. During foreign invasion and occupation the people experienced the deterioration of their rights. However, Emperor Akbar's benevolence and grace fortified human rights during the medieval face of Indian history. The compassion and grace of Sufi saints, the thought process of Kabir, Ramanujam and Thirumullar enhanced the value of individual and his worth. They preach the oneness of God and mankind and highlighted the need for compassion towards fellow beings.

The entry of British and the introduction of western system of education led to the awakening of Indian reformers and leaders. Saint Ramalingam preaches compassion and kindness towards all living organisms including plants. The denial of basic rights under the British intensified the freedom struggle. Mahatma Gandhi demanded rights and self-respect for the people of India. His novel idea of Satyagraha and honest way of fighting the national enemy enhanced the thought process of the masses. The Motilal Nehru report incorporated fundamental rights as a right to the people of India. The Indian Constitution included it and elaborated the list further.

India made it clear that the observance of human rights and democracy are two inseparable elements. Under internal emergency, there was a threat to the basic freedom enjoyed by the people of India. But people proved that the democracy and freedom should prevail over any authoritarian tendency. Despite this brief interlude democratic institutions functioned freely that guarantees the enjoyment of basic freedom. Since independence several efforts were taken to strengthen democracy and the institutions like the national and state commissions on human rights enhanced this process. Despite limitations and practical problems these institutions instil hope for the common man that they can get justice from the system. Acts like the Rights to Information Act facilitated the power of individual against corruption and other malice of society. Even though the whistle blowers are targeted people continue to assert their freedom and dignity. Being the largest dynamic democracy India proved that only under a democratic republic the people can enjoy the real benefits of human rights in modern world.

Since independence, the democratic India marched onward and enhanced the living condition of millions of the people. Great leaders like Nehru under trying circumstances laid the foundations for a prosperous India that would accommodate the aspiration and hopes of the common man. Despite the threat of divisive forces India pulled through enormous obstacles on its path to development and real freedom. It is fortunate that we have leaders like Nehru and Patel who have grand vision for an India that would claim its rightful place among the comity of nations. Only when men are liberated from the fear of hunger he can think about other rights and convenience. The leaders did their level best to assure that they have the opportunity to ward of any threat to the enjoyment of basic freedom. The onset of modern education and the inculcation of science and technological temper enhanced the capability of common man. As Gunar Myrdal observed in his Asian Drama, India slowly wriggled out of the feudal, medieval mindset and practices. It was a very painful process that threatened at times the very foundations of the nation.

The country passed through various phases experiencing ups and downs in its sojourn. Weakening of one party system led to the emergence of variety of forces that includes religious fundamentalism. Demolition of Babri Masjid was a black day for the secularistic credentials nurtured over the centuries and by great leaders. The pogroms at times conducted against the Sikh, Christian and Muslim minorities sullied the image of India. Despite centuries of understanding and the policy of live and let live these aberrations created a fear and a sense of insecurity in the minds of the minorities. A sense of fear is not a healthy sign for a vibrant democracy that protects and respects the rights of every individual. Politics based on vote bank and the naked desire for power is eating into the vitals of values nurtured over centuries.

After globalization, the emergence of commercialization and consumerist culture has profound influence on the core value. In addition to prosperity and development in number of basic sectors, the county's image enhanced considerably that the US President, Barack Obama, commented that India is not a developing country but already a developed nation. The market economy also led to the infusion of huge sums of money into the vast markets and on number of developmental projects. One cannot forget under what trying circumstances the nation is forced to adopt the market economy. Globalisation and market economy are forces that we cannot ignore. However, one cannot gloss over the difficulties and survival possibilities of the millions of the marginalized sections that gained nothing substantially in the transformation to market economy. Inclusive growth and sustainable development cannot be ignored in the desire to acquire wealth and status for a few sections of the society.

In the corresponding period after the onset of market economy, nearly two lakh farmers committed suicide that devastated the agricultural sector. Unfortunately, the media and the government failed to focus on this vital segment that provides food and employment opportunity to millions of unorganized, unlettered poor people. While changing from medieval to modernity we need not sacrifice the agricultural sector. Ways and means should be incorporated to find a balance between agriculture and industrialization. Food security emanating from our own source is strength and we cannot rely upon imported foodgrains with world's second largest population. The gains of green revolution should be remembered in providing food to millions of hungry mouth. Life free from hunger is an important fundamental right that must be respected.

The globalization process also facilitated the arrival of huge foreign resources to built mega projects in various sectors. Those in the helm of affairs never have such an opportunity to spend money in millions for every project. It also provided scope for corruption at all levels. Today one of the greatest threats to democracy and human rights is the institutionalization of corruption. Over the years, it slowly affects the practice of separation of powers. Our forefathers wisely divided the pillars of state power with checks and balances. Today there are incidents that strengthened the viewpoint that the administrative personel have close nexus with the legislators and criminals. This lethal combination can wreck any shield that protects democratic elements and human rights. The judiciary and media is the last resort for the civil rights group and the common man from the vested interests.

Judiciary is playing a proactive role in the recent years in upholding the values of democracy and human rights. Unfortunately, the malice of corruption had its impact in this segment too. While considerable number of learned judges and officials manning judiciary are doing a remarkable job of protecting the values enshrined in the Constitution, at least a part of the judiciary from bottom to top appears to be tainted. *The Hindu* dated November 11, 2010 reported on the former Union Law Minister, Shanti Bhushan and his son Prasanth Bhushan's open declaration that judiciary is corrupted at the highest level and their refusal to tender an apology on contempt charges. Already a removal proceeding was initiated in the case of V. Ramasamy, former Chief Justice of the Punjab and Haryana High Court who later became a Supreme Court Judge. Even though the motion for his removal failed, it created widespread apprehension. The indictment of Justice Soumitra Sen of the Kolkata High Court by the three member committee headed by Justice B. Sudershan Reddy, under Article 124 (4) read with Article 217 (1)(b) of the Constitution, paved the way for Parliament to take up the motion for his removal, as he was found guilty of collecting Rs. 33,22,800 from a purchaser of goods.

The former Chief Justice of India, S.P. Bharucha has commented that 80 per cent of the judges are honest and Justice V.R. Krishna Iyer also expressed his concern over corruption in judiciary. Since judiciary is the last pillar of hope for the common man, ways and means should be found to regulate judiciary from this negative trend. However, we come across a large number of honest, straight- forward and socially committed judges who uphold the values of judiciary. The Allahabad High Court judgment on Prime Minister, Indira Gandhi's electoral victory is a case in this point. There are number of trend setting verdicts passed by Justice B.N. Bhagwati, V.R. Krishna Iyer and other judges to uphold the value of human rights. Judiciary is playing a proactive role in the protection of human rights and on livelihood issues including environment.

Likewise, the press is also an important source of support for the people to fight against any arbitrary attempt on plucking their rights. The Indian press is known for its fearless presentation of facts during some of the critical years after independence. However, Pranjoy Guha Thakurta, an independent journalist and member of the Press Council of India pointed out that corruption in the mass media is as old as the media itself. To him, if there is corruption in the society it would be unrealistic to expect the media to be free from it. For the favours received in cash or kind the Indian media is planting informations disguised as 'news' to favour a particular individual, corporate entities, representative of political parties etc. In a seminar on "Abridging Freedom and Fairness of the Media: Combating Challenges" organised by the Rajasthan Working Journalists' Union, Editors and journalists were worried over the paid news syndrome which was exposed during the Assembly Elections of Maharashtra in 2009. P. Sainath, Rural affairs editor, *The Hindu* pointed out that "either we finish paid news, or paid news finishes us" and regretted that the main stream media give very little coverage to the suicide of 2 lakh farmers in Maharashtra, Karnataka, Andhra Pradesh, Madhya Pradesh and Chhattisgarh between 1997 and 2008. It is observed that there are attempts on the freedom of expression. The exploitation of media by vested interest and the extremist groups silencing the voice of criticism are other areas of serious concern. Pure commercial interest dilutes the focus of some media organisations. It is a regrettable development that worked against the ethics of journalism. The ever vigilant media and judiciary are the real watch dogs on the rights of the people and democracy.

The law enforcing agencies in India are working under trying circumstances. As the society advances the state is playing an all encompassing role. Development of science and technology led to variety of new crimes and terrorist strike that are hard to resolve. Communal animosity and increase in crime rate makes the position of policing vulnerable to criticism. The number of police personnel in relation to the vast population is inadequate. The weapon systems are rather outdated to match the sophistication of the lawbreakers. Their service conditions are far from satisfactory. Despite these limitations they are working round the clock to maintain law and order. But the politician, criminal and police nexus visible in the recent decades violates human rights flagrantly. Apart from individual rights violations like custodial killing and rape involving the law enforcing agencies, the role of army and police in communal violence is deplorable. The encounter killings involving minority communities only sullied the image of police force. Despite the dedicated service of large number of personnel in the law enforcing agencies, the violations committed by a section of these forces brought it under criticism.

What is the remedy to improve the human rights record of the law enforcing agencies? Even the senior police officials are sceptical on this front. However, forging partnership between people and police can improve the situation. All-over the world community policing is attempted in which the public is assisting the police in several ways which reduced riots and crimes considerably. It was attempted recently in 43 police station limits in Kerala as Janamaithri Suraksha following recommendations of Justice K.T. Thomas Commission on Kerala Police Performance and Accountability. The project was wholeheartedly accepted by the people of Kerala and all the MLAs have requested for its implementation in their constituencies. Despite its limitations such projects can be implemented in other parts of India as well. Awareness of the public, the proper use of RTI Act, and the support of civil rights group can also be incorporated to counter any move that affects human rights. Naturally, the media and judiciary have an important role to play in curtailing extra judicial killings and other rights violations. The important court rulings on the failure of law enforcing agencies and the conviction given to the erring police officials should be circulated or incorporated as a part of study material during the course of police training. Giving the essence of human rights theory and its practical operation in modern democracies can also be the part of syllabus for the trainees in law enforcing agencies.

Appendix I
Redressal Mechanism for the Protection of Human Rights

There are varieties of ways in which an individual or a group of people can protect their rights in India. Even though there is a redressal mechanism available, people are unaware of it. Lack of awareness and the hesitation to approach proper agency for the redressal of their grievance related to human rights is a common occurrence. Not only the marginalized people and the disadvantaged sections of the society is facing these sorts of problem, but even the educated people have no idea about the steps to be taken to redress grievances on human rights violations.

Public Interest Litigation: (PIL)

The PIL can be broadly defined to mean proceedings initiated in a court of law that related to an issue that affects the interest of the public. In recent years, the Public Interest Litigation lead to judicial activation that ultimately brings social justice to the disadvantaged sections of the society. It also encourages a system of participatory justice. The matters like environment, pollution and other social issues cannot be viewed as private wrongs restricted to the individuals involved. Earlier if a person approaches a court he/she should have suffered some personal injury or have been deprived of his/her legal rights. It restricted the availability of judicial machinery to a majority of people. In reality, the PIL prevents the government from acting in an arbitrary and autocratic manner.

One can approach the court with PIL whenever human rights violation are committed by the state authorities on an individual or a group of people as a collective. Whenever interest of women, poor and disadvantaged groups are affected, and the environment is threatened through pollution or other means anyone can approach the court. In addition to the above grounds, whenever the right to life and livelihood is threatened and the right to live in dignity and security is in danger, where neglect of responsibility and misappropriation is deducted, one can use the PIL. Besides, whenever social issues affecting large section of people in society and custodial injustice are observed, the concerned state and private parties can bring to accountability by this instrument. Normally, in the PIL the court takes up the cases not related to a particular petitioner's rights—but public at large into consideration. It is an instrument in the hands of people to effectively push the executive to do something or preventing it from doing something against the welfare of the people. Regarding India's experience with PIL shows that the Supreme Court contributed much for its reasonable use. On several PIL cases, the Supreme Court stressed that the liberty cannot be taken away except by due process of law and unequals cannot be treated equally to strike down arbitrary and unreasonable state action. The Supreme Court also declared that the right to life means right to livelihood and live in dignity, with safe environment enjoying the welfare measures that include the right to education. One must understand that anybody can bring Public Interest Litigation to the court's notice for action that may include issues of migrant workers, bonded labour, children, protection of water resources, and issues involving the construction of big dams. Likewise, issues related to the conditions in custodial institutions, right to education and issues of pollution and environment, the Public Interest Litigation has succeeded in several landmark cases that bring lot of hope to the common man. Today, the PIL is used to frame schemes, to give directions, monitoring and seeking reports on specific issues.

While using PIL as weapon to get justice, an informed decision is to be made regarding the issue at stake. It is prudent to consult all affected parties as well as the interested groups besides involving the experts for their advice. Collection of all relevant informations and photographs may be used. All the data and records should be kept in an organised manner. Engaging a competent lawyer is a necessity unless the person himself is capable of proper drafting. Since only a registered organisation can file a PIL, a person can file it in his personal capacity. A PIL can be filed in any of the following courts whether dealing with civil, criminal, constitutional and consumer issues. One must remember that the PIL should be used wisely. In certain cases, the court punishes those who seek this relief for trivial matters. Since the courts are handling variety of complex issues in today's context one must be very careful about the kind of issues taken to the court. Needless to say, that the process of litigation is expensive and time consuming in nature.

Other Methods of Redressal

One important step in the redressal mechanism is approaching the National Human Rights Commission by the victims or affected person. They can directly register their complaints or through some informed sources. The complaint may be written in English, Hindi or anyone of the languages included in the 8th Schedule of the Indian Constitution. The complaint may send through post or courier. Otherwise, it can be sent by fax to the number 91-11-23384863/ 23386521. Through e-mail the complaint may be send to *nhrc@ren.nic.in* for further action. The complaints may be on the violation of human rights by individuals, or group or even on an official who failed to do his duty that led to rights violations. Normally, the violations occurred within a year's period can be represented to the Human Rights Commission. The petition is completed with all the relevant details on the affected person's name, age, sex, caste, religion and the informations related to the date of occurrence and place of occurrence of rights violation. A fixed format is available through which the complaint can be forwarded. Normally, the complaints lacking clarity, lacking key informations like the affected party's name or cases under enquiry in the State Human Rights Commission are not normally entertained. If it is civil dispute related to property or agreement or related to service matter or cases already settled through the Commission or a court of law it would not be considered. For the petitions no charge is levied by the Commission.

Appendix II

Format for Complaint to the National Human Rights Commission

(a) Details of the complainant
   1. Name 2. Sex: Male/Female/Transgender
   3. State 4. Full Address
   5. District 6. Pincode

(b) Details of the incident
   1. Place of occurrence (Village/Town/City)
   2. State
   3. District
   4. Date of occurrence

(c) Details of affected person
   1. Affected person's name 2. Number of affected persons
   3. State 4. Full Address
   5. District 6. Pincode
   7. Religion 8. Caste (ST/SC/OBC/General)
   9. Sex: Male/Female/Transgender
   10. Age
   11. Whether Physically Challenged?

(d) Truth related to Human Rights/a brief report of the complaint.

(e) Security/Military personnel related complaint? Yes/No

(f) Whether this complaint was registered in a court of law or in the State Human Rights Commission earlier?

(g) Name, designation and address of the government servant against whom this complaint is lodged.

(h) Name, designation and address of the officials to whom the government servant is responsible to answer.

(i) Request/relief necessary.

Other Necessary Steps

The victims of human right must carefully preserve the evidence pertaining to the violation. In case if they are physically violated, they must approach the government hospital at the earliest, with sufficient witness and request the medical officer to examine them. They can also approach the police and make the complaint. If the crime is serious in nature, they have every right to demand the registration of the case and First Information Report (FIR). If the police officials are reluctant to register the case they can approach the higher officials, including the District Collector for redressal. Depending upon the nature of the crime, the support of the media and activists group can also be included to focus the violation to exert pressure. If the victims or the affected persons are illiterate or afraid to approach the law enforcing agencies, they can seek the support of several genuine human rights organisations available in each and every district. If women and children are affected they can approach the helpline numbers given in every place. Women can approach NGO organisations working for their welfare. A sustained campaign that includes petitioning, media exposure, dharna and fasting techniques would elicit required pressure on the police as well as on the culprit to respond. The matter can be taken up for representation in the legislature if the crime is serious and also affects a large number of people or a particular disadvantaged group or minority community. Sometimes, the political parties, especially the opposition may also show interest in pressurizing the government to take suitable action.

The following list of contact details can be used by the victims to represent their case.

CONTACT ADDRESS

National Human Rights Institutions

National Human Rights Commission
Faridkot House, Copernicus Marg,
New Delhi-110001,
Ph: 011-23382747
Fax No: 011-23384863 (Admn.)
23386521 (Law)
For Complaints-filling/status, General queires
MADAD: 91-11-23385368
Mobile: +919810298900
E-mail: nhrc@ren.nic.in
Website: *www.nhrc.nic.in*

National SC Commission

National SC Commission,
5th Block, 11th Floor, Lok Nayak Bhavan,

New Delhi-110 003.
Ph: No: 011-4620969
Fax No: 011-4625378

National Commission for Minorities

5th Floor, Lok Nayak Bhavan,
Khan Market, New Delhi-110 003
Fax: 011-24693302, 24642645, 24698410
Website: *www.ncm.nic.in*

National Commission for Women

4, Deen Dayal Upadhyaya Marg,
New Delhi-110 002.
Ph: 91-11-23237166, 91-11-23236988
Fax: 91-11-23236154
Complaints Cell: 91-11-23219750
E-mail: *ncw@nic.in*
Website: *www.ncw.nic.in*

National ST Commission

The Director, National Commission for Scheduled Tribes,
91, Satya Nagar,
Bhubaneshwar-751 007,
Orissa State.

State Human Rights Institutions

Andhra Pradesh

The Chairperson
"Gruhakalpa", M.J. Road,
Hyderabad-500 001
E-mail: *aphumanrights@ap.nic.in*
Tele (o): 24601571
Fax: 24601573

Assam

The Chairperson
H.O. Building, Bhangagarh,
Guwahati-781005
STD: 0361, Fax: 2529450/2527076,
Email: *hrca@sancharnet.in.*

Chhattisgarh

The Chairperson
Near Mantralaya, Raipur-492001
STD: 0771, Fax: 2235590.
E-mail: *cghrcryp@sify.com.*

Himachal Pradesh

The Chairperson
Pines Grove Building,
Shimla-171002.
STD: 0177, Fax: 224908

Jammu and Kashmir

The Chairperson
Dawn building,
Dalgate, Srinagar-119 001
STD: 0194, Fax: 454046,
Tele (o) 2481802, 2454046
Fax: 2454046

Kerala

The Chairperson
M.P. Appan Road, Vazhuthacaud,
Thiruvananthapuram-695 014
Tele (o) 0471-2337145
Fax: 0471-2337148
E-mail: *Kshrctvpm@vsnl.net.*

Madhya Pradesh

The Chairperson
Paryavas Bhawan, Arera Hills,
Jail Road, Bhopal-462 001
STD: 0755, Tele (o): 2764505,
Fax: 574028
E-mail: *mphrc@sancharnet.in*

Manipur

The Chairperson
Courts Complex, Lamphel,
Imphal-795 004
STD: 0385, Fax: 2410472,

E-mail: *mhrc@man.nic.in*

Maharashtra

The Chairperson
9, Hajarimal Somani Marg,
Near CST Railway Station,
Mumbai-400 001
Fax: 022-2885858, 22091804
Tele (o): 22071155/22073434

Orissa

The Chairperson
Orissa State Guest House,
Room Nos. 1, 2, 3, 4, Ground Floor,
Bhubaneshwar, Orissa.
Tele(o): 0674-23611334
Fax: 0674-2405094

Punjab

The Chairperson
SCO No. 20-21-22,
Sector 34A, Chandigarh,
Tele (o) 0172-2608520
Fax: 0172-2608520

Rajasthan

The Chairprson
State Secretariat, Jaipur,
Tele(o): 0141-2227868
Fax: 2227738
E-mail: *rshrc@raj.nic.in*

Tamil Nadu

The Chairpeason,
Thiruvarangam Haligai,
143, P.S. Kumarasamy Raja Salai,
Greenways Road,
Chennai-600028.

Uttar Pradesh

The Chairperson,

1/183, Vineet Khand, Gomati Nagar,
Lucknow-226010
Tele (o) 0522-2726742
Fax: 0522-2726743
E-mail: *uphrc@sancharnet.net.*

West Bengal

Shri Justice Mukul Gopal Mukherji
Bhabani Bhavan, Alipore, Kolkata-700027
Tele (o): 033-24797259
Fax: 033-24799633
E-mail: *wbhrc@cal3.vsnl.net.in.*

(3) EU-FNST-PWTN National Project on Prevention of Torture

Project National Office

No. 23, West Park Road,
Shenoy Nagar, Chennai-30.
Phone: +91-44-55252301
E-mail: *Chennai@pwtn.org*

Office of the National Director

People's Watch—Tamil Nadu
No. 6, Vallabai Road, Madurai,
Tamil Nadu-625 002
Tel: 91-452-2539520, 2531874
Fax: 91-452-2531874
E-mail: *info@pwtn.org*

STATE OFFICES

Andhra Pradesh

Door No: 8-3-988/10/10, SBH Colony,
Srinagar Colony, Hyderabad-73.
Andhra Pradesh
Phone No. 23736095
E-mail: *ap@pwtn.org*

Karnataka

C/o SICHREM, No. 35, Ground floor
Anjanappa Complex, Lingarajapuram,
Hennur Mail Road,

St. Thomas (town post),
Bangalore-560084, Karnataka.
E-mail: *Karnataka@pwtn.org*

Kerala

No. 11, Subash Nagar, Vallakkadavoo (p.o)
Triuvandrum, Kerala
E-mail: *Kerala@pwtn.org*

Orissa

294-A ground floor, Sahid Nagar,
Bhubaneshwar-07, Orissa.
Email: *Orissa@pwtn.org*

Rajasthan

Sameeksha, Near Pavansuth colony,
Mirshali, Opp. T.T. College,
Ajmer, Rajasthan-305001
E-mail: *rajasthan@pwtn.org*

Uttar Pradesh

S-2/335 D, Green Palace,
Bhojubir, Varanasi,
Uttar Pradesh.
E-mail: *up@pwtn.org.*

West Bengal

C/o MASUM, 26, Guitendal Lane,
Howrah-71101, West Bengal,
E-mail: *westbengal@pwtn.org*

Bibilography

Reports and Public Documents

Amnesty International. *Universal Jurisdiction: Improving the effectiveness of state cooperation*. AI Index: IOR 53/006/2007 June 2007, 1 July 2008.

Amnesty International. *Universal Jurisdiction: The Challenges for police and prosecuting authorities*. AI Index: IOR 53/007/2007 June 2007, 1 July 2008.

Ginkel, Hans Van, and Ramesh Thakur. "International Perspective on Global Terrorism." *U.N. Chronicle* (Online Edition) xxxviii: 3 2001.

Human Rights Advocacy and Research Foundation. *Basic Course on Human Rights Education for Teachers of Post Graduate Departments.* Chennai: Human Rights Advocacy and Research Foundation, 2003.

Human Rights Watch. *The Small Hands of Slavery: Bonded Child Labour in India.* New York: Human Rights Watch, 1997.

National project on presenting Torture in India. *Hand Book on Torture.* (Tamil) Madurai: National Project on Preventing Torture in India, ny.

Scheffer, Japp de Hopp. Minister of Foreign Affairs of the Kingdom of Netherlands and Chairman-in-Office of OSCE. "Human Rights and Terrorism." The Hague, September 18, 2003.

The White House Office of the Press Secretary. *Bush outlines U.S. Strategy against Terrorism*. October 28, 2005.

UNICEF. *Focus on Child Labour: The State of the World's Children 1997.* New York: Oxford University Press, 1977.

United Nations Department of Public Information. The International Bill of Human Rights. New York: U.N. Department of Public Information, 1993.

United Nations General Assembly. (Forty-ninth Session), Agenda item 100 (b). Resolution adopted on the report of the Third Committee (A/49/610/ Add. 2), 49/185 on Human Rights and Terrorism. 6th March, 1995.

U.N. Department of Public Information. *Human Rights: Children's Rights.* New York:

U.N. Department of Public Information, 1996.

United Nations General Assembly. (Fifty-seventh Session) Agenda item 109 (b) Resolution adopted on the report of the Third Committee. (A/ 57/556/Add. 2 and Corr.1-3), 57/219, on the Protection of Human Rights and fundamental freedoms while countering terrorism. 27th February, 2003.

United Nations Development Programme: Human Development Report 2006—*Beyond Security: Power, Poverty and the Global Water Crisis* (New York: UNDP, 2006).

Books

Adhidary, M.M., Acharya, S.K. and Ali, S.K. Musiar. *Empowerment and Entitlement of Rural Women in the Panchayat System*. Udaipur: Agrotech Publishing Company, 2009.

Ahuja, Ram. *Social Problems in India*. Jaipur: Rawat Publications, 1999.

Apter, David E. *Introduction to Political Analysis*. New Delhi: Prentice Hall of India, 1981.

Asshaha, Abdur Rahman. *Islamic Concepts of Human Rights*. Delhi: Sipra Publications. 2004.

Basu, L.N. *Human Rights in a Global Perspective*. Jaipur: Aavishkar Publishers, 2003.

Begum, Mehartaj S. *Human Rights in India: Issues and Perspectives*. New Delhi: A.P.H. Publishing Corporation. 2000.

Bhargava, Gopal. *Human Rights: Conflict Build Peace*. Delhi: Kalpaz Publications, 2003.

Bhatt, Umesh. *Human Rights: Achievements and Challenges*. Delhi: Vista International Publishing House, 2005.

Bhuimali, Anil. (ed.) *Globalization and Human Rights*. New Delhi: Serials Publication, 2006

Bluhm, William T. *Theories of the Political System*. New Delhi: Prentice-Hall of India Pvt. Ltd., 1981.

Busi, S.N. *Mahatma Gandhi and Baba Sahib Ambedkar: Crusades against Caste and Untouchability*. Hyderabad: Saroja Publications, 1997.

Chander, Prakash and Arora, Prem. *Comparative Politics and International Relations*. Gurgaon: Cosmos Bookhive (P) Ltd., N.Y.

Chandra, Bipan, Mukherjee, Mridula and Mukherjee, Aditya. *India Since Independence*. New Delhi: Penguin Books, 2008.

Chandra, Bipan, Mukherjee, Mridula and Panikkar, K.N. *India's Struggle for Independence*. New Delhi: Penguin Books, 1989.

Das, Wishan. *History of Great Britain—1485-1952*. New Delhi: S. Chand & Co.,1975.

Dev, Arjun, Dev, Indira Arjun and Das, Gupta., (ed.) *Human Rights: A Source Book*. New Delhi: National Council of Educational Research and Training, 1996.

Devanesan, A. *History of Tamil Nadu*. (Tamil) Marthandam: Renu Publications, 1998.

Durant, Will, and Durant, Ariel. *The Lessons of History*. New York: Simon and Schuster, 1968.

Gonsalves, Lina. *Women and Human Rights*. New Delhi: A.P.H. Publishing Corporation, 2001.

Gopalakrishnan, B. *Rights of Children*. Jaipur: Pavishkar Publishers, 2004.

Goswami, B., (ed.) *Human Rights and Reforming the Law*. Jaipur: Raj Publishing House, 2008.

Grant, A.J. and Temperley, Harold. *Europe in the Nineteenth and Twentieth Centuries—1789-1950,* Edited by Lillian M. Penson. London: Longman Group Limited, 1976.

Guha, Ramachandra. *Indhiya Varalaaru: Gandhikku Piragu*. (part I) (Tamil) Chennai: Kizhakku Pathippagam, 2009.

Gurr, Ted Robert. *Why Men Rebel*? New Jersey: Princeton University Press, 1970.

Habib, Irfan. *Essays in Indian History—Towards a Marxist Perception*. Aligarh: Tulika Books, 1995.

Harsh, Bhanwar Lal. *Human Rights Law in India*. New Delhi: Regal Publications, 2008.

Hill, C.P. *A History of the United States*. London: Edward Arnold Publishers, 1966.

Hitler, Adolf. *Mein Kampf* (*My Struggle*). New Delhi: Adarsh Books, 2003.

Iyer, Padma. *Human Rights of Women*. Jaipur: Pointer Publishers, 2006.

Jaffrelot, Christophe. *India's Silent Revolution: The Rise of the Low Castes in North Indian Politics*. Delhi: Permanent Black, 2003.

Kalimuthu, A.K. *Colonial Economy and the Lower Peasantry—Tamil Nadu Since 1801-1947*. Trichy: Archana Publications, 2004.

Kapoor, A.C. *Principles of Political Science*. New Delhi: S.Chand & Co., 1995.

Kartikeya, K. *Women Movements and Human Rights*. New Delhi: Navyug Publishers, 2008.

Kepel, Gilles. *Jihad: The Trial of Political Islam*. London: I.B. TAURIS, 2003.

Ketelbey, C.D.M. *A History of Modern Times from 1789*. Bombay: Oxford University Press, 1976.

Llewellyn, J.E. The Legacy of Women's Uplift in India. New Delhi: Sage Publications, 1998.

Mangai, A. Ethirolikum Karavoligal; Aravanigalum Manithargale. (Echoed Hand Claps; the Aravanis are also human beings) (Tamil) Chennai: Bharadhi Puthakalayam, 2009.

Mcwilliams, Wayne C. and Piotrowski. *The world since 1945: A History of International Relations*. New Delhi: Viva Books, 2012.

Mehra, Shweta. *Human Rights: A Gandhian Perspective*. New Delhi: Sarup & Sons, 2006.

Mehta, Lyla. *Politics and Poetics of Water*. New Delhi: Orient Longman, 2005.

Merry, Sally Engle. *Human Rights and Gender Violence*. New Delhi: Oxford University Press, 2009.

Moinuddin, S.A.H. *Divorce and Muslim Women*. Jaipur: Rawat Publications. 2000.

Muni, S.D. (ed.) *Responding to Terrorism in South Asia*. New Delhi: Manohar Publishers, 2006.

Narasimha, Roddam and Kumar, Arvind. (ed.) *Science and Technology to Counter Terrorism*. Washington, DC.: The National Academies Press, 2007.

Omvedt, Gail. *Dalits and the Democratic Revolution: Dr. Ambedkar and the Dalit Movement in Colonial India*. New Delhi: Sage Publications, 1994.

Pachawri, S.K. *Women and Human Rights*. New Delhi: A.P.H. Publishing Corporation, 1999.

Palanithurai, G. and Mohanasundaram, K. *Dynamics of Tamil Nadu Politics in Sri Lankan Ethnicity*. New Delhi: Northern Book Centre, 1993.

Panda, Bhavani Prasad. *Human Rights: Development and Environmental Law*. Delhi: Academic Excellence, 2007.

Panigrahy, Rajib Lochan and Bhuyan, Dasarathy. (ed.) *Women Empowerment*. New Delhi: Discovery Publishing House, 2006.

Ramphal, R.C. *Perspectives in Human Rights*. New Delhi: Rajat Publications, 2001.

Rawat, Gyanendra Singh. *The Status of Dalit and Human Rights in India*. New Delhi: Sumit Enterprises, 2005.

Roy, Rekha. *Women's Rights in India*. New Delhi: Akansha Publishing House, 2006.

Sahu, Ashima. *Human Rights Violations and the Law*. Jaipur: Pointer Publishers, 2007.

Saksena, Anu. *Gender and Human Rights: Status of Women Workers in India*. Delhi: Shipra Publications, 2004.

Sathianathaier, R. *History of India. Vol. 1*. Madras: S. Viswanathan, Printers & Publishers, 1985.

Sharma, S.K. *World Crisis in Human Rights*. Jaipur: Sublime Publications, 2007.

Sharma, Vinod. *Human Rights Violation: A Global Phenomenon*. New Delhi: A.P.H. Publishing Corporation, 2002.

Singh, Gurucharan. *Pollution to Purity of Environment*. New Delhi: Deep & Deep Publications, 2005.

Singh, Ruma Ghosh, Raj, Nikhil and Sekar, Helen R. *Hard Labour at a Tender Age*. Noida: V.V. Giri National Labour Institute, 2002.

Singh, L.K. *Ecology, Environment and Tourism*. Delhi: Isha Books, 2008.

Smith, Vincent A. *The Oxford History of England*. London: Oxford University Press, 1933.

Southgate, George W. *A Text Book of Modern European History—1789-1960*. London: J.M. Dent and Sons Ltd, 1974.

Subramanian, S. *Human Rights: International Challenges. Vol. 2*. New Delhi: Manas Publications, 2004.

Suchinmaya, Rachna. *Gender, Human Rights and Environment*. New Delhi: Atlantic Publishers, 2008.

Symonides, Janusz. (ed.) *New Dimensions and Challenges for Human Rights*. Jaipur: Rawat Publications, 2003.

Thorat, Sukhadeo. *Ambedkar's Role in Economic Planning: Water and Power Policy*. Delhi: Shipra Publications, 2006.

Tiwari, Jyotsna. (ed.) *Scope and Categories of Human Rights*. Delhi: Isha Books, 2006.

Upadhyaya, B.S. *Women in Rigveda*. New Delhi: S. Chand & Co., 1974.

Articles

Agnihotri, Indu. "Towards Equality." *Frontline*, April 9, 2010.

Ahmed, Ishtiyaq. "Refugee Problems in India." *Third Concept*, 10:110-11(1996): 27-30.

Anuradha, C.S. "Women Political Leadership and Perception: A Case Study of South Asia." *International Journal of South Asian Studies*, 1:1, (2008): 189-194.

Anshuman, Kumar. "D Companies", *The Week*, January 22, 2012.

Ardharujina, T.R. "Mercy Petitions: Inhuman Procrastination." *The Hindu*, June 30, 2010.

Bandyopadhyoy, Jayanta, and Babu, Rajesh R. "Regulating the Stuff of Life." Review of Water and the Laws in India, by ed. Iyer, Ramasamy R. *Economic and Political Weekly* XLV: 17 (April 24-30, 2010): 30-31.

Batra, Bikramjeet. "Justice or Revenge?." *Frontline*, June 4, 2010.

Biju, M.R., "Eco Tourism in Kerala." *South Asian Journal of Socio-Political Studies*, 5 (December 1, 2004): 102.

Bunsha, Dionne. "Clouds of Misery." *Frontline*, August 1, 2008.

Bunsha, Dionne. "Withering Heights." *Frontline*, July 18, 2008.Chandrasekhar, C.P. "Liberalising loot." *Frontline*, July 16, 2010.

Chomsky, Noam. "Dominance and its Dilemmas." *Frontline*, November 21, 2003.

Dharmalingam. "Female Beedi Workers in South Indian Village." *Economic and Political Weekly* XXVIII: 27 and 28 (July 3-10, 1993), 37-44.

Dorairaj, "Seeking Identity." *Frontline*, January 1, 2010.

Dorai Raj, S. "Kilns of Bondage." *Frontline*, July 17, 2009.

George, Annie, Vindhya, U., and Ray, Swamy. "Sex Trafficking and Sex Work: Definitions, Debates and Dynamics—A Review of Literature." *Economic and Political Weekly* XLV: 17 (April 24, 2010), 64-73.

Ghosal, Bidisha, "Silent Sufferers", *The Week*, September 14, 2008.

Jodha, Surinder S. "Dalits in Business: Self-Employed Scheduled Castes in North-West India." *Economic and Political Weekly* XLV:11 (March 13, 2010): 41-48.

Kamat, Anjali. "Turning the Clock Back on Lebanon." *The Hindu*, July 20, 2006.

Katakam, Anupama. "In Cold Blood." *Frontline*, October 9, 2009.

Katju, Markandey. "The Ideal of Women's Emancipation." *The Hindu*, February 18, 2009.

Kennedy, David. "Terrorism and Human Rights." *Harvard Human Rights Journal* (Spring, 2002): 1.

Krishnakumar, B. "Feminisation of Panchayats." *Frontline*, June 6, 2008.

Krishnakumar, R. "The Village and the behemoth." *Frontline*, January 15, 2010.

Kothari, Ashish. "Sustainable Future?" *Frontline*, January 15, 2010.

Laquer, Walter. "The Terrorism to Come." *Public Review* (August and September 2004): 51.

Mahaprashasta, Ajoy Ashirwad. "Mining Tussle." *Frontline*, July 16, 2010.

Malar, Kavin, "Vachathy Pain", (Vachathy vali-Tamil) *Ananda Vikadan*, October 12, 2011.

Mohanasundaram, K. "Human Rights and the Child Labour." *Third Concept* 14:157 (2000): 21-24.

Moddie, Mandira. "Development: Dreams within Reach." *The Hindu*, June 13, 2010, Magazine section.

Muralidhar Reddy. "A Sinking feeling." *Frontline*, October 23, 2009.

Muralidharan, Sukumar. "POTA: Untold Stories." *Frontline*, April 9, 2004.

Subramanian, T.S. "Bail for Nedumaran." *Frontline*, January 30, 2004.

Nayar Kuldip. "They Left Behind their Homes ... and Hopes." (India: Special issue) *The Hindu*, August 15, 1997.

Nazakat, Syed and Pushkarna, Vijaya. "Pardoning President". *The Week*, June 17, 2012.

Parthasarathy, Indira. "Existential Dilemmas." Review of Venomous Touch: Notes on Caste, Culture and Politics, by Ravikumar. *The Hindu*, Book Review, June 6, 2010.

Pudukone, Neil. "Climate Change in India: Forgotten Threats, Forgotten opportunities." *Economic and Political Weekly* XLV: 22 (May 29-June 4, 2010): 47-54.

Ragavan, R.K. "A Judicial Murder." *Frontline*, October 21, 2011.

Rajalakshmi, T.K. "Fire of Aggression." *Frontline*, September 23, 2005.

Rajalakshmi, T.K. "Women as Victim." *Frontline*, January 4, 2008.

Ram, N. "Interview of President Chandrika Kumaratunga." *Frontline*, January 1, 1999.

Ramachandran, R. "Lethal Aftermath." *Frontline*, July 2, 2010.

Ramakrishnan, Venkitesh, "Plunder and Profit." *Frontline*, July 16, 2010.

Rona, Gabor. "Legal Frameworks to Combat Terrorism: An Abundant Inventory of Existing Tools." *Chicago Journal of International Law* 5:2 (Winter 2005): 499.

Rosenthal, Elisabeth. "Gateway for trash." *Frontline*, October 23, 2009.

Sainath. "Thirst for Profit." Frontline, April 21, 2006.

Sharma, Kalpana. "Invisible Environmentalists." *The Hindu*, June 13, 2010, Magazine section.

Satyarthi, Kailash. "Child Labour: A major cause for poverty." *Health for the Millions* (November-December 1998): 29.

Singh, Kirti. "Left in the Lurch." *Frontline*, April 9, 2010.

Sreedhar, R. "The way ahead." *Frontline*, July 16, 2010.

Srinivasan, Sarada and Bedi, Arjuna. "Daughter Elimination: Cradle Baby Scheme in Tamil Nadu." *Economic and Political Weekly* XLV: 23 (June 5-11, 2010): 17-20.

Subramanian, T.S., "Reprieve from Death", *Frontline*, September 23, 2011.

Suroor, Hasan. "Striking at London." *Frontline*, July 29, 2005.

Subramanian Nirupama. "The LTTE's Baby Brigade." *Frontline*, December 7, 2001.

Swami, Praveen. "Catch them Young." *Frontline*, December 7, 2001.

Swamy Praveen. "Maximum Terror and its Mechanics." *Frontline*, July 28, 2006.

"The Auction", *The Week*, March 18, 2012.

"The Case Against Death Sentence." (editorial) *Economic and Political Weekly* XLV: 20 (May 15-21, 2010):8.
Tiwari, Deepak. "*Women for Sale*", *The Week*, January 26, 2003.
Tripathi, Purnima S. "Child Rights: Audit Shock." *Frontline*, June 4, 2010.
Varadarajan, Siddarth. "Beware the New Order Israel is Imposing." *The Hindu*, July 29, 2006.
Velayudhan, Meera. "Cut off by Caste." *Frontline*, April 9, 2010.
Venkat, Vidya. "From the Shadows." *Frontline*, February 29, 2008.
Venkat, Vidya. "Sex-reassignment surgery." *Frontline*, February 29, 2008.
Venkataraman, K. "Alien invasion." *Frontline*, July 3, 2009.
Venkatesan, J. "Gas Leak: Centre to File Curative Petition." *The Hindu*, June 27, 2010.
Venkatesan, V. "In the Normal Course." *Frontline*, December 2, 2005.
Venkatesan, V. "For a New Law." *Frontline*, July 16, 2010.
Vijaya Pushkarna, "Dead man waiting", *The Week*, September 25. 2011.
Viswanathan, A. "Temple Car and Caste Tension." *Frontline*, August 15, 2003.
Viswanathan, S. "A Silent Revolution." *Frontline*, June 6, 2008.
Viswanathan, S. "The Fall of a Wall." *Frontline*, June 6, 2008.
Viswanathan, S. "Untouchability Unlimited." *Frontline*, March 28, 2008.
Yadavar, Swagata. "Lethal Prescription", *The Week*, June 10, 2012.
Zaide, Annie, "India's Shame", *Frontline*, September 22, 2006.

Conference Proceedings

Das, Sumita. "The Role of UNHCR in Sri Lankan Tamil Refugees Repatriation during 1992-1995." Proceedings of *South Indian History Congress*, 22nd Annual Session, 2002.
Moosvi, Shireen. "Domestic Service in Pre-colonial India: Bondage, Caste and market." *Proceedings of the Indian History Congress,* 64th session, 2003 (Patna: Indian History Congress, 2004).

Website Reference

Amnesty International. (Australia) *www.amnesty.org.au*.
Hijra. (South Asia) Wikipedia, the free Encyclopedia.
http://www.un.org/Women Watch/daw/sitemap/ index. html.
http://www.hrea.org/index.php?base_id=14.
The European Human Rights System.

Index